GRAPHIC DESIGN MATERIALS & EQUIPMENT

GRAPHIC DESIGN
MATERIALS&
EQUIPMENT

An international directory
JONATHAN STEPHENSON

CHARTWELL
BOOKS, INC.

A QUARTO BOOK

Published by Chartwell Books Inc
A Division of Book Sales Inc
110 Enterprise Avenue
Secaucus, New Jersey 07094

ISBN 1-55521-078-3

This book was designed and produced by
Quarto Publishing plc
The Old Brewery, 6 Blundell Street
London N7 9BH

SENIOR EDITORS Polly Powell
                     Henrietta Wilkinson
EDITOR Mike Darton

ART EDITOR Vincent Murphy
DESIGNER Hugh Shermuly
PHOTOGRAPHER Paul Forrester

ART DIRECTOR Moira Clinch
EDITORIAL DIRECTOR Carolyn King

Quarto Publishing plc would like to acknowledge the generous
assistance of Langford & Hill Ltd, Graphic Art Suppliers, London, who
made available all the materials and equipment photographed in this
book.

Typeset by Facsimile Ltd and Burbeck Associates
Manufactured in Hong Kong by Regent Publishing Services Ltd
Printed by Leefung-Asco Printers Ltd, Hong Kong

CONTENTS

INTRODUCTION 6

HOW TO USE THIS BOOK 7

GRAPHIC MEDIA 9

Pencils • Pens • Nibs • Calligraphy Instruments • Pastels • Chalks
Crayons • Brushes • Airbrushes • Compressors • Paints
Inks • Paper • Board • Films

DESK EQUIPMENT 89

Rulers • Drawing Aids • Compasses • Erasers • Sharpeners
Cutting Instruments • Tapes • Adhesives
Instant Lettering • Color Specifiers

STUDIO EQUIPMENT 155

Drawing-boards • Light-boxes • Studio Furniture • Cameras •
Enlargers • Photocopiers • Computer graphics

INTRODUCTION

Writing a book on graphic artists' and designers' materials and equipment poses several problems. The first is the definition of graphic art. Strictly, it refers to commercial artistic activity in support of printing processes, but the boundaries of graphic art now extend way beyond this narrow definition. And in its broadest sense graphic art arguably includes such activities as illustration, advertising design, packaging design, book and magazine design, some aspects of product design, the preparation of exhibitions and displays, and design activities in support of television and other media presentations. In other words, graphic art has now become a generic name which encompasses the majority of commercial artistic endeavors.

It follows that the materials and equipment used in graphic art must be varied in type and extensive in number. Any attempt to catagorize them is further confused by the fact that so many of the materials used in graphic art are shared by other artistic disciplines such as fine arts, architecture and technical drafting. The solution has had to be arbitrary decision-making, and items have been included or excluded on a personal assessment of their foreseeable relevance to graphic design.

A second problem area is created by the complexities of graphic materials and equipment supply. Many items are supplied internationally, but they are often marketed locally by distributors. This makes it very difficult to determine which manufacturers are actually responsible for specific products. If any misattribution of products has occurred in this book, it is highly regretted: all that can be said in defence is that the information given here has been extracted from materials supplied by manufacturers, distributing agents and suppliers of graphic artists' materials and is believed to be a reasonable interpretation of the facts supplied by them.

This in turn raises the question of what information is of most value to the reader — that specific products are available, or that product types are available of which specific examples are quoted. The question has been answered by the sheer size of the product ranges on offer. Many manufacturers' catalogs contain more pages of detailed information than there are in this book. Furthermore, manufacturers' ranges tend to change from year to year, and to place too much emphasis on individual products would be to invite a situation in which the material in the book could differ greatly from the actual product ranges on the shelves of graphic artists' materials suppliers.

How to use this book

To try to overcome this, a solution has been reached which presents the information throughout the book in four main categories:

The main text sets out to describe and explain graphic artists' materials and equipment by type. This information is relevant to all the available materials whether or not they are specifically listed in this book.

In the caption text, and in the charts on materials, some manufacturers and their products are listed, and the reader's attention is drawn to particular products where they are of special interest.

Information is presented visually in the form of illustrations, so that the product types and the specific products referred to can be readily identified.

The book contains summary charts and end matter on the suppliers of materials themselves. These are based substantially on information obtained from questionnaires, and they are offered as supplementary information products.

Acknowledgements

This book could not have been produced without the information supplied by the manufacturers, distributors and retailers whose products are listed in the text. My thanks are particularly extended to those manufacturers who supplied additional information on technical matters over and above what was necessary in relation to their own products. I should also like to thank my wife, Tricia, for her help and support while this book was being written, and my daughter Amy, aged 2¾, who insisted on helping too. An acknowledgement is also due to Polly Powell for her part in the book's production, and for her assistance with information-gathering in the early stages. I will extend my final thanks to Mike Hutchinson and Ann Hickman whose assistance helped bring this book to completion.

The publishers would also like to thank the following for their help: Sebastian Noakes, Aesthedes Ltd; Mike Morrison, Alan Stevenson and Nick Mole, Agfa Gaevert; Michael Orchard, Altus; Mary Ainsworph, Apple Computers; Muriel Drury, Grant Equipment Supplies; Ken Howkins, Halco; Caroline Maughaun and Mark Owens, Harris/3M; Hewlett Packard; Alan Rodgers, Honeywell Bull; Deborah Lines, Quantel; and Richard Beer of Scangraphic.

In particular, thanks to Keith Lockwood, Cliff Mason and all the staff at Langford & Hill, who kindly supplied the graphic materials for photography; and to Laura Beck of QV Typesetting for the charts.

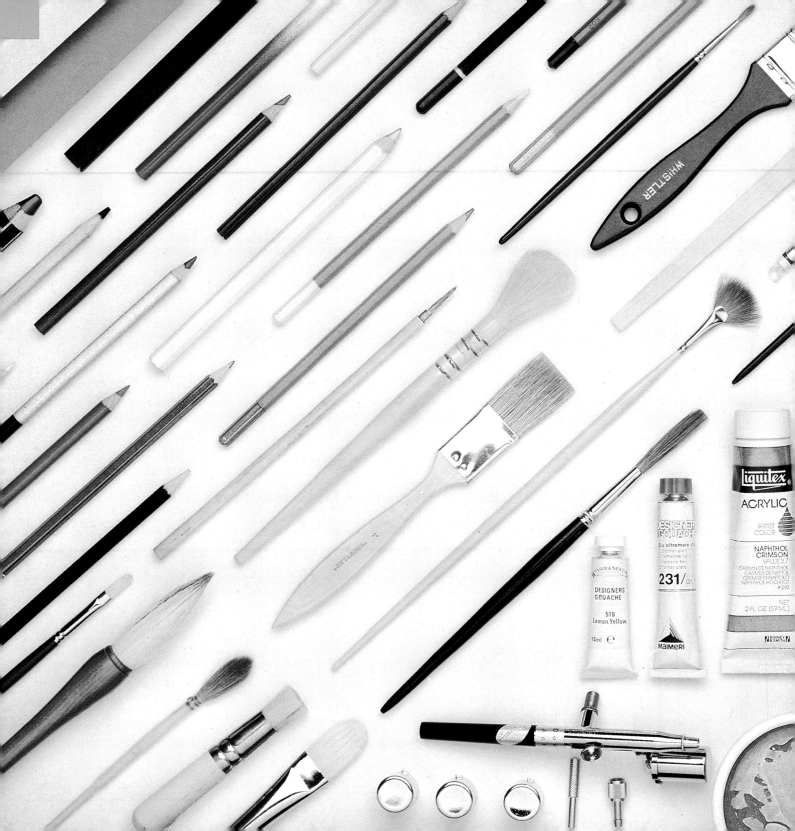

SECTION ONE

GRAPHIC MEDIA

Pencils • Pens • Nibs
Calligraphy Instruments
Pastels • Chalks • Crayons
Brushes • Airbrushes
Compressors • Paints • Inks
Paper • Board • Films

PENCILS, PENS AND CRAYONS

Pencils, pens and crayons are drawing instruments and are extremely important items of the graphic artist's equipment. Because of their low cost and apparent simplicity they are seldom given much thought, but they can be surprisingly sophisticated and are frequently made with a particular application in mind. Those which are specifically intended for graphic or fine-art use are obviously discussed here, but a broader view is necessary, and several items are considered which are likely to find applications in graphic art, even though they are not designed primarily or exclusively for that purpose.

In this chapter the relevance of particular products or product categories to graphic art has been determined by a consideration of their intended use, their potential use, their quality, the degree of control that they allow the user, and the permanence of the marks they make. Although it is acknowledged that this last factor may frequently be less important in some areas of graphic art than others, and is generally more important to fine artists, it is increasingly being taken note of and is in any event a consideration where certain specific purposes are intended for the finished artwork.

PENCILS
Wooden-cased pencils

The traditional pencil probably originated in England a little over 300 years ago, although one of the first recorded manufacturers was a carpenter named Staedtler in Nürnberg. These early pencils contained a stick of pure graphite, a naturally occurring form of carbon. A major source of graphite was Borrowdale in Cumberland. Pencil-making still continues in Cumberland today, although local supplies of graphite have been effectively exhausted for some time. Graphite has since been discovered in other locations, and the modern pencil industry is supplied with its raw materials by countries such as Korea, Sri Lanka, Germany and Mexico.

At a fairly early stage in the history of pencils, attempts were made to replace pure graphite with leads made from powdered graphite bound with glue or gum. The period of hostility between England and France following the French Revolution caused pencils to be made in the way that they are today. The supply of graphite from England to France was interrupted, so a French chemist named Conté began to investigate ways of extending pure graphite to make it more economical and efficient to use. In 1795 he obtained a patent for his process, which involved mixing powdered graphite with clay and baking it. From this the wooden-case pencil with a composite lead, which is used today, came into being.

Nowadays it is usual to treat the pencil leads with waxes, after firing, to improve their performance and to increase the permanence and stability of their mark. Various manufacturers have their own special recipes for this process, and there are some slight differences in their products as a result.

The wooden surround of a wooden-cased pencil is generally made from cedar, which is straight-grained and soft enough to sharpen easily. There are different varieties and qualities of cedar wood available, some of the best coming from California. The cylinder of lead should be glued in place within its wooden casing so that it cannot slip out of position when pressure is applied to the point. The wooden cases are round or hexagonal in section. Hexagonal pencils are intended for office or studio use because they are less inclined to roll on a desk top or a drawing board. Carpenters' pencils are traditionally rectangular or oval in section, with a rectangular lead instead of a round one.

PENCIL DEGREES

Graphite pencils are made in many degrees of hardness and blackness. In all, 20 grades exist extending from 9H to 9B, with HB and F in the middle of the range.

Pencil leadings available in Rexel Cumberland's Derwent Graphic range.

Pencil degrees

One advantage of a composite lead is that it can be made in differing degrees of hardness and blackness. More clay and less graphite gives a lead that is gray rather than black, but which is hard, enabling it to be sharpened to a fine point, and slow-wearing, so the pencil line remains fine and controlled. More graphite and less clay gives a lead which is darker and richer in shade, approaching black, but which is soft so that the point wears quickly, giving a less even and less precise line.

Each set of properties is suited to particular applications, and it is usual for manufacturers to produce pencils in varying degrees of hardness and blackness, designated H and B respectively. Typically, a range might be available in grades 6H to 6B, with HB as its middle quality, but ranges can extend as far as 9H and 9B. A grade F is included in ranges between HB and H.

One manufacturer's grades will not necessarily correspond to those of another. A 4B from one source might be equivalent to a 3B or a 5B from another. Very hard pencils are of most use to draftsmen, and very soft pencils are best suited to fine-art sketching. Graphic designers are likely to find a middle range extending from around 4H to 6B satisfactory for most purposes.

Pencils for artists and designers

The graphite content of a pencil not only governs the intended hardness or blackness of the finished product but also relates to the use of the pencil. Some pencils are manufactured specifically for graphic artists and designers. Such pencils are likely to contain higher-quality graphite in their leads than pencils that are made for more general use in offices and schools. They may contain purer graphite or more finely milled graphite, and will make a richer mark in consequence.

Artists' and designers' pencils commonly have thicker leads than low-grade pencils. A fairly standard size for a pencil lead is 2mm in diameter, but artists' pencils often have leads of 3mm or even 4mm in diameter. This allows the user a greater variation of point thickness and permits a more varied line, which is particularly useful for freehand drawing. A pencil made for a graphic artist or for a fine artist consequently costs more than an ordinary pencil, but it is a higher-grade product and can be expected to perform better.

Some manufacturers make their artists' pencils round and their designers' pencils hexagonal, but there is no accepted convention concerning such finishes. A few manufacturers make flat pencils for artists and graphic designers, with an oblong section and a flat, square-ended lead. These make a broad, flat mark which may be varied by tilting the angle at which it is used so that it works on either the broad or the narrow part of its lead. These pencils are similar to carpenters' pencils but are manufactured in qualities appropriate to artists.

Top quality graphite pencils include the Derwent graphic and the Derwent sketching from Rexel Cumberland, the Castell 9000 from Faber-Castell, the Turquoise drawing pencil and the Venus from Berol, the Tombow Mono 100, the Criterium from Conté, the Orlow Technico 6300 from Lyra, the Stabilo-micro from Schwan-Stabilo, the Technograph from Caran d'Ache, the Rowney Victoria, the Mars-Lumograph 100 from Staedtler, the Kimberly drawing pencil from General, the Microtomic drawing pencil from Eberhard-Faber and the RS 800 from Royal Sovereign. A flat version of the Derwent sketching pencil is also available, and the Berol Turquoise is also made in a version for use on drafting film called the Turquoise Filmograph. A graphite pencil with a wide lead is included in the Stabilotone range from Schwan-Stabilo.

1 Flat-leaded sketching pencil
2 Sketching pencil
3-19 Graphite pencils
20 Jumbo pencil

*Selection of colored pencils, including a Lyra thick-leaded pencil (**top**).*

Colored pencils

Colored pencil leads are similar in principle to those of graphite pencils. Instead of graphite and clay, however, mixtures of pigment and clay are used. Colored pencil leads are dried but not usually fired in a kiln (as are graphite leads), so the clay acts substantially as a filler or extender of the pigment, rather than as the structural element of the lead. Colored pencil leads are also treated to a greater extent with waxes and additives, which are necessary to insure that they have the desired softness to draw and write smoothly.

As with graphite pencils, some grades of colored pencil are produced especially for artists, graphic artists and designers. Good-quality colored pencils have a high proportion of pigment in their leads and make use of pigments that are recognized as suitable for artistic use. This means that they will be lightfast and stable to an acceptable degree. Colored pencils are not produced in different degrees of hardness and softness, but different ranges vary in composition, and both hard and soft colored pencils do exist.

Colored pencils intended for artists and designers often have thick leads, but it is not unusual for manufacturers to offer good-quality ranges of thin-lead pencils which can be quite useful for small-scale or detailed work. In use, colored pencils can be overlaid to create visual blending of the colors, but they cannot be mixed like paints. They are therefore usually produced in a wide range of colors, shades and tints.

The Derwent Studio and the Derwent Artists from Rexel Cumberland have wide leads, and both ranges offer 72 colors. The Polychromos from Faber-Castell is also available in 72 shades. The Berol Prismacolor, which offers 60 colors, and the Berol Verithin, which comes in a range of 40 colors, are also popular with graphic designers. Other high quality colored pencils include the Lyra Rembrandt, the Mars Lumochrom and the Norris Unipoint from Staedtler, the Rowney Coloured pencils and the Stabilo Thin-lead colored pencils from Schwan-Stabilo. Oversized colored pencils and thick-lead pencils are available from Lyra and Berol.

Water-soluble pencils

The water-soluble pencil, known sometimes as a watercolor pencil, is similar in appearance to an ordinary colored pencil, but the lead contains a water-sensitive binder. The pencil can be used in a conventional way, but when the marks are gone over with a wet brush, a wet sponge or even a wet finger, they become a watercolor wash and can be redistributed on the surface of the paper. By wetting the pencil itself, or by only partially wetting the pencil drawing, a drawn image can be retained, but the pencil marks will be substantially altered in character. These pencils allow a combination of drawing and painting techniques to be employed at the same time and are particularly suited to mixed techniques where some color is washed in and some color is left as drawing. Water-soluble pencils may also be used in combination with graphite and ordinary colored pencils (which resist water) to create some interesting effects.

Water-soluble pencils commonly contain powerful organic pigments mixed with fillers. The amount of pigment they contain varies not only from shade to shade but also from one manufacturer to another. The results obtained from different ranges vary considerably, and some are undoubtedly of better quality than others.

Water-soluble pencils contain less pigment than high-grade watercolor paint, so there is a limit to the strength of color that can be achieved with them, but their convenience and the unusual techniques that they lend themselves to make them potentially very useful. It is important to use a suitable paper with watercolor pencils if wet methods are to be employed. The leads of water-soluble pencils are usually very soft and are inclined to break if mishandled. A few ranges exist that are sensitive to turpentine and spirit rather than water, and some are sensitive to both types of solvent.

The short, fat Stabilotone pencils from Schwan-Stabilo are very useful for graphic artists, and the Derwent Watercolor pencils from Rexel Cumberland also offer many varied possibilities. The Prismalo I and II ranges from Caran d'Ache have a particularly good reputation as watercolor pencils.

Other respected brands include the Albrecht Dürer pencils from Faber-Castell (also available as separate leads), the Conté Aquarelle, the Lyra Aquarelle and the Staedtler Karat and Aquarelle pencils.

Water-soluble pencils, including a Stabilotone jumbo pencil (**bottom**).

Colored drawing pencils and specialist pencils

Several manufacturers produce colored drawing pencils intended specifically for tonal drawing. These are not the same as ordinary colored pencils and have wide, crayon-like leads. They are available in basic colors (including black and white) and selections of earth colors and the sanguine shades.

Pastels are also available in pencil form as a convenient alternative to the potentially messy and fragile pastel crayon. Compressed charcoal is also made into pencil leads, but charcoal pencils seldom give such satisfactory results as the natural product. Hard-leaded charcoal pencils are particularly unresponsive, but, as with pastel pencils, there is much to be said for the cleanliness and convenience of the pencil form.

Some pencils are manufactured using black pigments, rather than graphite, to color the lead. These give an exceptionally rich, dark line. All-surface, glass and china pencils have very waxy and often crumbly leads that will adhere to most surfaces. They are available in dense blacks and in a limited selection of colors.

The Faber-Castell range of Pitt Artists' pencils, the Derwent Drawing and the Conté white, sanguine and sepia pencils, are all crayon pencils. The Conté pastel pencils and the Carb-Othello pencils from Schwan-Stabilo have soft pastel-like leads which can be blended and mixed on the paper surface. Charcoal pencils and black pencils with pigmented leads are available from several manufacturers including Conté, Grumbacher, General, Eberhard-Faber and KIN. Specialist pencils include types such as the Berol China Marker and the "All" Stabilo pencil which writes on almost any surface.

Mechanical pencils

The leadholder is the simplest form of mechanical pencil. This holds a fairly standard pencil lead, usually 2mm in diameter, within its body. In effect, a leadholder is simply a pencil with a renewable point of a constant weight and size. Its lead works in all major respects like that of a conventional pencil, but with a leadholder the very last small piece of the lead can be used and new leads may be fitted as required.

Most leadholders take 2mm leads, but if you want to use soft leads between 4B and 8B a holder is required that will accept 3.15mm leads. The Mars Pan Technico from Staedtler, the Universal from Faber-Castell and the 0003 leadholder from Caran d'Ache will take the fatter leads. Lyra, Schwan-Stabilo, Berol, KIN and Alvin, among others, include leadholders in their ranges. Shorter versions such as the Mars Technico 782 are more suitable for carrying around.

Selection of clutch pencils.

The fine line leadholder is an advance on the ordinary type. This is a mechanical pencil which holds an extremely thin lead. There is no need to sharpen these pencils, since the diameter of the lead represents the point size: A fine line leadholder therefore has a constant point as well as a constant weight and size. The mechanisms for these leadholders are usually more sophisticated than those of the standard type so that the lead can be fed forward in a more controlled way.

Propelling leadholders work by winding the lead forward as the pencil barrel is twisted. More modern mechanisms advance the lead by a precisely measured amount as it is required. One type of mechanism works by a shake or a flick of the wrist, and another is fully automatic: spring-operated; it feeds the lead through when the pencil is lifted from the paper surface.

Pencil leads

The leads used in fine line leadholders are of such small diameters and potentially so fragile that they cannot be made from a conventional mix of graphite and clay. Instead, the clay component is replaced by a plastic polymer which gives the lead considerable strength and flexibility. For use on paper, fine leads containing mixtures of graphite and carbon are used which give rich, dense lines.

However, technical pencils are frequently used on drafting film, and special leads are required for this, as graphite leads not only are inclined to smudge but also may prove too reflective where photography and detailed reproduction are required. Special film leads, therefore, do not contain graphite and are made either of carbon and dye bound with a polymer or of sophisticated carbon-polymer structures. Recently the handling properties of film leads have improved, and forms are available that perform like graphite leads but without the technical problems that are associated with the use of graphite on film.

Polymer-graphite leads are graded in a similar way to conventional graphite pencils, in degrees of hardness and blackness. Film leads are also graded, but these grades do not correspond to those of graphite leads. Different manufacturers use different grading systems, and there is not necessarily any relationship between them. Film-lead grades are best related to the type of drafting film being used. Fine leads are also available in a small selection of colors. Typical sizes for fine leads include 0.3mm, 0.5mm, 0.7mm and 0.9mm diameter, and a separate leadholder is required to hold each lead size.

2mm and 3.15mm leads are available to fit leadholders. Most are graphite leads, but some colored leads are made. Fine leads are available in 0.3mm, 0.5mm, 0.7mm and 0.9mm diameters to fit compatible leadholders. Faber-Castell's Super Polymer leads and Pilot's Neo X-S enjoy a good reputation, as do Pilot's PF film leads. Pentel Colored leads are made in a small selection of colors for fine line leadholders; other similar ranges are also available.

Drafting pencils

Many fine line leadholders are intended for drafting work and are available with point sizes that correspond to technical drawing standards. The lines they produce are of a constant size because the width of these lines corresponds to the diameter of the lead. The drawing point of a drafting pencil is protected by a sleeve consisting of a narrow tube enclosing the lead. This extends approximately 4-5mm from the end of the pencil and insures that the point may be positioned accurately against a ruling edge and that its position, relative to the edge, will not waver as it is drawn along. Many drafting pencils have a fixed point, meaning that the sleeve does not move and only as much lead is exposed beyond the sleeve is available to draw with.

However, there are pencils that have sliding and half-sliding points. These types of pencil cushion the lead against heavy-handedness and allow the mechanism that holds the lead to slide back against the lead as it is used, in effect making more lead available to draw with. In a half-sliding pencil, the mechanism can move back only so far, which means that these pencils, like fixed-point pencils, are suitable for accurate drawing against a ruling edge. Full-sliding pencils are not, because the lead will retract fully, allowing the pencil body to mount the ruling edge.

The Shaker (or Rocker as it is sometimes called), which is manufactured by Pilot, advances the lead by a flick of the wrist. The TK-Matic from Faber-Castell is a fully automatic pencil that advances the lead every time the point is lifted from the paper, so that the point length is kept constant. Other technical pencils include the Pentel PG 500 series, the Niji Grip 300 Cartridge pencil (which takes a lead refill cartridge) and the Contématic, which is disposable. Fine line leadholders and drafting pencils are also offered by Rotring, Schwan-Stabilo, Lyra, Staedtler, Uni, Berol, Alvin and Marabu.

PENS
Dip pens

The simplest form of pen is the dip pen. It can be used for drawing as well as for writing and is most suited to application onto paper.

Reed pens have been used for centuries and can be traced back to ancient Egyptian times. They are not used much now except by calligraphers, but the bold expressive lines that they make can lend themselves to certain types of illustration or to special lettering, where something with character is required. Any dry reed, piece of stout grass, cane or even a drinking straw can be converted into a reed pen with a few quick cuts from a sharp knife, but they are available ready-made; bamboo pens from the Far East can be obtained from some art stores.

Quill pens are cut from the wing feathers of birds and are round and hollow at their bases just like a reed. The principle is exactly the same, but the differences are that a quill is flexible and can be cut to a more delicate point. Quill pens have also been in use for many years and are first recorded in the 7th century. Like reeds, quills are used little now, but they are available ready-cut from a few specialist suppliers and are, of course, relatively easy to make for yourself.

The major advantage of the quill is its flexibility, which makes it particularly responsive to individual handling. Feathers of different sizes will lend themselves to different points. Crow and hawk were traditionally favored for drawing because of their small size, but turkey, goose and swan are more likely to be available commercially now. These are best suited to writing and only to drawing on a reasonably large scale.

A major disadvantage of the quill pen is that it wears down quickly and needs to be recut at the point. To overcome this problem early attempts were made to replace quills with pen nibs made of other materials including horn, tortoiseshell and metal. The technical problem was to combine flexibility with durability, and it was some time before this was achieved satisfactorily. One solution was to tip pen nibs with hard-wearing semiprecious stones, a principle that is still employed for some specialized technical pens, but the obvious solution was to produce a workable metal nib.

QUILLS AND REEDS

Cut quills and reeds are available through specialist retailers. Cut quills are included in the range of products offered by Sennelier.

Reed and quill pens.

Metal nibs

Metal nibs were first produced cheaply and efficiently by John Mitchell in 1828, and their design was subsequently improved by Joseph Gillott in 1831. Modern dip pens consist of a holder which carries a metal nib. These nibs are replaceable and available in a variety of shapes and sizes for different purposes. Typically metal pen nibs are made from a steel similar to spring steel and are designed with a fine slit running from the point into the body of the nib. Smaller slits at the sides of the nib are often an additional feature. These slits give the nib flexibility so that it can respond to movements of the hand.

Drawing nibs

Drawing nibs have elongated points which are likewise designed to give the nib increased flexibility. Small drawing pens are called mapping pens and have fine tips. These nibs are sometimes round in section and require a different type of holder. However, mapping pens are also made semi-circular in section for use with standard penholders. Drawing pens and extremely fine mapping pens are more easily damaged by heavy-handedness than are others.

DIP PENS

Metal pen nibs in a variety of patterns are manufactured by Rexel. Metal nibs are also offered by Hellerman, Osmiroid, Sennelier and Hunt Speedball. All these companies offer drawing nibs and some lettering nibs, but the Rexel range of lettering nibs is the most extensive.

1 Mapping pen with nibs
2 Calligraphic nibs
3 Round hand calligraphic nibs
4 Italic drawing nibs with holder
5 Mapping penholder with nibs
6 Calligraphic nibs
7 Five line music nibs

Writing nibs tend to have much shorter points than drawing pens and are often cut square at the tip, even when the point of the pen is very small. Various designs exist. When the point size is relatively large a writing nib is called a calligraphy or lettering nib. The most common calligraphy nib consists of a square point cut at a slight angle to suit the natural tilt of the hand. Special calligraphy nibs are necessary for left-handed users. They come in a variety of sizes and deliver a broad line that tapers to a narrow line as the angle of the pen is changed. They can, therefore, be used for italic and other forms of decorative lettering.

Another type of lettering nib has a flattened ball at its point set at an angle to the body of the nib. These nibs deliver a completely even line however the pen is directed, and several sizes are available. There are some variations on this type of nib which have a tilted square at their points.

A copperplate nib has an angled shaft that tilts the pen point more obliquely to the paper than the hand itself. The resulting script is extremely elegant. There are also several slightly exotic types of nib which have more than one point. These include shadow nibs for calligraphy, which mirror the main line with a second, finer line, and fan-shaped, multipointed ruling nibs that lay down parallel lines.

Ruling pens

A different principle is used for dip pens that are intended for ruling lines and groups of lines, although several pens of this type can be used for lettering. Instead of a conventional nib made from a single piece of steel, two pieces of metal converge to form a narrow gap. The gap itself is, in effect, the pen point, and the supply of ink is retained between the two pieces of the nib by surface tension.

The system may be employed in two ways. In a ruling pen of the type used in technical drawing both pieces of the pen come to a point. The pen delivers ink from the gap between the points, and the gap can be adjusted to give a line of any desired width, within the capacity of that particular pen. Alternatively, the two sides of the pen may end in a flat line with their edges ground away to insure a broad, flat edge. If this edge is cut into, the pen point will produce several lines. Depending on how it is cut, different groups of lines may be produced. Pens of this type are available which rule lines in pairs, in groups of even-sized lines, in groups of lines with varying widths and in groups of lines with varying gaps between them.

Reservoir pens are similar in concept to dip pens. For example, calligraphy nibs are often fitted with a small piece of metal that sits over the back of the nib tapering toward the point, but which is drawn down toward the point as the pen is used. In fact the principle is the same as that described for ruling pens, but here the two parts of the pen — the nib and the reservoir attachment — act only as an ink-feed system and not as a pen tip.

More sophisticated reservoir pens are made for technical use and as precise lettering pens. These include funnel pens, which deliver ink down a tubular nib from a reservoir that sits immediately behind it.

The term "reservoir pen" is occasionally used to describe fountain pens and technical pens that carry a substantial supply of ink and need filling only occasionally.

Graphos nibs from Rotring (pen now discontinued)

RULING AND RESERVOIR PENS

Coit and Automatic pens are types of ruling pens, sometimes known as brush pens, Technical reservoir and lettering pens include the Rotring Graphos, Hellerman's funnel pens and the Keuffel & Esser Leroy standard pens.

Fountain pens

Fountain pens are primarily writing instruments and are engineered with that function in mind. Because writing inks can be corrosive and because fountain pens are designed for long life, it is necessary to manufacture their nibs from durable materials such as stainless steel. This can be at the expense of flexibility, and a fountain pen, although a good writing tool, will not necessarily make a satisfactory drawing instrument. There are, however, a few fountain pens that are specifically designed for artistic applications.

Calligraphy pens are fountain pens with a selection of interchangeable nib units, housing both the nib and the ink feed, and are suitable for decorative lettering. They are often supplied in sets and some include an elongated sketching nib. Separate sets are available for right- and left-handed users, although at least one manufacturer supplies blank nibs, together with instructions for grinding the nibs to fit the individual tilt of the user's hand.

Sketching pens are art pens with specially designed nibs for drawing. These nibs claim a high degree of flexibility and deliver ink smoothly to the paper. Some sketching pens outwardly resemble an ordinary fountain pen, while others have an extended barrel, shaped to resemble the nib holder of a dip pen. Sketching pens with this shape combine the convenience of a fountain pen with the feel and balance of a traditional drawing pen.

FOUNTAIN, CALLIGRAPHY AND SKETCHING PENS

Fountain pens are widely available, and fine examples are produced by Parker, Cross and Waterman, among other manufacturers. Calligraphy fountain pens with interchangeable nib units are made by Osmiroid, Shaeffer, Platignum and Reform. The Rotring Art pen and the Pelikan Calligraphy pen have elongated pen bodies and include sketching nibs in their range of points. The Osmiroid series includes a shadow calligraphy pen.

Technical pens

A technical pen is a fountain pen that delivers ink down a fine metal tube instead of via a more conventional nib. They were first experimented with in the early part of this century by a German businessman named Wilhelm Riepe, but were not fully developed as a drawing instrument until the 1950s. Modern technical pens are extremely sophisticated and are increasingly easy to use and maintain. They deliver a uniform line of a precise width with great accuracy.

Technical pens are primarily technical-drawing instruments for draftsmen, architects and engineers, but have been adopted by graphic designers because of the crisp lines they make and the high standard of performance that they offer. As with drafting pencils, the point sizes available relate to certain technical-drawing standards, although pens are made with more point sizes to choose from.

In total there are 19 point sizes in use; these relate to two separate technical drawing standards. The ISO standard requires 9 point sizes between 0.13mm and 2.00mm and the DIN 15 standard uses 10 sizes ranging from 0.10mm to 1.20mm. Pens matched with the ISO standard are now most common. A few pens offer points corresponding to both standards, and some of the pens on the ISO standard do not include all 9 point sizes.

In practice technical pens require a good surface to work on and are inclined to snag or produce feathery lines on poor paper. Of practical use to the graphic designer is the fact that they deliver an even dot from the tip of the pen, if just touched against the paper. This factor allows neat stippling techniques in pen drawings. They are designed to take technical pen inks, which are very rich in coloring matter and are slightly thicker in consistency than ordinary ink. Several of the liquid colors now available to designers can be used in technical pens.

Poor maintenance and irregular cleaning can cause technical pens to clog up, although more modern designs often claim ease of maintenance as a feature. Special stands are available which hold pens while they are in use, and these can prevent the tips from drying out. Ultrasonic cleaning equipment can be used to dislodge ink from badly clogged pens and to thoroughly clean them.

Among the variations offered by different manufacturers are technical pens that take ink cartridges, pens with anti-leak caps, pens for lettering and stenciling and pens with hard-wearing tips. The points of all technical pens extend away from the main nib unit, allowing them to be placed close up against rules and templates with precision.

Constant use will wear down the points of technical pens, particularly if used on drafting film, and special pens with wear-resistant tips are made. Tungsten-carbide points are harder-wearing than stainless steel, but ceramic and jewel-tipped points are the most durable.

Special inks are made for work on drafting film, but since these may corrode pen mechanisms several technical pens are available that have specially treated components. These components are commonly gold-plated. Special-application technical pens can be significantly more expensive than regular technical pens and are not necessary for most graphic work.

Technical pens are also referred to as stylo-tip pens, and as "Rapidographs" — the brand name of the first really successful technical pen which found its way into popular use.

TECHNICAL PENS

Rotring makes the Rapidograph ISO and the Isograph. Staedtler makes the Marsmatic 700, and Faber-Castell makes the TG1-S. Other technical pens include the Pentel Ceranomatic, the Lyra Lyragraph 9000, the Keuffel & Esser Leroy technical pen, the Reform Refograph ISO, the Holbein Trim Graph, the KIN Rapidograph and the MG-1 technical drawing pen from Mecanorma. Most of these pens are available either individually or in sets. Spare points are available separately. Versions of many technical pens are made for use with drafting film and etching inks. These are commonly indicated by "F" added to the pen name. Typical examples are the Isograph "F" from Rotring, the Marsmatic 709 and the TG1-J from Faber-Castell ("J" in this instance indicates that the point is jewel-tipped).

Technical pens from the Rotring, Staedtler, Faber-Castell, Reform, K-E Leroy and Pentel ranges.

India ink pens

India ink is a traditional medium that has been popular with artists but has until recently been excluded from use in either fountain or technical pens. This is because it contains shellac, which is very difficult to remove once dry. However, India ink is popular because it is permanent and lightfast. The worst that can happen when it is used with a dip pen is that a cheap nib may have to be thrown away. If it clogs a fountain or technical pen — which it is inclined to do — the consequences are more serious. A few manufacturers claim to have overcome the problems associated with the use of India ink, and there are both fountain and technical pens on the market that are specially adapted for use with it. These are the only pens (other than cheap dip pens) that should be used with this type of drawing ink.

1 Scraper from an Osmiroid
  India ink pen
2 India ink pen with lid
3 Illustrator fine India ink pen

Some pens are specially adapted for use with India ink. A good example is the Osmiroid India ink pen, which includes two sketching nib units. Illustrator Pens produces an India ink rolling-ball pen which is available in three point sizes and which produces a permanent black line.

Technical pens for graphic designers

Graphic designers' technical pens outwardly resemble true technical pens and can perform to some extent in a similar fashion. They use a different operating system from that of a true technical pen. Since graphic artists have little use for the more specialized functions of technical pens, many will find that this type of pen satisfies their requirements. Most of these pens have tubular nibs in several sizes which are fed by a grooved plastic filament connected to an ink wick. At least one model available has a ceramic tip. These pens cannot be refilled with ink, but refill units that include a new tip can be bought. A modest selection of point sizes and ink colors is available with this type of pen.

Pentel manufactures the Ceramicron and Pilot make the Ceramigraph, both of which have ceramic tips. Marabu produces the M1 technical pen for graphic designers. Refill units are available in a limited selection of ink colors.

1

PILOT CERAMIGRAPH 0.50 PSC-05 JAPAN

1 Pilot Ceramigraph with parts
2 Pentel Ceramicron

Markers

Pens with felt, fiber or plastic tips are now widely used. Early versions of these marker pens were first introduced in the 1940s, but the principle is, in fact, extremely old and can be traced back to the ancient Egyptians and Chinese. Pens of this type rely on capillary action, a natural phenomenon whereby liquids creep along narrow gaps. The tips of these pens are in reality one end of a wick along which the ink flows. Their points are made of materials such as felt or compacted fibers of manmade materials. They may also be made from plastic scored on a microscopic scale to produce tiny channels along which ink can run. The different points can claim a variety of individual properties, but the average user will be able to appreciate only the most obvious differences between them. Differences in the size and shape of different points are more readily apparent and are of more practical importance.

Fine points for drawing markers are commonly sleeved in a metal tube. This supports the tip and carries it clear of the pen body, allowing close-up use against a ruling edge. The principle is the same as that for technical pens and drafting pencils. Fine porous-tipped pens like this are available in nominal point sizes. The lines they produce are less exact than with other types of pen with specified point sizes, and the tip wears and spreads with use. Other fine-point markers are unsheathed at their point and are necessarily broader at their base to support the tip. A more expressive line with some variation from fine to very fine can be achieved with this type of pen tip.

Bullet points are for more varied use. They are made with a point that is rounded rather than sharp and come in various sizes. The lines they produce are not particularly fine, and by using the pen at an angle one can produce a much broader line. Bullet points

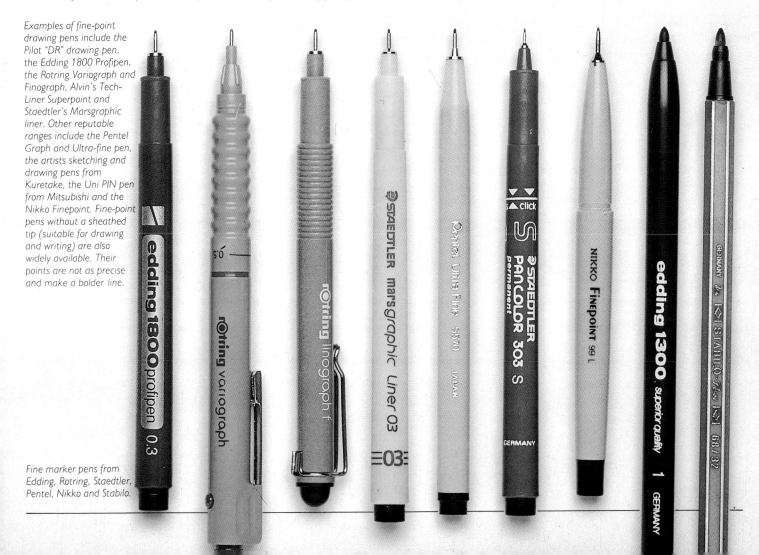

Examples of fine-point drawing pens include the Pilot "DR" drawing pen, the Edding 1800 Profipen, the Rotring Variograph and Finograph, Alvin's Tech-Liner Superpoint and Staedtler's Marsgraphic liner. Other reputable ranges include the Pentel Graph and Ultra-fine pen, the artists sketching and drawing pens from Kuretake, the Uni PIN pen from Mitsubishi and the Nikko Finepoint. Fine-point pens without a sheathed tip (suitable for drawing and writing) are also widely available. Their points are not as precise and make a bolder line.

Fine marker pens from Edding, Rotring, Staedtler, Pentel, Nikko and Stabilo.

are more suited to coloring than to drawing but, if the point is of a modest size, a reasonable combination of linear and flat effects is possible. Several manufacturers supply these pens in a generous selection of colors.

Square-cut points can be divided into two types: lettering and calligraphy points and chisel points. Lettering and calligraphy points are a fairly recent introduction and consist of a flat, square-cut porous point that imitates the effect of a standard calligraphy nib. They can be used for italic lettering and for various decorative scripts. Chisel points are usually made of a softer material in a chunky, square-sectioned tip that is cut obliquely — like a chisel — to give a point that can be used either on its thin edge, when it works very like a lettering pen, or on the cut face for large strokes that cover areas quickly. The thin edge of a chisel point allows more control when working up to a line and the flat face is best for bold coloring.

Brush points are made of manmade material and are soft and flexible but strong enough not to break or tear easily. The point is shaped like the tip of a round, fine-haired brush and tapers to a point that is fine but very flexible. The tip is intended to be handled like a brush, and the marks it makes are like brush strokes but less subtle.

PROFESSIONAL MARKER PENS

The Stabilayout pen from Schwan-Stabilo and the Edding 600 are professional marker pens with chisel points. The Design art marker from Eberhard Faber, the AD marker from Chartpak and the PANTONE®* markers from Letraset all come in a choice of point shapes, sizes and colors. Magic Markers from Royal Sovereign are available in two forms; the slimgrip in 48 colors and the fat and functional Studio Magic marker 86 in 130 colors.

Other ranges include the Graphic marker from The Graphic Marker Co. and the Illust marker from Holbein. The Berol Prismacolor is also available in a broad selection of colors. Other useful pens include the Edding 1414 Colorpen, the Pentel N50 and the Berol Toughpoint. Large tips are available on pens such as the Pentel Jumbo felt-tip, the Inscribe 770 and the Berol Flo-Master and Flo-Master Magnum.

Thicker marker pens, including those from Schwan and Pentel.

*Pantone Inc's check-standard trademark for color reproduction and color reproduction materials

Porous-tip inks

Porous-tipped pens are nearly always disposable. They contain their own inks which are provided by the manufacturer. These may be of varying quality, and it is necessary to select a pen carefully when specific properties are desired from its ink.

Both spirit-based and water-based dyes are used in inks for this type of pen, and in the cheaper ranges it is quite possible that many of these will not be lightfast. Several ranges of drawing pens, coloring pens and ink markers are made specifically for graphic designers; these are more reliable and many are permanent. The manufacturers of these quality products usually indicate whether the inks are waterproof and lightfast on the body of the pen or by providing instructions on the packaging.

Special-application inks are also available. These include all-surface inks which will write on anything, fluorescent highlighting inks for picking out text, and white opaque for blanking out. Metallic inks are also available, and some pens lay down a contrasting line of metallic ink enclosed by a colored border. Color-matched inks are available in some ranges as part of an overall color-specification system.

OTHER MARKERS AND PENS

Calligraphy tips are a feature of the Nikko HI-Graphic pen system, the Edding 1255 and the Pentel JMC calligraphy markers include the Berol Italic pen and the Speedball Elegant Writer. Special application markers and pens include all-surface pens such as the Staedtler Pan Color fiber-tip pens, highlighters such as the Berol Highlighter, opaque white pens such as the Texta from Inscribe, overhead projection markers, for example the Schwan-Stabilo-OH pen, and metallic ink pens such as the Super Color gold and silver pens from Pilot. Contrast markers, also from Pilot, produce a metallic line with a colored edge. A particularly useful pen is The Silver Genie from Griffin, which can be used to clean and correct photographic materials. Examples include the Letraset Drop-out marker and the Non-reproducing "India Ink" pen from Illustrator Pens.

BRUSH PENS

Brush pens include the Marsgraphic 3000 from Staedtler (which is available in a good selection of colors), the Pentel SF 20 brush pen and the GFL Color Brush, and the Berol Colorbrush. The Tombow brush pen is a combination pen which has a brush tip at one end and a fine tip at the other, both of which are fed from the same ink reservoir.

Selection of brush-point pens from Tombow, Edding, Staedtler and Berol.

Ballpoint and rolling-ball pens

The idea of delivering ink from a small rolling ball fitted in a socket at the end of a pen was first conceived at the end of the 19th century, but it was not until 1937 that a really practical pen was introduced. Its inventors were Ladislao and Georg Biro. The ballpoint pen is strictly a writing instrument and has a very limited use in graphic art, although it can be used for jotting down quick sketches. The problem with ballpoint pens is the quality of their ink.

A recent development of the ballpoint principle has, however, produced the rolling-ball (rollerball) pen. This is an improved system that makes use of a more conventional liquid ink and which can carry permanent inks. The line from these pens is smooth and fairly even, and it allows a degree of individual touch by the user. Rolling-ball pens are free-flowing in use and can take sharp changes in direction without faltering. There are several on the market that are acceptable for graphic work, and there is at least one that is designed for graphic artists.

Rolling-ball pens use liquid ink and deliver a neat flowing line. Several models are rechargeable using a refill pack, and several ink colors are available.

Examples include the Pentel Ball and Superball, the Edding 77 Rollingpen, the Nikko Rollerpoint, the Zig Ball from Kuretake, the Pilot Hi-Tecpoint V5 and BX5/3, the Uni-ball

Exceed from Mitsubishi and the India ink pen from Illustrator Pens. Rolling-ball pens from the Pentel, Edding, Nikko, Pilot, Zig and Illustrator ranges.

OTHER DRAWING MEDIA
Charcoal and graphite sticks

Charcoal is wood burned in a restricted supply of air. After burning, what remains is mainly carbon. The charcoal retains the shape of the original wood, and when made from twigs and small branches it produces convenient drawing instruments. Charcoal is fairly soft and will leave a mark when dragged over paper or any surface with a slight grain.

Drawing charcoal, usually made from willow, is supplied in a number of grades commonly described as thin, medium, thick and scene-painters'. Extra-large sticks are also available from some suppliers. Charcoal is supplied also in compressed form. This is evenly shaped and sized, and is produced in several degrees of hardness.

As an alternative to wooden-cased pencils, graphite can be obtained in stick form. This is processed graphite in the form of an oversized lead or crayon. The graphite content is extremely high, and graphite sticks are generally available only in a small selection of the softer pencil grades. They are sharpened in much the same way as a pencil, although care should be taken to avoid wastage. They are best suited to bold, expressive drawing and to large-scale works.

Natural charcoal is supplied by P.H. Coate & Son, Daler-Rowney, Faber-Castell, Burton Holt, Grumbacher, Holbein, Winsor & Newton, KIN and Sennelier. Most manufacturers and suppliers include it in their ranges. Compressed charcoal sticks are supplied by Conté, Faber-Castell, Burton Holt, Grumbacher, Sennelier and KIN. Graphite sticks are available in two shapes: both Faber-Castell and Conté offer the ½-inch diameter stick with a hexagonal section; and Faber-Castell offers a narrow pencil-like graphite stick. KIN also includes a graphite stick in its range.

1 Medium
2 Thin
3 Scene painters'
4,5 Compressed
6,7 Graphite sticks

Chalks, crayons and pastels

The divisions between drawing chalks, pastels and crayons are not clear-cut. In theory there may be slight differences in the hardness and in the quality of line, but the variations that occur from manufacturer to manufacturer render any attempt to qualify them as individual types impossible. They all consist of pigment mixed with a base, such as chalk, bound together in stick form by a weak medium. The variations in the type of binder and in the exact composition of the base can give rise to slightly different handling properties from one manufacturer to another.

Drawing chalks are made, in a restricted range of colors, for use in tonal drawing. These colors include the red earths — known as the sanguine shades — and black, white and brown. Drawing chalks are likely to be thinner than pastels and crayons, and may be harder and more intensely colored. They are often square in section.

Crayons are sometimes indistinguishable from pastels but may be slightly harder. They are produced in a wide range of colors which include bright, strong colors, mixed shades and tints. Insofar as they can be separated from artists' pastels, crayon ranges tend to concentrate on strong colors and may have less shades and colors. They are often thinner in section than artists' pastels.

Pastels are noticeably soft and are commonly round in section, although some are square. They are produced in extensive color ranges in which each strong color is sometimes available in a series of reduced shades and tints. A separate pastel is theoretically available for every color value that needs to be represented.

Drawing chalks, crayons and pastels all function at their best on slightly textured surfaces. All types produce very fragile color layers which are easily disturbed, and it is usual to fix them with a spray of fixative solution. The sticks themselves are quite fragile. For some ranges holders are available. These not only protect the chalk, pastel or crayon to some extent from undue pressure but also make its use cleaner and more controlled.

The Pitt Artists' Crayons from Faber-Castell are designed for tonal drawing and are available in a restricted range of colors. A similar selection of crayons is available from Conté as part of their Crayon Carrés range. The Neopastel from Caran d'Ache is also a colored artists' crayon. Eberhard Faber make Nupastel Color Sticks, and Lyra makes a modest selection of soft crayons. Faber-Castell makes the Polychromos pastel range

and Conté offers the Conté soft pastels. The Grumbacher, Rowney, Talens Rembrandt and the Lefrance & Bourgeois Girault ranges of soft pastels are all available in a very good selection of colors. However, the most extensive selection is that offered by the Sennelier A L'Ecu range which runs to more than 500 different colors, shades and tints. Pastels are also offered by Holbein, Maimeri and J. M. Paillard.

Pastels, crayons and chalks including those from Rowney and Caran d'Ache.

Soluble color sticks, oil pastels and wax crayons

Color sticks are an alternative to watercolor pencils. They are obviously suited to large-scale work where color needs to be applied strongly and broadly. They may be held as they are or fitted into a holder for protection and convenience. Like watercolor pencils, they can be used for drawing and for various mixed and painting techniques.

Oil pastels resemble ordinary crayons or pastels, but they are bound with waxes and oils, giving them a rather different feel. When built up on the surface of a drawing they take on a greasy appearance and are inclined to smear if the application of color becomes too thick. In thinner layers they give results not unlike those achieved with crayons and pastels, although they are less able to produce subtlety and softness. Oil pastels can be thinned and converted into washes by applying solvents such as turpentine. They offer a combination of drawing and oil-painting techniques, and one product claims to be oil paint in stick form.

Wax crayons are made mostly for children and have limited use for graphic artists. They are essentially sticks of dyed wax which produce a rugged, greasy line but work on most surfaces. Some ranges are of a better quality and are an acceptable tool for graphic artists. Their main use in this field is in mixed techniques, and they are particularly suitable for combination with watercolor on paper. Areas covered by wax crayon will reject watercolor, and interesting effects can be created.

Oversized leads are offered as a companion to the Albrecht Dürer watercolor pencil range by Faber-Castell, and can be mounted in a special holder. Neocolor II Aquarelle crayons are water-soluble and are available in a selection of 40 colors from Caran d'Ache. Oil pastels are offered by Inscribe, Holbein, Sennelier and Talens. The Sennelier range and the Talens Panda oil pastels both enjoy an excellent reputation among artists. Neocolor I Wax-Oil Crayons from Caran d'Ache are described as painting crayons. Stick painters such as the Edding 650 and 950 are an oil-paint paste in stick form which are used like crayons. They are quick drying and water resistant. Talens marker crayons are suitable for almost any surface.

Soluble color sticks, oil pastels and wax crayons from Edding, Lyra, Caran d'Ache and Panda.

PENCILS, PENS AND CRAYONS

SUPPLIER	Manufacturer	Distributor	Wholesaler	Retailer	Areas where products are available	Local variation in product range	Graphite	Artists/Designers	Charcoal	Leadholder	Technical/Fine Lead	Colored	Watercolor	Spirit-Soluble	Pastel	Special Application	Dip	Reservoir/Ruling	Fountain	Calligraphy/Lettering	India Ink/Pigmented Ink	Technical	Rolling Ball	Fiber Felt/Plastic Tip	Markers	Special Application	Colored	Wax	Watercolor	Spirit Soluble	Pastels	Oil Pastels
Abelscot-Marchant	•	•	•		W	No	•	•	•	•	•				•			•			•	•										
Alvin	•	•	•		US	No	•	•	•	•	•		•		•	•	•	•	•	•	•	•	•	•	•	•						
Automatic Lettering Pen Co	•				N/S	N/S									•		•															
Berol	•				W	Yes	•	•	•	•	•	•			•			•	•				•	•	•							
Burton Hart	•				W	No			•																							
Cannon & Corin	•	•			A C S UK	No											•		•			•	•	•								
Caran d'Ache	•				W	No	•	•		•	•	•	•		•		•					•		•		•	•	•	•	•	•	
Chartpak (AD Marker)	•	•			E UK US	Yes																		•	•							
P.H. Coate & Son	•				W	No			•																							
Colt Pen Co	•				N/S	N/S											•		•													
Conté	•	•			W	No	•	•	•		•	•			•						•	•	•	•			•				•	•
Daler-Rowney	•	•			W	Yes	•	•	•		•		•		•				•						•						•	•
Drafton		•	•		E UK US	No			•	•									•					•	•							
Eberhard Faber	•				C UK US	No	•	•	•		•							•		•	•	•	•					•				
C.W. Edding	•				W	No					•						•	•		•	•	•	•	•								•
Faber-Castell	•				W	N/S	•	•	•	•	•	•	•	•		•				•	•	•	•					•				
Sam Flax	•	•	•	•	W	No	•	•	•	•	•		•	•	•	•	•	•	•	•	•	•	•		•			•		•	•
General Pencil Co	•				US	No	•	•	•			•																				
The Graphic Marker Co	•				UK US	No																		•	•							
Griffin Manufacturing Co (Grifhold)	•	•			W	N/S			•								•			•												
Grumbacher	•	•			W	Yes	•	•	•			•													•					•	•	
Helix	•				N/S	N/S											•					•										
Esmond Hewerman	•	•		•	UK	No	•	•		•	•	•				•	•	•	•	•	•	•	•	•								
Holbein	•		•		W	No	•	•												•				•								
Illustrator Pens	•				N/S	N/S																•										
Inscribe	•	•			N/S	N/S				•	•											•	•	•						•	•	
Jakar International		•			UK	No	•	•	•	•	•	•					•	•		•	•	•						•				
Keuffel & Esser (Leroy)	•				N/S	N/S											•		•													

SUPPLIER	MANUFACTURER	DISTRIBUTOR	WHOLESALER	RETAILER	Areas where products are available	Local variation in product range	PENCILS Graphite	Artists/Designers	Charcoal	Leadholder	Technical/Fine Lead	Colored	Watercolor	Spirit Soluble	Pastel	Special Application	PENS Dip	Reservoir/Ruling	Fountain	Calligraphy/Lettering	India Ink/Pigmented Ink	Technical	Rolling Ball	Fibre Felt/Plastic Tip	Markers	Special Application	CRAYONS Colored	Wax	Watercolor	Spirit Soluble	Pastels	Oil Pastels
KIN Rapidograph	•	•			US C	No	•	•	•	•	•							•	•	•	•				•	•	•	•			•	
Kuretake Co	•				N/S	N/S					•									•	•	•	•									
Langford & Hill		•		•	UK	No	•	•		•	•	•	•				•	•	•	•	•	•	•	•	•						•	•
Letraset (Pantone)	•				W	N/S																	•	•	•							
Lyra GmbH	•				N/S	N/S	•	•		•	•	•	•							•	•	•									•	
Erwin Martz (Marabu)	•				N/S	N/S					•									•												
Mecanorma	•				UK	N/A														•					•							
Microflame		•			N/S	N/S	•	•	•	•	•	•	•	•	•	•	•	•	•	•	•	•	•	•	•	•	•	•	•	•	•	
Mitsubishi Pencil Co	•				W	Yes	•				•									•	•	•	•									
Osmiroid	•				W	Yes												•	•	•	•	•										
Ron Owens		•			UK	No	•	•		•	•								•	•	•	•								•		
Pebeo	•				W	No		•					•																			•
Pelikan	•				W	N/S		•										•	•	•						•	•	•	•			
Pentel	•				W	No			•	•				•				•	•	•	•	•								•	•
The Pilot Pen Co	•	•			W	Yes					•							•	•	•	•	•	•	•	•						•	
Platignum	•				W	No	•										•	•	•				•	•	•		•	•				
Reform	•				W	N/S												•			•											
Rexel (Cumberland/Derwent)	•				W	Yes	•	•			•	•	•		•			•			•	•	•		•							
Rotring		•			W	Yes					•							•	•	•		•										
Royal Sovereign	•				UK	N/S	•	•	•				•							•	•											
Schwan-Stabilo	•				W	N/S	•	•		•	•	•	•		•	•				•	•	•										
Sennelier	•				N/S	N/S	•		•																						•	•
Staedtler	•				W	No	•	•		•	•	•	•		•	•		•	•	•	•	•		•			•					
Talens	•				W	N/S																		•	•					•	•	
Tombow	•				UK US	Yes	•	•		•	•							•	•	•	•	•	•	•						•		
Winsor & Newton	•	•		•	W	Yes	•	•	•		•							•						•				•			•	•
Yasutomo & Co	•				N/S	N/S					•							•			•	•	•	•								

KEY: **A** = Australia **C** = Canada **E** = Europe (excluding UK) **S** = Scandinavia **UK** = United Kingdom **US** = United States **W** = Worldwide **N/S** = Not Stated

BRUSHES AND AIRBRUSHES

Brushes are still very commonly used, although there are now several alternative means of applying color to artwork. A brush, for example, allows the user as much control as a pen or a pencil, and also allows for personal expression where it is required. For the illustrator or the fine artist such a degree of control may be essential. For the graphic artist, who is required to produce precise lines or precise divisions between areas of color, to create perfectly flat applications of paint or textured effects within it, or to retouch photographic images, a brush may often serve a more exact and specialized purpose. And in that case, especially, it helps to have the right brush for the job.

Varieties of brush are made for almost every purpose in which a brush might conceivably be put to use. There are, accordingly, types to meet the needs of artists, designers, decorative artists, china painters, make-up artists, signwriters, calligraphers and commercial decorators. Of course, not all of these would be of help to a graphic designer, but there is considerable overlap in some areas — and a signwriters' brush designed for smooth and neat lettering might, for instance, be extremely useful for graphic work.

With sufficient knowledge and skill relating to techniques and materials there is little that can be done with an airbrush that cannot be done with a conventional brush. The reverse is not the case, however. An airbrush is an implement with a specific application that particularly lends itself to use in graphic art: what it does it does well. Desired effects may be achieved in a systematic way, and it is a happy feature of airbrush work that the means by which the results have been attained should not necessarily be immediately apparent — hence its usefulness in photographic retouching and hyper-realist illustration. It is increasingly popular as a medium in its own

right, and produces a distinctive type of image that lends itself to reproduction.

Yet the airbrush is not really a brush at all. Its relationship to the conventional brush extends no further than the fact that they are both a means of delivering color in the form of paint or ink. The way in which that delivery is made, and the mode by which it may be controlled, differ considerably; nevertheless, the fundamental similarity of purpose is sufficient reason for their inclusion together in the same chapter. And because an airbrush cannot function without an air supply, that too is dealt with here.

BRUSHES

There are countless variations and several alternative ways of classifying brushes. Important considerations include the purpose for which the brushes are intended; the size, and more significantly the shape, of the brushes; and even the type of hair that is

used. When brushes are being selected or bought it is helpful to be able to assess how appropriate they are for any specific purpose. To do this it is necessary to appreciate the relative merits of the various features that a brush may or may not possess.

1 Decorators' flat
2 Quill-mounted round
3 Short-handled brush
4 Long-handled brush (soft hair)
5 Long-handled brush (bristle)
6 Round
7 Mop
8 Filbert
9 Fan
10 Flat
11 Bright
12 Slant-cut or sword

Brush shapes

The round is perhaps the most useful and most common brush shape. Made in softer hair, the brush shape is often pointed so that the round body of hair finishes in a very delicate tip. A brush of this type may be used either for fine, linear strokes or for broader strokes and flat washes. In stiffer hair (and in some soft-hair brushes) the round may instead be given a rounded tip rather than a true point. Such a shape can deliver a controlled brush-stroke or a wash, but not a fine line. Some special-application rounds have a tip that has been cut straight across, or one that has been drawn out into a long and extremely fine point for laying lines.

Flat brushes leave a square-edged brush-mark. This may be drawn out into a broad line which, with some practice, can be used up against an edge if it is not too intricate. A large flat brush is good for filling in areas. Flat brushes may have either long or short hair, or long or short bristle. Versions with longer hair or bristle are more flexible and offer a greater variation of brush-stroke. They are also potentially useful for lettering. The short flat types can really offer only a small, squarish brush-stroke and do not hold much color, so they are suitable only for specific applications. Short flat brushes made for artists are often referred to as "brights."

The filbert is a compromise between the round and the flat. This is a flat brush which, instead of having a square end, has a curved and rounded tip when viewed from the top. It makes a flat mark of a distinctive shape that is considerably less harsh in effect than the mark made by a square-ended flat brush. If the brush is turned on its side, however, a much more linear mark is possible. And by varying the angle of tilt and the bias toward the brush's flat shape or its edge, a variety of brush-marks can be produced, and a comparatively detailed edge line can be followed. Filberts, consequently, can be very useful general-purpose brushes.

Slant-cut brushes are usually flat in format, through which the tip has been cut across at an angle rather than left square. These are useful brushes for lettering and are able to make some distinctive marks. They are seldom included in ranges intended for artists and designers (and when they are, they may occasionally be described as "sword brushes"). Rounds cut off at an angle or cut straight across may, when the hair is short, be used to deliver dots or ovals of color. Stiff-haired short rounds, cut across, are used for stenciling.

Fan-shaped brushes are used for blending wet paint, and are frequently included in ranges for artists. Many other brush shapes exist, but they are mostly variants of those described here and depend for their further specialization on the use of different hair-types or combinations of length, section and point.

SERIES 16 · ARTISTS' SABLE · WINSOR & NEWTON · ENGLAND

ISABEY 6165 MARTRE PURE FRANCE

L. CORNELISSEN & SON

Types of hair

Soft-haired brushes are used mostly with thin and very liquid paints or inks, and are associated with detail and fine finish. Stiff-haired brushes are used with thicker paints that require something stronger to manipulate them, and often lend themselves to broad techniques.

In practice, the division is not quite so clear-cut, and both soft- and stiff-haired brushes have some applications with each type of medium and technique. Only the best grades of highest-quality hair can be considered for some applications, whereas for others cheaper qualities are perfectly adequate. Special hair types are required for some highly specialized brushes.

Sable is undoubtedly the best soft hair for brushmaking; sable hair is obtained from the sable marten, a relative of the mink. It is a reddish-brown or yellow-brown hair that is fine, but strong and springy. The very best sable is known as red sable or Kolinsky sable. This makes exceptionally good brushes, although they are invariably expensive. Sable hair tapers naturally to a fine point so that brushes made from it have a very delicate and accurate tip. The natural resilience of the hair gives it a long life: if well cared for, sable brushes last a lifetime. The springiness is also an advantage in use, in that it keeps the brush-tip firm but flexible, allowing a greater degree of control than either a very stiff or a very soft brush-point.

The best brushes use Kolinsky sable either for the entire range or as an admixture in the smaller sizes. Good-quality sable, only slightly inferior to Kolinsky, is commonly used as the material for artists' and designers' brushes in order to moderate cost, and is perfectly adequate for all but the most exacting purposes.

Poorer grades of sable are to be found in brushes intended for model-makers, for leisure painters and for craft use. Their lower cost may at first sight make them an attractive proposition, but they seldom perform well enough to justify their use in fine or graphic art. The fact that both good and average-quality sable brushes are often marked simply as sable brushes can be misleading. Red sable brushes are generally

1 Sable
2 Squirrel
3 Ox
4 Pony
5 Synthetic (golden)
6 Bristle
7 Goat
8 Synthetic (white)
9 Badger

marked "Kolinsky."

Squirrel hair is much softer than sable, and a brush made from it cannot hold its shape in use or be as easy to control as a sable brush can. The hair is most commonly a dark brown. Squirrel is, however, much cheaper than sable, so it finds favor as a hair suitable for educational and student use. (A large wash brush in squirrel is a fraction of the cost of an equivalent brush in sable.) It does make good wash brushes, especially in the larger sizes, because the sheer bulk of the brush can give the tip some solidity. This increases the potential for control, although very fine control is still not possible.

Ox hair is strong and springy, but the individual hairs are quite coarse. It is not suitable for use in fine-pointed brushes, therefore, but it is a very good hair for use in square-cut flat brushes. Ox hair is generally yellowish brown with some lighter-colored hairs mingled in. It is taken from the ear of a species of cow, yet for some unaccountable reason is occasionally referred to as camel hair, a term used indiscriminately for various soft hairs. Brushes made with ox hair

frequently have a long hair-length in comparison with similar brushes made from sable; this increases their flexibility and allows them good color-carrying capacity.

Pony hair is commonly dark brown or black. It is a coarse hair that is not particularly responsive in use but makes acceptable round and flat brushes for laying areas of color on a reasonably large scale. It is used mostly for low-priced brushes in fairly large sizes, as artists' and designers' brushes.

Pony hair may be used in mixed-hair brushes too. These are blends of natural hair types which are intended to provide reasonable performance at a modest or even a very low price. Mixed-hair brushes vary considerably in quality, and the description can mean almost any combination of natural hair types. The better mixes make acceptable general-purpose brushes, but are of little use for demanding work in which precision and detail are required. What is meant exactly by terms such as "imitation squirrel hair" is uncertain, but it is reasonably safe to assume that some variety of mixed hair is referred to.

Bristle is the main stiff hair used in brushmaking. This is obtained from pigs and is now for the most part imported from China. For artists' and designers' brushes only the white bristle of a particular species of boar is used, but coarser black bristle and mixed qualities of bristle may be used in brushes intended for other purposes. The best bristle is obtained from an area around the pig's backbone, and this has to be collected and selected by hand. (Because bristle brushes contain pig hair they are commonly referred to as hog tools.)

Bristle is much harder-wearing, tougher and springier than any of the soft hairs. In use it is far more resistant to manipulation: bristle yields and flattens in response to the movement of the hand only if the hair is of a reasonable length. Even then its give depends on the angle at which it is held and the pressure that is applied to it. Bristle brushes are more commonly used with the stiffer mediums such as oil or acrylic, but they may be used with fluid media if a broad technique is employed. The only real difficulty that might arise in such use is that

BRUSH SIZES (SOFT HAIR)

Quality soft-haired brushes are sized according to the width of the ferrule. A good range is likely to run from size 0-12, but some ranges start at size 000 and may extend to size 14. Cheaper hair types are supplied in a restricted range of sizes. Although sizing is fairly standard, there may be some variation between products from different manufacturers.

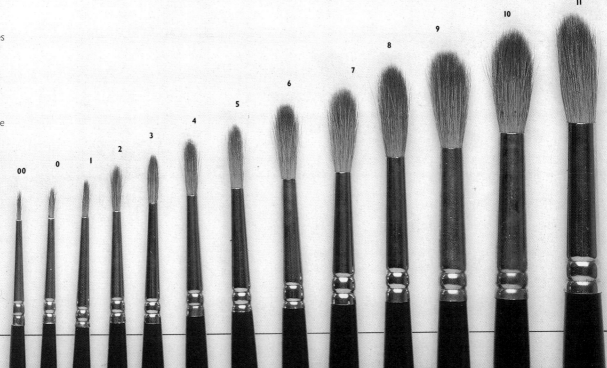

00 0 1 2 3 4 5 6 7 8 9 10 11

the stiff bristle could damage a sensitive painting surface if it is used too vigorously. A good bristle brush is likely to get softer and more responsive after a period of use. Fine points are impossible on hog brushes, but most are constructed with an edge or a point of sorts that allows a mark of a definite size and shape to be made.

One of the main differences between bristle and hair is found at the end of each individual strand. Hair tapers out to a fine point, but a bristle splits into several small points (called flags) at its tip. The best bristle brushes have these intact. On lower-grade bristle brushes — particularly those intended for educational or industrial use — the brush has often been shaped by cutting and trimming the bristle ends, and the result is a brush that has less shape and that holds less color. These are sometimes referred to as "fitch" brushes, although the meaning of that term — which once described a brush made from a particular type of hair — is no

longer applied in a predictable way. For large areas and commonplace jobs these cheaper bristle brushes may be perfectly adequate.

Goat hair is white and coarse. It is not a particularly stiff hair, but it is too sturdy to call soft. Its use in brushmaking is limited but it does occur from time to time in larger brushes and in oriental brushes.

Badger is a rare and expensive hair best classified as stiff. It is usually two-tone, showing shades of gray and white. Its main use is in making blending brushes for evening out the effects of brush-marks and for producing softened color changes. The badger is a protected species in many countries, so the supply of badger brushes is limited. Yet at least one badger-hair brush is made specifically for artists; larger badger-hair brushes for decorators can be made to order by the brushmakers; and the hair is still ordinarily used in high-quality shaving-brushes (which, not surprisingly, can make very useful items of equipment for artists, graphic artists and designers).

Synthetic fibers have been introduced in an attempt to control costs and to overcome shortages in supplies of high-grade natural hair. The main target has been to replace

sable with something that can give a similarly high performance at a lower cost. Qualities have been produced that bridge the gap between the finesse of fine hair and the sturdy qualities of bristle.

Beware of extremely cheap synthetic brushes in which the filaments have cut ends. These are solely for educational use (although, incidentally, they are of no more use to children than they are to graphic designers.)

For a synthetic fiber to work well in a brush it must be drawn out to a tapering point just like a natural hair. Some reasonable, though by no means perfect, substitutes for sable are now available. These are often a golden yellow in color, which loosely resembles sable but is easily distinguished from it; others may be plain white. Plain white synthetic fibers are also used in brush shapes that are commonly associated with bristle, but they are again easy to distinguish from the real thing. For certain purposes these give quite satisfactory results. A few manufacturers are also combining real sable and synthetic hair in an attempt to achieve the desired balance between cost and quality.

BRUSH SIZES (BRISTLE)

Quality bristle brushes are sized according to the width of the ferrule. A good range may run from 1 to 12. It is not unusual for bristle ranges to offer only alternate sizes or to exclude less popular sizes. Larger sizes may be found in ranges for scene painters and decorators. Sizing is fairly standard between manufacturers, but Continental manufacturers use smaller standard sizes. Cheap bristle brushes (hog-fitch) may be slightly oversized compared to other bristle brushes.

Brushes for special applications

Depending on the circumstances, almost any brush may prove useful to a graphic artist . . .

Small soft-haired brushes officially made for signwriters are excellent for laying even lines and for lettering. These have a much longer extension of hair from the ferrule than either artists' or designers' brushes and end in a flat-edged tip known as a chisel edge.

Stencil brushes may obviously be useful, and lacquer brushes may also find applications. Paste brushes in small sizes are useful for applying glues and pastes in the studio, and a very clean mop brush can be used to dust off artwork without causing damage.

Oriental brushes are interesting because they are made somewhat differently stiff hair, like bristle or goat, is built into points in them to create a very flexible and quite fine-tipped instrument. They are intended for oriental calligraphy — but they do have other possibilities.

1 Mop brush
2 Stencil brush
3 Signwriters' chisel-edged brush
4 Soft-haired lacquer brush
5,6 Oriental brushes

Artists' and designers' brushes

Brushes intended primarily for artists and designers are generally made of sable or of white bristle. In the case of sable brushes there are in fact some slight differences between those intended for fine artists and those intended for graphic artists. The typical sable brush is round and pointed. An artist's version has a good body of hair coming to a very fine point, and extends from the ferrule far enough to make it flexible yet able to withstand the broad action of a wash stroke. A designer's brush is very similar, but the hair extends farther from the ferrule so that the head of the brush is longer. This gives greater flexibility to the point and makes the brush more suitable for laying lines or for following contours. For tight control over the point the length of hair extending from the ferrule needs to be shorter. Brushes made in this fashion are offered to artists as miniature-painting brushes, but brushes with even shorter hair are made for graphic artists and are known as retouching brushes.

Pointed rounds, flats, brights and filberts are usually made in sable, particularly in the smaller sizes, and are offered as artists' and designers' brushes. Fan-shaped brushes for blending are made in both sable and bristle. Alternative ranges in synthetic fibers are now offered by many manufacturers, following the accepted shapes and sizes of traditional artists' and graphic artists' brushes. Bristle brushes nearly always have long stick-like handles when they are supplied to artists, whereas sable and other soft-haired brushes are mostly on short handles. The reason is traditional: short-handled brushes are commonly associated with watercolor and gouache, and long-handled brushes are associated with oil, and so it has become the practice of manufacturers to offer some versions of their fine soft-haired brushes with long handles. Long-handled sable brushes very like designers' points are still supplied to artists as sable "riggers," a name that has stuck from the time when such brushes were used

for the rigging on marine paintings.

Brushes are categorized in size by numbers. Typically, a range might run from 0 to 12, although it is not unusual to find ranges in bristle that offer only alternate sizes. There is no relationship between sizes in sable or soft hair and sizes in bristle.

1 Quill-mounted designers' sable	8 Larger sized miniature brush
2,3,4 Miniature painting and retouching brushes	9 Kolinsky sable round
5 Short-haired sable flat	10 Ox-hair flat
6 Sable writer	11 Wash brush
7 Short-handled sable filbert	12 Long-handled sable flat

AIRBRUSHES

The airbrush was invented toward the end of the 19th century. Although the exact date on which a practical airbrush was introduced is open to debate, it is a matter of recorded history that one Charles L. Burdick, an American living in Britain, was granted a patent for their manufacture in 1893. He set up a business called the Fountain Brush Company in London and began producing his product, which he called an aerograph. Burdick was an inventor and engineer, but in his spare time was apparently an artist working with watercolors. His aim was to create a device which could deliver one color on top of another without disturbing the lower one, a procedure that is difficult in watercolor. His invention fulfilled this requirement satisfactorily, and it is still a technical feature of the airbrush that is highly valued.

The first aerograph had a platinum nozzle and a color-cup within its body. The air hose had a simple push-on fitting. Between 1900 and the 1920s, various facets of the design were improved, and by the end of that period several rival manufacturers had entered the field. Burdick's invention included the centralized needle and matching nozzle that are still part of modern airbrush design, but the atomizing system now employed in airbrushes was originally developed for other purposes. It was the brainchild of Dr Alan De Vilbiss, an ear, nose and throat specialist who was looking for a system of delivering medicines that would improve on the ordinary swab. His own invention was made around 1890. Later, he and Burdick became friends and in 1931 pooled their ideas and resources to form an airbrush-manufacturing company that still exists and that is still one of the best-known names in the market.

How an airbrush works

An airbrush works by compressed gas, which has a low volume and therefore a high pressure. If it is released suddenly, its volume expands rapidly and its pressure drops. Allowing compressed air to escape through a narrow gap produces this effect, and if the flow of air is continuous the area of reduced pressure remains static. If a liquid is then fed into that area of reduced pressure, it is drawn out and becomes semi-gaseous itself, splitting into minute particles, or atomizing.

Atomization may occur internally or externally — that is, it can occur inside or outside the airbrush. External atomization is found only in very basic airbrushes in which the paint-feed is at the tip of the airbrush, immediately outside its body, and the stream of air is blown across it. At this point it has already begun to expand and its take-up dispersion of paint is imperfect. The atomization process is less thorough, and the resulting spray is not as fine or as even as it could be.

With internal atomization, the paint-feed is placed in the airflow at the point at which the pressure of the air first drops, usually just inside the nozzle opening. The air is still partly compressed at this point, and further expansion occurs as the air leaves the tip of the airbrush, causing the atomization process to continue and resulting in a very fine and even spray.

The flow of paint and air may be controlled by a variety of mechanisms, all dependent on very finely engineered parts. The smoothness of operation relies to a great extent on the fine machining of the channels through which air and paint flow. The gas need not be air, although that is most common; carbon dioxide and other special gases are sometimes used. Nor need the colorant be paint as such: ink or any liquid colorant may in theory be used. In practice, however, certain properties are required of the coloring matter in order to allow efficient working. It must be fine enough and liquid enough to pass through the airbrush without causing blockages, and should not contain binding media that might foul the delicate parts of the mechanism.

Types of airbrush

Most airbrushes employ one of three mechanisms for their operation: the single-action, the double action, or the independent double-action.

The single-action has a control button on the top of the airbrush. When this is depressed the air supply is activated, but there is no separate control over the supply of paint. As a result, neither the paint-to-air ratio nor the delivery pattern of the spray can be varied. The desired control has as a result to be exercised by moving the airbrush toward or away from the work surface. Some single-action airbrushes have a separate control for altering the paint ratio, but this has to be set prior to use, so that the supply of color cannot be altered during the actual painting process.

The double-action mechanism — also known as the fixed double-action system — has, instead of a control button, a lever on top of the airbrush, which can be depressed by the user's finger. As the lever is depressed it activates first the air valve and then the supply of paint; the first part of the movement thus allows the air to flow on its own, and further depression of the lever activates the paint supply, releasing the color into the stream of air. The amount of paint that is delivered into the constant airstream can be varied: the paint may be fed in gradually, or may be tailed away, by depressing or releasing the lever gently at the point at which the color supply is first activated. This permits a more sophisticated approach to technique than is possible with a single-action airbrush. However, the air-flow and paint-flow cannot be controlled separately or simultaneously.

The independent double-action mechanism allows the user the most control. It has a combined control button and lever mounted on top: pressing down on it

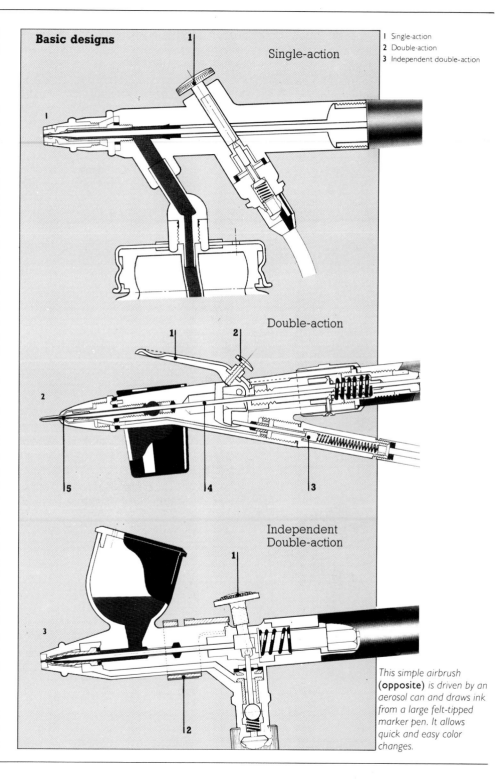

Basic designs

1 Single-action
2 Double-action
3 Independent double-action

Single-action

Double-action

Independent Double-action

*This simple airbrush (**opposite**) is driven by an aerosol can and draws ink from a large felt-tipped marker pen. It allows quick and easy color changes.*

activates and controls the air supply, and pulling back on it activates and controls the color feed. Both air and color supply can be varied independently, so the ratio between air and paint may be varied as desired, and some very subtle effects may be achieved by appropriate adjustments of the air-to-paint ratio. Because the controls on independent double-action airbrushes are very sensitive, it is usual to fit them with a stop in the form of an adjusting screw or cam ring. This means that the flow of paint and air can be kept at a constant, or may be returned to a preset level during operation, if required.

Three other types of airbrush should be mentioned. The first is an unsophisticated product which is inexpensive and convenient for general studio use. This is the felt-tip airbrush, presently offered by at least two manufacturers.

The felt-tip airbrush is a small holder consisting almost entirely of an air nozzle fitted over a felt-tip pen: the air supply is from an aerosol can. When the control lever is depressed, air jets across the tip of the pen, using it as an ink feed. Changing the color of the ink is a very simple process: the pen in the holder is simply changed for another one — and because these slip-over airbrushes correspond with extensive ranges of designers' marker pens, the choice of colors is extensive.

The turbine airbrush is at present offered by only one manufacturer. In this airbrush the air supply is fed through a turbine which in turn operates the motion of a needle. This needle moves backward and forward, passing alternately into the color supply and into the airstream. Every time the needle enters the paint supply it picks up a tiny amount of color which it then releases into the airflow as it next encounters it. The movement of the needle is related to the speed of the turbine, and because the user may control the speed of the turbine very accurately, very fine control is possible over the whole delivery system. A distinct advantage of this type of airbrush is that it may be used to spray a very fine line.

A canister airbrush again makes use of an unusual mechanism, and is also at present offered by only one manufacturer. This has an integral color-mixing facility and is fed from a canister containing basic colors. A control dial can be set as required, and various shades and tints may be produced as a result. This has distinct advantages over other airbrushes which can accommodate only one color at a time.

Regardless of whether it is single-actioned, double-actioned or independent double-actioned, an airbrush may be supplied with color by either of two different feed systems; which varies from model to model. Gravity-feed systems have a reservoir for color mounted on top, and the paint is fed into the brush under its own weight. The capacity of the reservoir — which is sometimes in the form of a cup — is not large, but such reservoirs are easily refilled during use. Airbrushes fitted with this type of paint feed are usually quite light and easy to handle, which makes them particularly suitable for detailed work. The alternative form is siphon-feed, in which the color is drawn up into the airbrush from a color container that is located either below or to one side of the airbrush. Siphon-feed airbrushes can carry more color and facilitate comparatively quick and easy color changes.

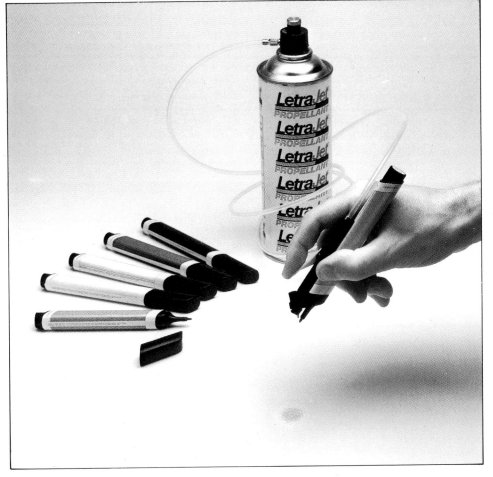

They are especially useful when large areas have to be sprayed, but they are sometimes a little too bulky and heavy to allow really delicate handling.

TYPES OF AIRBRUSHES

1 Badger 400 touch-up gun
2 De Vilbiss MP spray gun
3 Paasche air eraser
4 Thayer and Chandler Model C
5 Badger 200
6 Paasche VLS
7 Paasche H3
8 Badger 110 LG
9 Paasche Turbo
10 De Vilbiss Super 63
11 De Vilbiss Sprite
12 Conopois
13 Olympos SP-B

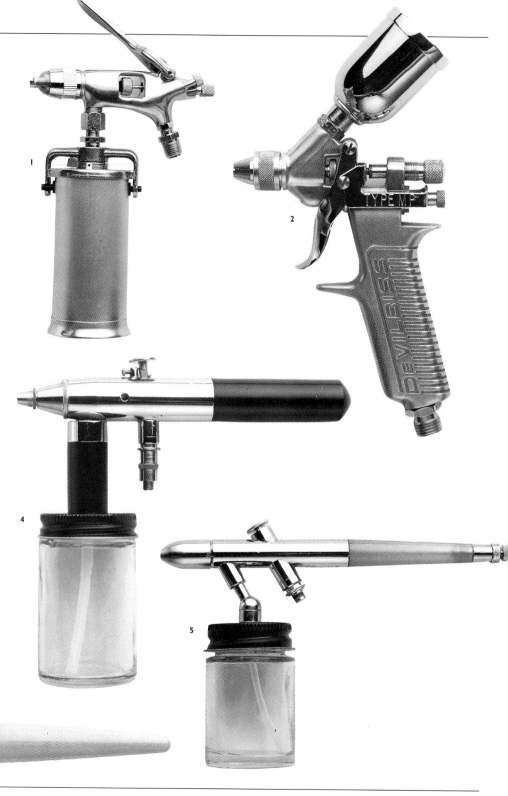

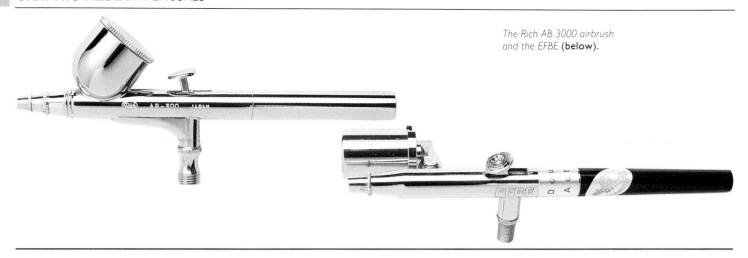

The Rich AB 3000 airbrush and the EFBE (below).

Air and gas supply

Ideally, the supply of air to an airbrush should be even, at a constant pressure. There are two main sources of supply: containers of one sort or another of compressed air or gas, or power-driven compressors which manufacture the pressurized air as and when it is required.

Containers of compressed air or gas are expensive to use if they are used more than minimally — but they are a much cheaper starting-point than a compressor. Aerosol cans for the purpose generally contain either carbon dioxide or a gas such as freon — as opposed to air — and may be used to power most types of airbrush. They constitute handy back-up power supplies as well, of course, and are often thus kept for emergencies like compressor failure by professional airbrush users.

Aerosols come in different sizes, but the capacity of all aerosol gas supplies is limited — cans require frequent changing. One particular disadvantage is that as a can uses up its contents, the pressure at which gas is expressed steadily reduces. This can be overcome to some extent by fitting a pressure-regulator, only to be subject to the limitation that once the pressure falls below a certain point the supply dries up even though there may still be a fair amount of gas remaining in the container.

Believe it or not, one semi-professional dodge is to use old car tyres in a similar fashion to provide a supply of compressed air: if they can be refilled at a convenient garage they can be a very cost-effective way to power an airbrush; they may, indeed, also be fitted with a pressure-regulator to overcome the fact that the pressure drops as the air is expelled.

A third type of power supply in a container is a cylinder of compressed gas. In effect this is a scaled-up aerosol which contains considerably more gas and at a much greater pressure. Compressed gas cylinders are used industrially for a variety of

AIRBRUSH ACCESSORIES
1 De Vilbiss air line
2 Badger air line
3 Paasche air line
4 Filter
5 Pressure regulator
6 Combined filter/regulator
7 Paasche moisture trap

purposes and are available with any of a large number of different gases in them. However, carbon dioxide is most favoured for powering airbrushes — and is likely to be considerably safer in use than some other gases currently marketed. A pressure-regulator *must* be fitted to a gas cylinder — the pressure in it is so high to begin with, and must be released in a controlled way.

There are quite a few types of compressor, some more sophisticated and more expensive than others.

The diaphragm compressor is the most basic, and pumps air using a flexible diaphragm. The air supply is not even: it pulses, and this can affect the spray pattern noticeably, particularly if delicate work is being attempted. An advance on this is the storage compressor.

A storage compressor has a small storage tank for the compressed air set between the input from the pump and the output to the airbrush. This arrangement ensures that the air supply is not directly from the pump mechanism itself, but from a pressurized container that the pump is constantly refilling

with more air. The only disadvantage with storage compressors is that those currently on the market are not constructed for very heavy duty and have to be rested for periods to prevent them from overheating.

Piston compressors are better. These use a piston tightly fitted into a cylinder to compress the air, and work rather like a car engine in reverse. The piston is driven usually by an electric motor, and compresses the gas in the cylinder. Many piston compressors are lubricated and cooled by oil, and it is essential that the level is kept to the required mark — like simple storage compressors, piston compressors may overheat if run for long periods.

The automatic compressor is another form of storage compressor and the most sophisticated. When the tank is full, the compressor shuts off automatically, and only comes back into action when the pressure in the storage tank falls below a set level. This means that the compressor is not running continually, so that because the engine operates only intermittently there is little risk of overheating.

Airbrush propellants from Frisk and Letraset.

COMPRESSORS

1 Simair SAC 110
2 Badger 180 Automatic
3 Simair SAC 330
4 Dawson McDonald & Dawson D351 VM

BRUSHES AND AIRBRUSHES

SUPPLIER	MANUFACTURER	DISTRIBUTOR	WHOLESALER	RETAILER	Areas supplied, or in which goods are available	Variation in range of goods	Soft-haired	Stiff-haired	Designers	Artists	Retouching	Lining	Stencil	Blending	Mop	Lettering	Oriental	Airbrushes	Compressors	Propellant Cans	Marker Brushes	Cleaning Materials
Abelscot-Marchant	•	•	•		W	No												•	•	•		•
The Airbrush Co		•	•		E UK	No												•	•	•		•
Alvin	•	•	•		W	No				•					•							
The Art Factory	•	•			W	No	•	•	•	•	•	•	•		•							
Art Material International	•	•	•		W	N/S												•	•	•		•
Atlantis		•		•	N/S	N/A	•	•		•	•	•	•		•	•	•					
Badger	•				W	No												•	•	•		
Berol	•				W	No				•												
BFE/Drafton		•	•		E UK US	No	•	•	•	•	•	•	•	•	•	•						
Calder (Ocaldo)	•				W	No	•	•	•				•		•							
Conopois	•	•	•	•	A E UK	No												•	•	•		•
Conte	•				W	Yes	•	•	•	•					•							
Daler-Rowney	•	•			W	No	•		•	•	•			•	•							
Eberhard-Faber	•				C US	No		·												•		
Sam Flax	•	•		•	W	No	•	•	•				•	•		•		•	•	•	•	•
Habico	•				W	N/S	•	•	•	•	•	•	•	•	•	•						
Hamilton	•	•			UK	N/A	•	•	•	•	•	•	•	•	•	•						
Handover	•				A UK US	No	•	•	•	•	•	•	•	•	•							
Holbein	•		•		W	No	•	•	•	•	•	•	•				•	•	•	•		•
Jakar International		•			UK	No				•												
KIN Rapidograph	•	•			C US	No	•	•		•										•		•

SUPPLIER	Manufacturer	Distributor	Wholesaler	Retailer	Areas supplied, or in which goods are available	Variation in range of goods	Soft-haired	Stiff-haired	Designers	Artists	Retouching	Lining	Stencil	Blending	Mop	Lettering	Oriental	Airbrushes	Compressors	Propellant Cans	Marker Brushes	Cleaning Materials
Langford & Hill		•	•	•	W	No	•	•	•	•	•	•	•	•	•	•	•	•	•	•	•	•
Langnickel	•				W	No	•	•	•	•	•	•	•	•	•	•	•					
Lukas	•				W	No	•	•	•	•						•	•				•	
Maimeri		•			UK	No	•		•	•	•	•	•			•						
Marabu	•				W	No	•	•	•													
Microflame			•		N/S	N/S					•	•	•	•	•	•	•	•	•	•	•	
Pebeo	•				W	No			•	•												•
H.W. Peel & Co	•	•			W	No	•	•	•	•												
Pelikan	•				W	No	•	•		•						•					•	
Salis International (Dr. P.H. Martins)	•				W	No												•	•			
ETS Max Sauer (Raphael)	•				W	No	•	•	•	•	•	•	•	•	•	•	•					
Schmincke	•				W	No																•
Simair	•	•			A C E UK US	No												•	•			
D. Simons			•		W	No	•	•	•	•								•	•	•	•	
Talens (Dr. P.H. Martin)	•				W	No	•	•	•	•	•	•	•	•	•	•	•	•				
Winsor & Newton	•	•		•	W	No	•	•	•	•	•	•	•			•						•

KEY: A = Australia **C** = Canada **E** = Europe (excluding UK) **S** = Scandinavia **UK** = United Kingdom **US** = United States **W** = Worldwide **N/S** = Not Stated

PAINTS AND INKS

Designers can now use any of several alternative means of applying color to artwork. There are, for example, extensive ranges of pens and pencils, pre-printed papers and computerized paintboxes. Yet the traditional coloring media — paints and inks — still constitute an area of materials that are essential to graphic designers.

Within this field, certain products and product ranges are aimed specifically at graphic artists; others are not, and may be aimed instead (at least officially) at applications in fine art. These fine-art materials should nevertheless be regarded as available to designers if they should wish to use them, and may prove suitable to a greater or lesser degree, depending in each instance on the particular applications that they are put to. There is no clear-cut division, for all paints and all inks are generally products of a similar type.

Subtle differences do obtain, however, between the requirements of fine and graphic artists, and the differences are reflected in the product ranges. Permanence, for example, may be of considerably more importance to fine artists, who may wish their work to last, than to graphic designers, whose work may have fulfilled its purpose as soon as it is recorded photographically. This may not, of course, apply to the work of an illustrator, which may readily be assessed both as an example of fine art and as a piece of commercial artwork.

Graphic designers need colors that correspond, roughly at least, to those which can actually be reproduced in print; graded tones or special qualities of finish may also be required for specific purposes such as photo-retouching. Colors that are visually striking — such as fluorescents, metallic colors, or bright and vivid variants of the primary colors — are frequently particularly suited to the work of graphic artists, and consequently tend to feature more often in the various ranges intended for designers.

The paints and inks considered here include both fine art and graphic design products. It is reasonable to regard them all as graphic artists' materials, but it has to be acknowledged that some are inevitably of limited interest in this field. High-quality artists' oil-color, for example, despite all its virtues, is impractical for everyday studio use, and probably appeals mostly to illustrators. Gouache has always been regarded as a graphic artist's medium, although it is evident that some ranges are more clearly intended for use in graphic art than others. Products such as acrylics may well be as much use to designers as to fine artists. Transparent liquid watercolors, colored inks and dyes, and specialized drawing inks, however, are certainly designers' products, as are process colors and retouching colors.

Pigments and dyes

The basic coloring matter in all paint and ink is pigment or dye. In a wider, more general context the word "pigment" can refer to any coloring matter, but here we are restricting it to its more technical meaning of a solid material, usually in the form of a finely-ground colored powder. A dye, on the other hand, is generally liquid, although it may occur as a solid in a concentrated form. A liquid dye can in fact be converted into a solid pigment by a simple chemical process — indeed, a number of reliable modern colorants are made in this way — but it is usual to regard them as totally separate categories of material. The two types of coloring matter work differently, and each lends itself to particular uses.

Paints combine tiny particles of pigment with binding materials. Although the paint may be used in a very liquid state, the colored pigment within it is at all times solid; it behaves like a liquid only because of the finely-crushed state of the pigment particles, and because of their even dispersion within the liquid medium. When the paint dries, the color seen represents a layer of solid pigment that sits on top of the surface to which it has been applied. Solid applications of color, texture and impasto are possible only with paints that contain a solid ingredient.

A dye behaves like a liquid because it *is* a liquid, and can behave in no other way. Dyes actually penetrate the surfaces to which they are applied, staining them with the color of the dye.

In practice there are notable differences between colorative materials containing pigments and those containing dyes: although several pigments are in fact transparent or semi-transparent in use, many are not, but dyes are almost invariably transparent. Because dyes permeate and stain the surfaces to which they are applied, they can be very difficult to remove from areas of artwork in which they have been wrongly placed. (This applies also to pigments based on dyes.) Dyes may also migrate — that is, they may move from the place where they are put into an adjacent area or through a superimposed color. It would be wrong to overstate this risk, but migration can occasionally cause problems, particularly when solvents are used in the preparation of the work. Dyes offer some extremely rich, glowing colors, but often at the expense of permanence.

Paint manufacture

All paints were originally made by hand, and modern manufacturing processes for artists' and designers' paints are still essentially just mechanized versions of the old hand process. This is significant because in terms of paint-making technology the methods used for the preparation of artists' and designers' materials are rather old-fashioned.

A major reason for this is that such materials are available in a base state, from which the user can alter them by thinning or mixing to achieve desired results. They are different from the commercial and technical colorists' requirements in that they are specifically *not* ready-finished products to be simply applied without further modification. The higher the quality of a range of artists' and designers' paints, the more likely it is to have been produced by traditional methods.

Attempts to introduce newer technology into this area of paint-making have been limited (and have sometimes provoked an unfavorable reaction from artists). However, the exceptional performance of certain materials, and the very particular application intended for some graphic designers' products, are possible only as a result of the modern science of paint chemistry.

Most artists' and designers' paint is made following a basic process. Pure, finely powdered pigment is mixed with a binding material, which acts like a glue, in sufficient quantity to fix the paint when it is applied. Additional ingredients — such as stabilizers, preservatives and wetting agents — are put in if required, and the resulting paste or slurry is then put through milling equipment which breaks it down.

For artists' and designers' paints the Triple Roller Mill is generally used. This is a machine with three cylindrical rollers set in a line and rotating at different speeds. The gaps between the rollers are very small, and as the pigment paste is fed into the machine it is forced between them, breaking down any oversized particles and insuring a smooth,

even distribution of pigment particles within the medium. The finished paint is scraped from the last roller by an adjustable blade, and, if necessary, the process is repeated until a desired consistency and quality is achieved. Variations in the process and ingredients determine what type of paint is being made; such considerations are discussed below.

Paint qualities

Although there is no formal standard for artists' materials, it is the accepted practice of most manufacturers to produce specific types of paint in a choice of at least two qualities. Some produce more than this and may offer as many as four different versions of one type of paint. The exact differences between such ranges are not always made clear, but there is generally a top-quality range which may be designated an artists' or designers' range, and there are ranges intended for less professional users (such as students, leisure painters and amateur artists). The top ranges should contain only the finest ingredients, prepared to the highest quality, and should be capable of performing well in the most demanding applications.

In reality there are often variations in quality between the ranges of one manufacturer and those of another, because of the differences in the pigments used and the extent to which additions such as stabilizers are included in the composition. In principle, however, they should all be of an approximately similar standard. Ranges of such quality are mostly priced individually — the cost of each color reflecting the actual cost of the pigment that it contains — and some are very expensive. They can nonetheless be economical to use if used properly, and the highest quality is thus preferred by many practicing artists, illustrators and designers.

It is difficult to be specific about paints of lesser quality; no manufacturer seems prepared to give full details of the ingredients

Tempera paint is made by mixing powdered pigment, as shown here, with an egg solution. The wide range of pigment means that tempera can be produced in vivid colors.

of such ranges, although a few publish some details about their composition. A feature of these ranges is that they usually constitute a one-price range: all colors are for sale at the same fixed price per tube. The selection of colors is usually smaller than that of the professional ranges, and many of them may be substitute colors — that is, they may not contain the expensive pigment after which they have been named, but contain a similarly-colored substitute more economical to use. Such substitution is commonly indicated by the terms "Hue" or "Imit.," placed near the name in smaller lettering. Sometimes these substitutes are based on inferior pigments or dyes, but most often they are a combination of cheap but reliable colors and powerful modern pigments that are strong enough to maintain their coloring power when extended.

It is reasonable to assume that extenders (or fillers, which are solids with little coloring power of their own) are added to several, if not all, of these ranges. It is also reasonable to assume that expensive binders are replaced by less costly products when possible without an excessive loss of quality. Most of these ranges give acceptable results for many purposes and are certainly attractive from the point of view of their price, but are decidedly less satisfactory for certain purposes than the Artists' or Designers' ranges. For the sake of convenience, the term "Sketching Quality" has been applied to such colors in the text and charts, although this may not coincide with individual manufacturer's descriptions of their products, and should be interpreted only as meaning that these are not the top-quality products in any range. Substantial variations may occur between them.

GOUACHE

Gouache paints are often aimed specifically at designers. Most major manufacturers of artists' colors supply them, but the most extensive selection is offered by Schmincke. In addition to their finest artists' gouache they offer five other ranges including airbrush gouache and retouching gouache (matte and gloss finish) for use on photographs. Schmincke's HKS Designers' colors include a range of gouache paints linked to the HKS color specification system, which includes papers, marker pens and painting inks.

TEMPERA

Tempera is used by some suppliers as an alternative name for gouache. Genuine tempera colors are offered by Daler-Rowney and Sennelier. Many tempera painters prefer to prepare their own colors using pigments. These can be bought from Sennelier, Schmincke, Maimeri, Winsor & Newton, or from specialist suppliers such as J.P. Stephenson or L. Cornelissen.

POSTER COLORS

Poster colors feature in the ranges of a number of major manufacturers, but they are not always clearly distinguishable from gouache paints. Winsor & Newton and Rowney both offer good ranges.

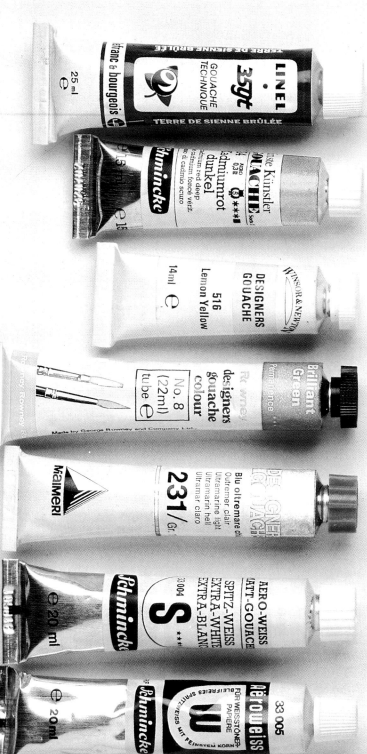

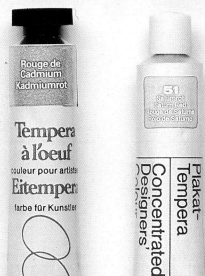

Gouache, tempera and poster colors

Gouache, tempera and poster colors are all similar paint types. In fact, there are differences between them, but the techniques by which they are applied and the end results that they produce do not differ greatly. To some extent the names are interchangeable in any case, and in some countries one product known as gouache may somewhere else be known as tempera. All are water-based paints and are quick-drying. Most of them dry to give a matte finish, or one with a slight sheen, although at least one version produces a gloss finish.

Gouache is, in theory, body color — that is, it is watercolor made opaque by the addition of either white pigment or an opaque filler. If Chinese White, for example, is mixed with ordinary watercolor, the result is a gouache finish. There is no fixed composition for gouache paints, and although most of them generally contain a gum binder, like watercolors, they may alternatively be prepared using various glues or starches. In practice, gouache ranges vary considerably between those of one manufacturer and those of another, in both color strength and opacity. It is therefore advisable to try out samples from a few ranges in order to assess the suitability of any specific product for a particular method of working. Good opacity is frequently more important than strength of color — but it is as well to have both if possible.

Gouache is commonly available in tubes and jars; most gouache ranges are aimed specially at designers. Some manufacturers make a point of recommending their products for airbrush use. At least one range is made especially for photo-retouching; another includes colors specifically matched to the three color-values used in color printing; and several ranges of greys are marketed. Gouache paint quickly dries out: it is advisable always to replace the tops of containers immediately after use, and to keep them clean and tight-fitting.

Tempera paint is now regarded strictly as paint that uses natural egg as a binding medium, although various egg emulsions and natural proteins may in fact alternatively be used as binders. Many fine artists who work in tempera prefer to prepare their own paint in the traditional manner, mixing pigment and egg directly as it is required, but there are some ready-made tempera ranges. Tempera paint is very like gouache in use, but is perhaps better for building up layers of superimposed color: it is less easily disturbed once it has dried. Very soft and subtle effects may be achieved using tempera.

"Poster color" is the term sometimes applied to gouache sold in jars, although it may occasionally refer conversely to a slightly different quality of paint when it is offered as a range in its own right, separate from the same manufacturer's gouache range.

Gouache, tempera and watercolor paints from Linel, Schmincke, Winsor & Newton, Rowney, Maimeri and Pelikan.

GOUACHE, EGG-TEMPERA AND POSTER PAINTS

MANUFACTURER/ DISTRIBUTOR	RANGE	NUMBER OF COLORS	TUBE	TUBE SIZES	POT/JAR	POT/JAR SIZES	PERMANENCY RATING
Calder (Ocaldo)	Designer's Gouache Color	42	●	21ml*	●	37ml	N/S
	Designer's Poster Color	40	(12 colors)	21ml	●	15, 57, 250ml	N/S
Caran d'Ache	Gouache	20	●	10.4cc*			N/S
Conté	Designer's Gouache	28	●	21ml			N/S
	Conté Poster Color	22			●	23ml	N/S
Daler-Rowney	Designer's Gouache Colour	60	●	22ml*			★(14) ★★(7) ★★★(39)
	Rowney Poster Colour	41			●	14ml*	N/S
	Egg Tempera Colour	28	●	22ml			★★★(14) ★★★★(14)
Grumbacher	Designer's Gouache	53	●	24ml*			+(13) ++(6) +++(19) ++++(15)
Holbein	Artist's Gouache	63	●	15cc			★(2) ★★(30) ★★★(26)
	Holbein Poster Color	17	●	11cc			N/S
Lascaux	Lascaux Gouache	27			●	30ml	N/S
LeFranc & Bourgeois	Linel Technical Gouache	38	●	25ml*	●	200ml*	★(3) ★★(13) ★★★(20)
Lukas	Designer's Gouache	64	●	20, 55ml*			★★(37) ★★★(19)
Maimeri	Designer's Gouache	60	●	20, 60ml	●	500ml	N/S
	Studio Tempera Colors	24	●	10, 20ml			N/S
Marabu	Tamma Poster Color	24				15ml	N/S
	Plakat Tempera Color	45	●	7, 20ml			N/S
Marcus Art	Multimedia Gouache	10	●	38ml			N/S
Pebeo	Extra Fine Gouache	74	●	20ml*	●	250ml	★(2) ★★(11) ★★★(53)
Pelikan	Designer's Color Gouache	64	●	20ml	●	50ml	N/S
Sennelier	Extrafine Gouache	62	●	10, 21ml*	(55 colours)	332ml	★(5) ★★(21) ★★★(26)
	Egg Tempera 'Sennelier'	31	●	18ml*			★(1) ★★(15) ★★★(15)
Talens	S. Series Poster Color	22	●	10ml*			N/S
	Ecola Poster Paint	14	●	16ml*	●		N/S
	Extra Fine Designer's Color	65	●	22ml*			+(3) ++(16) +++(42)
Schmincke	Afro Finest Gouache	60	●	15ml*			★★★(16) ★★★★(22) ★★★★★(22)
	Speciality Gouache	11	●	N/S		N/S	N/S
	Matt Gouache	13	●				★★★(4) ★★★★(7) ★★★★★(2)
	Glossy Gouache	30	●	20ml			★★(5) ★★★(9) ★★★★(14) ★★★★★(2)
	HKS Designer's Colors	84	●	N/S			★(13) ★★(52) ★★★(13)
	Academie Gouache	8	●	N/S			N/S
Winsor & Newton	Designer's Gouache	80	●	14ml*	●	100ml	C(15) B(14) A(39) AA)12)

KEY: * Larger sizes available   **N/S** Not Stated   **★ + AA** Manufacturers' individual marking for permanency rating   **(37)** Number of colors available in that range, luminous colors excluded

Liquid masks

A liquid mask is a fluid that can be applied temporarily to artwork to protect or preserve an area from subsequent applications of color. Generally, such masks are painted on, although some may instead be applied with a pen. When dry they form an inpenetrable film which has a tight, but easily released grip on the underlying surface. Later they may be removed by rubbing, leaving the area beneath untouched. Most liquid masks seem to be latex-based. It should be noted that they become increasingly difficult to remove the longer they are left in place. It is, therefore, advisable to complete the sequence of work in which they are involved within a reasonable timescale.

Liquid masking media of this type can sometimes damage or discolor the surface of the work or underlying paint, and in some instances masking films are preferable. Films do not, however, give a tight enough seal to mask very liquid paint or ink effectively.

Red liquid masks serve a different purpose. These are for correction and alterations, and for masking off areas of film during printing processes in which effective blockage of the sensitizing light is required.

Liquid masks are supplied by Winsor & Newton and Grumbacher. Luma Liquid Mask is a particularly good product. Plumtree Red Liquid Opaque can be used on prints and negatives.

Opaques and retouching colors

Opaque whites and blacks are very dense paints. These are especially suitable for correcting artwork and for photographic retouching; mixtures of the white and the black can be used for intermediate grays. Dense whites of this type may also be useful in combination with gouache to insure extreme opacity, or to prevent the migration of strong colors from lower layers of paint. Inks, dyes and marker-pen coloratives may also present some problems if they have to be erased — high-density opaque whites are available specifically adapted for such use.

Retouching colors are paints or inks intended specifically for retouching photographic images. They appear either as part of a standard range or as a designated variant of a normal product range. Various paints, dyes and inks lend themselves to particular styles of photo-retouching, so despite the fact that they have a common purpose, retouching colors do not form a readily coherent group.

Manufacturers of opaque whites and blacks include Steig, Luma and Winsor & Newton; well known brands are Pro-white, Graphic White, Q-white, Luma, Bleedproof White, Pen-opaque, FW white and black, Winsor & Newton's Process black and white and Schmincke's Deck-Weiss. Schmincke offers a selection of retouching blacks and grays as part of their specialized selection of gouache colors.

Acrylic and vinyl colours

Acrylic and vinyl colours were first offered in a form suitable for artistic use in the 1950s and were initially applied to murals. The binding medium in acrylic colours is plastic which has much greater flexibility than other, more traditional, paint binders. This also has appeals to artists, for in theory such paint should be quite durable.

But the main attraction of acrylics for artists and graphic designers has to be their physical handling properties — and one property in particular: they dry very quickly. Moreover, although water may be used to thin the paints, once dry they are no longer water-soluble, so subsequent layers may be applied with speed. In this way they can be used to imitate many of the media and the techniques used by traditional artists: oil, watercolour, tempera and gouache. This makes acrylics ideally suitable for use in graphic design, where time and practicality are always major concerns.

Since their first introduction, acrylic paints have been substantially improved, thanks partly to advances in the chemistry of the plastic resins on which they are based, and partly to improved production methods. Not all the resins that find their way into this type of paint are genuinely acrylic, however, so the name has now come to represent a type of paint generally, as well as having a specific meaning. Vinyl and polyvinyl acetate (PVA) colours are essentially the same thing as acrylics, although they do differ in minor ways.

All these paints differ from traditional artists' and designers' colours in the way they are made and in how they operate. The binding media are plastics in their simplest compound form — monomers (the building blocks of plastic molecules) — prepared as a colloidal suspension in water (an emulsion). A potential chemical reaction is set up within this emulsion which, when triggered, causes the monomers to link up and form long plastic molecules which surround and enclose the pigment also dispersed in the water. It is the drying of the paint that triggers the reaction — although because the water content is not in fact a solvent, the paint does not dry in the normal sense. The water evaporates, the reaction takes place — and a layer of plasticized colour is formed. Many monomer emulsions are alkaline, so preventing certain pigments from being used in acrylic paints, but manufacturers have also wisely taken this factor as an excuse to drop some superfluous traditional pigments. Present day ranges generally consist of strong modern pigments, which are extremely reliable and are also those most suitable for use in this kind of paint.

The colour strength varies between different brands of acrylics. This is in part due to the fact that the texture of the paint does not depend on its pigment content in the way that the texture of some other media does. Differences in the actual amount of pigment used can thus occur between similar colours in different ranges. As with gouache, it is advisable for an artist or designer to try out a few samples for comparison before committing to a particular range.

The standard presentation of acrylics is in a form similar to artists' oil colour: a thick paste that may be applied as it is or thinned before use. Some, however, are available in a softer, more fluid form which, for many graphic art uses, is more desirable. Acrylic additives are also available for use with watercolour and gouache, converting those paints into waterproof and flexible versions of the parent material.

Liquitex was the first brand of quality acrylics offered in America in the 1950s, since when it has remained a market leader. Liquitex acrylics are available in two forms: as a soft paste and in a more fluid formula suited to large, flat applications of colour. Another respected brand is the Hyplar range from Grumbacher. Lascaux Acryl and Lascaux Studio are two further acrylic paint ranges with an international reputation. Rowney introduced acrylics in the UK first, and offer the Cryla and the Cryla Flow ranges. Cryla has a consistency like oil colour whereas Cryla Flow has a much softer fluid form that is favoured by designers. Winsor & Newton, Talens, Maimeri, Pebeo and Holbein also produce ranges of acrylic colours for artists. Vinyl and PVC colours are supplied by many of the manufacturers of acrylic paint. They are commonly sold in pots and are a less expensive alternative for covering large areas.

Acrylic paints from Maimeri, Liquitex, Winsor & Newton, Rowney and Talens.

ACRYLIC AND VINYL PAINTS

MANUFACTURER/ DISTRIBUTOR	RANGE	NUMBER OF COLORS IN RANGE	TUBE SIZES			POT/JAR	SETS	MANUFACTURER'S PERMANENCY RATING
Binney & Smith	Liquitex Acrylic Color	72	22ml	59ml		•	•	N/S
Calder (Ocaldo)	Artist's Acrylic Colours	43	37ml	225ml			•	N/S
Daler-Rowney	Cryla Acrylic Colour (+ Cryla Flow)	45	33ml	120ml		•	•	***(33) ****(12)
Alois K. Diethelm (Lascaux)	Lascaux Acryl	45	15ml	45ml	200ml	•	•	N/S
	Lascaux Studio	27	15ml	45ml	200ml	•	•	N/S
Grumbacher	Hyplar Acrylic Colors	40	59.1ml	150ml			•	**(1) ***(20) ****(19)
Holbein	Acrylic Polymer Color	70	20ml	40ml			•	**(18) ***(21) ****(23)
Lukas	Lukas Cryl	30	20ml	35ml	115ml	•		**(5) ***(25)
Maimeri	Versil Acrylic Color	32	60ml			•	•	*(4) **(28)
Pebeo	Extrafine Acrylics	34	37ml	150ml		•	•	**(5) ***(29)
Talens	Rembrandt Acrylics	41	40ml	50ml		•	•	++(6) +++(35)
Winsor & Newton	Acrylic Colour	37	20ml	60ml	120ml		•	A (25) AA(12)
	Vinyl Colour	21				•		*(1) **(1) ***(14) ****(5)

KEY: **N/S** Not Stated ★ + **AA** Manufacturers' individual marking of permanency rating **(22)** Number of colors available in that range, luminous colors excluded

Oil paints and alkyd colors

Artists' oil colors are prepared as relatively stiff pastes. They may be used straight from the tube — the common practice since the end of the 19th century — or they may be modified with thinners or other media to alter their consistency and behavior. The richness of effect and intensity of color that is achievable with oil paint exceeds that of all other media, but their long drying-time makes them unsuitable for many day-to-day activities in graphic art. They are, however, used on occasion by airbrush artists and by illustrators, and if applied thinly with appropriate additives to accelerate drying, they can be made to conform to a businesslike timescale.

In addition to strength of color, two further distinct advantages offered by oil paints are the fact that they may be physically blended as they are applied, making graded tones easy to achieve, and the fact that the color alters considerably less than that of any other medium on drying. This last fact makes for a high degree of control by the artist over color values.

Oil paint consists of two main ingredients: pigment and a drying oil. For the latter, linseed oil is most commonly used, but poppy oil and safflower oil also occur in artists' oil colors. These are oils which dry more slowly, but which are favored because they have less tendency to yellow and darken on aging. High-quality oil color for artists should ideally contain nothing but the primary two components, yet small amounts of stabilizers (and sometimes also driers) are frequently added. The practice varies between one manufacturer and another.

The sketching ranges that many manufacturers offer are more likely to contain extenders, stabilizers and driers, and are less likely to use expensive oils. They usually perform reasonably well, but lack the finesse of the higher-grade qualities for use in sophisticated artistic techniques. Far more extensive color selections are offered in the artists' ranges than in the sketching ranges.

Several variations on the basic oil-paint recipe are possible, some of which are intended to improve the drying and aging properties of the paint, others to improve its handling properties. Different white pigments, for example, exhibit markedly different properties in oil — their opacity, tinting strength and drying-time vary considerably, and in addition are affected by the oil in which they are ground. Because of this, many oil-paint ranges offer a choice of whites each suitable for specific applications. One manufacturer adds a resin varnish to the paint to reduce its oil content and to improve the clarity of the colors. This is a semi-traditional practice thought still to be desirable by some authorities. A similar modern product is alkyd paint.

Alkyds are synthetic resins blended with oils, and are used extensively in modern paints, mostly outside the sphere of fine or graphic art. At present only one manufacturer offers a range of alkyd colors for artists, but alkyds are widely used in primings and media that accompany many ranges of traditional oil colors. They dry quite quickly, and are therefore of practical use to graphic designers.

Another recent innovation is oil paint that contains a pre-treated oil which easily emulsifies with water. These colors may be diluted either with conventional thinners (such as turpentine or mineral spirit) or with plain water. It is possible that the availability of alkyds and emulsifiable oil colors will improve in future.

OIL COLORS

Many manufacturers offer oil colors in more than one quality. For example, Winsor & Newton offer an artists' range, and their Winton range includes a smaller number of colors at a more economical price. Some manufacturers differentiate between their quality ranges by using terms such as extra-fine or finest. Lefranc & Bourgeois, Maimeri, Talens, Pebeo and Sennelier are among the manufacturers who use these terms. Grumbacher, Maimeri and Talens each offer three or four qualities of oil colors as separate

ranges. Winsor & Newton's Artists' range and Holbein's Extra Fine Artists' Colors offer the widest selection of oil color whites. Schmincke's Mussini Oil colors use additions of varnish to reduce their oil content. This reputedly gives greater clarity and brilliance to the colors.

Fine and extra-fine oil colors from Lefranc & Bourgeois, Talens, Schmincke and Winsor & Newton.

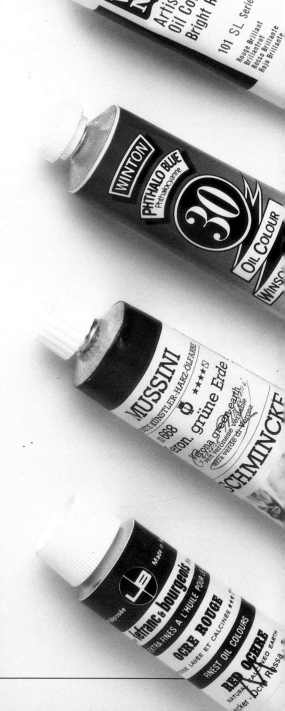
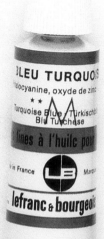

Alkyd colors from Pelikan and Winsor & Newton.

OIL PAINTS

MANUFACTURER/ DISTRIBUTOR	RANGE	QUALITY	NO. OF COLORS	NO. OF WHITES IN RANGE	TUBE SIZES	SETS	MANUFACTURER'S PERMANENCY RATING
Calder (Ocaldo)	Academy Oil Colors	Artists	56	3	21, 37, 225ml	•	N/S
Conté	Louvre Oil Color	Sketching	51	3	21, 38, 54ml	•	★★(11) ★★★(40)
Daler-Rowney	Artist's Oil Color	Artists	87	3	22, 38, 57, 115ml	•	★★(13) ★★★(47) ★★★★(27)
	Georgian Oil Color	Sketching	53	3	8, 22, 38, 57, 115, 225ml	•	★(1) ★★(14) ★★★(28) ★★★★(10)
Ferrario	Vandyke Oil Colors	Sketching	77	3	23, 60ml	•	N/S
Grumbacher	Finest Oil Colors	Artists	72	3	37, 150ml	•	++(6) +++(27) ++++(39)
	Artist's Pre-Tested Colors	Artists	59	3	37, 150ml	•	++(5) +++(27) ++++(27)
	Gainsborough Oils	Sketching	54	3	11ml	•	+(5) ++(12) +++(19) ++++(18)
	Golden Palette Oils	Sketching	36	3	37, 150ml	•	++(3) +++(18) ++++(15)

Continued

MANUFACTURER/ DISTRIBUTOR	RANGE	QUALITY	NO OF COLORS	NO OF WHITES IN RANGE	TUBE SIZES	SETS	MANUFACTURER'S PERMANENCY RATING
Holbein	Extra Fine Artist's Oil Colors	Artists	122	8	50, 110, 330ml	●	★(3) ★★(19) ★★★(68) ★★★★(32)
	Pop Oil Colors	Sketching	36	1	80, 160ml		★(3) ★★(6) ★★★(18) ★★★★(9)
LeFranc & Bourgeois	Extra Fine Artist's Colors	Artists	137	3	5.5, 15ml	●	★(27) ★★(49) ★★★(57)
	Fine Oil Paints	Artists	79	4	25, 40, 60, 250ml	●	★(19) ★★(31) ★★★(29)
Lukas	Sorte 1 Fine Oil Color	Artists	84	4	24, 35, 55, 115ml		★(3) ★★(33) ★★★(58)
	Studio Fine Oil Colors	Sketching	72	4	7.5, 20, 55, 115, 350ml		★★(36) ★★★(36)
Maimeri	Artist's Extra Fine Oil Colors	Artists	110	5	20, 30, 60, 150, 350ml	●	★(34) ★★(75)
	Classico Oil Colors	Sketching	63	3	20, 60, 150, 350ml	●	★(33) ★★(30)
	Brera Oil Colors	Sketching	34	2	60, 150, 350ml	●	N/S
	Studio Oil Colors	Sketching	24	1	10ml	●	N/S
Pebeo	Extra Fine Oil Paints	Artists	75	4	20, 37, 55, 150, 250ml	●	★(14) ★★★(61)
	Studio Fine Oil Paints	Sketching	40	2	20, 37, 150ml	●	★★(6) ★★★(34)
Sennelier	Extra Fine Oil Paints	Artists	110	4	18, 36, 58, 110ml	●	★(12) ★★(49) ★★★(49)
	Decorateur Oils	Sketching	34	1	25, 36, 58ml		N/S
Schmincke	Mussini Oil Colors	Artists	119	4	15, 35ml	N/S	★(2) ★★(12) ★★★(27) ★★★★(28) ★★★★★(49)
J.P. Stephenson	Artists' Oil Colours	Artists	27	2	38ml		★★★(14) ★★★★(13)
Talens	Rembrandt Oil Colors	Artists	121	4	17, 40, 60, 150ml	●	+(4) ++(34) +++(83)
	Van Gogh Oil Colors	Sketching	53	3	22, 60, 150ml	●	++(22) +++(31)
	Amsterdam Oil Colors	Sketching	27	2	22, 60, 150, 200ml	●	++(13) +++(14)
Winsor & Newton	Artist's Oil Colours	Artists	110	7	21, 37, 60, 120ml	●	C(2) B(14) A(57) AA(37)
	Winton Oil Colours	Sketching	45	3	21, 37, 60, 120, 200ml	●	★(4) ★★(6) ★★★(25) ★★★★(9)
	Griffin Alkyd Colors	Artists	40	2	20, 60, 120, 200ml	●	B(4) A(23) AA(13)

KEY: N/S Not Stated ★ + **AA** Manufacturers' individual markings for permanency ratings **(22)** Number of colors available in that range, luminous colors excluded

Painting media

The function of a medium is to modify the properties of paint. Both oil and acrylics are presented to the user as a paste; they may thus need to be thinned for certain methods of working. Diluents can of course do that simply enough — turpentine or mineral spirit for oil, and water in the case of acrylics — but to maintain the substance of the paint layer a medium is required.

Ready-made media are available for oil paint, although many artists choose to prepare their own for themselves from mixtures of various oils and thinners. Alkyd media are of particular interest because they impart to the paint those properties especially associated with alkyds — like fast drying. Gel media for impasto effects with oil, again based on alkyds, are also practical where the slow drying of thick applications of oil paint would be a disadvantage. Acrylic dries quickly and thoroughly, even in thick layers, but the use of a medium in impasto techniques can reduce the amount of expensive paint that is used. Gel media and liquid media are essential with acrylics if such colors are to be used to imitate the effects of oil paint.

One of the most useful products and one that accompanies most acrylic ranges, is a retarding medium. The fact is that acrylics actually dry too fast for some methods of working, and can damage brushes and palettes by drying on them even while they are in use. The addition of a small amount of a retarding medium to the paint slows the process down significantly.

Acrylic media are beyond the capacity of artists to prepare for themselves, and because the exact chemical composition of the manufacturers' ranges for acrylic paints may vary, it is as well to match the media with the products supplied by the same manufacturer. Media are also available for use with other paints such as gouache and watercolor, but they are only rarely employed and in general have a very limited appeal to graphic artists and designers.

Three examples of thinning media: the gloss varnish for acrylic paint, liquin — a quick-drying resin-based medium — and mineral spirit for oils.

Watercolors

Watercolor paint has been in use in one form or another for a considerable time. In its earliest form it was used chiefly as a body color, very much in the way that gouache is used today. The modern translucent watercolors, and the methods by which they are applied, derive from the 18th century, when watercolor painting evolved as an art form.

The material soon became popular; so much so that a number of manufacturers both in Britain and on the Continent can claim a present-day historical link of some sort with the first commercial producers of the late 18th century. This is significant both because the way in which high-quality watercolors are manufactured has not altered a great deal since those times, and because it is generally agreed that this type of paint requires considerable experience and understanding on the part of the manufacturer if the very best results are to be achieved.

Watercolor paints of the highest quality for artists contain the finest pigments and a gum binder (most frequently gum arabic). They also include a third ingredient, now ordinarily glycerine, although it used to be sugar or honey. This retains a small amount of moisture in the paint and prevents the blocks of paint from splitting through over-drying. The glycerine content also encourages the paint to take up water and form a wash when in use. Some colors may also contain a wetting agent such as ox gall, or a modern equivalent, to improve the flow of the color during application, and all are likely to contain a preservative to prevent the gum (which is a plant extract) from being attacked by mold.

The balance of one ingredient with another is very important in watercolor paint; different pigments require slightly different recipes for the preparation of the paint, and in some instances may require modified production methods. For grinding pigment initially, the grinding equipment used to produce high-quality watercolors for artists commonly employs stone rollers to avoid muddying the color. Another common process involves simply an automatic slab and muller, which duplicate the original hand-grinding process. At least one manufacturer still hand-grinds certain colors in order to insure that the quality is correct and that the color is not bruised by excessive grinding, which, in relation to a few sensitive pigments, can actually change the hue.

After preparation and dispersion (grinding), the watercolor is in the form and consistency of a soft paste which is dried under controlled conditions until it becomes like toffee. At this stage it can be cut into strips and pressed into blocks which are set into pans and half pans. If the paint is to be marketed in tubes, however, it is dried only until it has the right consistency to remain stable in the tube: thick but fluid. Tube colors sometimes contain more glycerine than pan colors in order to retain a higher degree of moisture.

Artists' ranges offer a very good selection of colors, and the translucence and brilliance of the paint are normally of a high order, although of course some pigments are naturally more translucent than others. The traditional use of certain fugitive colors in watercolor paints has meant their continued presence in several ranges, but if permanence is an important issue there is no real need to use them: acceptable and reliable alternatives exist in most manufacturers' selections. Watercolors should never contain white pigment, at least in theory, but sometimes some of the colors in less well-known ranges do, and it may affect their translucence quite significantly.

High-quality artists' watercolors can be very expensive, yet the additional performance obtainable from this grade of material is well worth the expense. Sketching-quality watercolors offer much smaller color-ranges, and the translucence and brilliance of the paints is less than that of most artists' ranges. At the same time, sketching watercolors can still be forceful colorants because of the tendency of some manufacturers to use particularly powerful organic pigments (and perhaps, occasionally, dyes) as the coloring matter in these ranges.

Both artists' and sketching watercolors may be available as tube or pan colors; pan colors are less usual in the sketching qualities. Pans and half pans are useful for small-scale works, whereas tubes are much more practical for large areas of wash and for artists such as graphic designers who use the paint in quantity.

WATERCOLORS

Watercolors are sold in tubes or pans, but best quality ranges are often packed in small tubes of about 5ml. Slightly larger tubes are used for secondary ranges. Pans and half-pans vary slightly in size from one manufacturer to another and may fit only into boxes supplied by the same manufacturer. Full-pans are less common, and some suppliers do not offer them at all. The continental double-pan is of a similar size to the full-pan made elsewhere. Pelikan's new pan paints have a wide lip designed to retain a small amount of wash while the paints are in use.

Acquarelle watercolors in tubes and blocks from Winsor & Newton, Maimeri, Schmincke, Lefranc & Bourgeois and Talens.

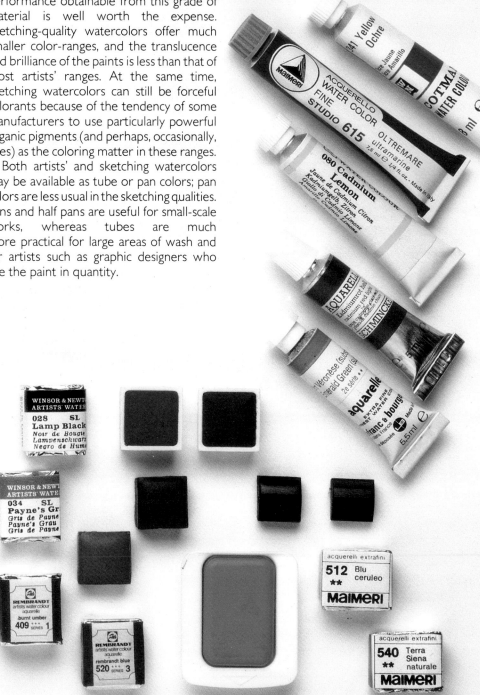

WATERCOLOR PAINTS

MANUFACTURER/ DISTRIBUTOR	RANGE	QUALITY	AVAILABILITY ½ PAN	WHOLE PAN	TUBE SIZE	SETS	NO. OF COLORS ½ PAN	WHOLE PAN	TUBE	MANUFACTURER'S PERMANENCY RATING
Calder (Ocaldo)	Artist's Watercolors	Artists			5ml	•			38	N/S
	Academy Watercolors	Sketching			7.5, 21ml	•			28	N/S
Conté	Extra Fine Watercolors	Artists	•		5, 10, 21ml	•	60		60	N/S
Ferrario	Ferrario Artist's Watercolors	Artists		•				48		××(16) ×××(32)
	Students Watercolor	Sketching			7.5ml				24	N/S
Grumbacher	Finest Watercolor	Artists			5.3, 16ml	•			56	++(9) +++(26) ++++(21)
	Academy Watercolors	Sketching			7.4ml	•			55	+(4) ++(13) +++(22) ++++(16)
Holbein	Extra Fine Watercolors	Artists			5, 15cc	•			84	*(6) **(38) *** (40)
LeFranc & Bourgeois	Extra Fine Watercolors	Artists			5.5, 15ml				99	N/S
Lucas	Artist's Watercolor	Artists (80%)	•	•	7.5cc	•	60	60	60	**(26) ***(34)
Maimeri	Artist's Extra Fine W/color	Artists	•	•	5, 7ml	•	51	51	51	*(21) **(30)
	Studio Fine Watercolors	Sketching			5, 7ml	•			31	N/S
Pebeo	Extra Fine Watercolors	Artists	•		8.5ml	•	47		47	***(47)
	Studio Five Watercolors	Sketching				•				N/S
Pelikan	Transparent Watercolors	Artists (80%)				•				N/S
Rowney	Artist's	Artists	•	•	5ml	•	65	29	65	*(2) **(22) ***(22) ****(19)
	Georgian	Sketching	•		8ml	•	24		33	N/S
Schmincke	Fine Artist's Watercolors	Artists	•	•	5, 15ml		100	100	100	**(5) ***(15) ****(38) *****(42)
Sennelier	Extra Fine Watercolors	Artists	•		8.5ml	•	80		80	*(6) **(21) ***(46)
Talens	Rembrandt Artist's Watercolors	Artists			5ml	•			72	++(16) +++(56)
	Talens Watercolor	Sketching			8ml	•			36	++(10) +++(26)
Winsor & Newton	Artist's Watercolour	Artists	•	•	5ml	•	85	85	80	C(6) B(13) A(43) AA(23)
	Cotman Watercolours	Sketching			8, 21ml	•			39	*(2) **(13) ***(13) ****(11)

KEY: N/S Not Stated   *** + AA** Manufacturers' individual markings for permanency ratings   **(22)** Number of colors available in that range, luminous colors excluded

Liquid watercolors and liquid designers' colors

Interestingly, the forerunners of modern watercolor paints were the liquid colors used in staining prints and maps. The medium has now come full circle — liquid colors are once again in fashion. They are particularly favored by graphic artists and designers because of their suitability for use in pens and airbrushes, as well as with conventional brushes.

Although all similar in function, liquid colors may be divided into separate types. Some are difficult to distinguish from inks in that they appear to be strong translucent colors, most likely dyes in origin, very like some ranges of colored drawing-inks. One noteworthy feature, however, is that they tend not to contain shellac, as inks often do, and so they are less likely to clog technical pens and airbrushes. Some are sold as dyes; some are described as liquid watercolors or as concentrated watercolors.

However, descriptions like the last two are applied also to a very similar, but quite distinct, product: a liquid color based on a very fine suspension of pigment rather than dye. These are quite fluid enough to use in pens and airbrushes, and because they contain pigment, offer a great degree of permanence. The ranges of dye-based colors frequently contain some very charming, glowing and brilliant colors that unfortunately are not light-fast, and must therefore be restricted to applications in which permanence is not of the essence.

Among the products that fall within the general description of liquid designers' colors there are also those made specifically for photo-retouching, and others like liquid acrylics which because of their flexibility are suitable for use on surfaces such as acetate. Most liquid colors are supplied in bottles fitted with pipette tops which allow the highly concentrated color to be dispensed in accurately-measured quantities for dilution and for controlled and repeatable mixing of colors.

1 Talens Ecoline
2 Dr. P.H. Martins Radiant Concentrated Water Color
3 Lefranc & Bourgeois Fluidline

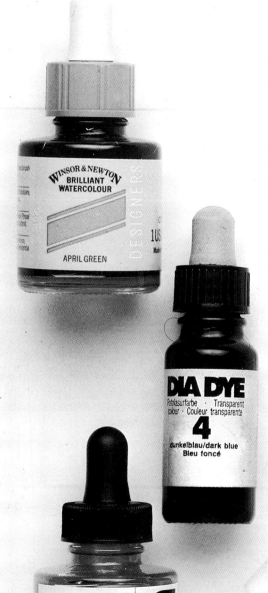

Inks

Drawing-inks may obviously overlap with liquid colors in composition, presentation and function. Many contain shellac or a similar ingredient to make them waterproof, which in turn makes them most suitable for use with a traditional dip pen or on a brush. India ink is, strictly speaking, Chinese stick ink, although the name is now applied more or less flexibly to a variety of rich black inks, all of which are opaque and light-fast, and most of which are waterproof. These are pigmented inks and contain very fine particles of carbon black in suspension.

Those which contain shellac should not be used in a technical pen; instead, special inks should be used, sometimes confusingly also referred to as India ink. These are rich preparations of black pigment once again, but specifically formulated for that kind of use. A small assortment of colored inks are also available for use in technical pens and, subject to the manufacturer's recommendations, several of the liquid designers' colors may be applied using technical pens as well.

Metallic colors based on heavy pigments appear in some drawing-ink ranges. These frequently settle out and must be well shaken before use. They are likely to clog no matter what implement is used to apply them with, and frequent cleaning of pens and brushes during their use may be necessary in order to achieve a smooth effect.

Writing-inks are often of uncertain composition and are not to be recommended for any application in graphics other than their normal use in writing instruments. Special inks are available for use in drafting films; different formulations are available for use on matte and uncoated drafting films. Those for use on uncoated drafting films are called etching inks or drafting film inks and should be used only with certain pens.

Concentrated watercolors from Winsor & Newton, Dia Dye and Luma.

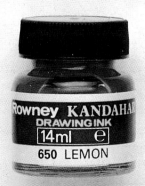

Aerosol sprays

Aerosol spray colors are convenient for large-scale work — on posters or displays, for example — and on items where the soft, smooth effect of a spray is required but the subtlety of an airbrush is unnecessary. Only a few aerosol spray-paint ranges are made specifically for use by artists and designers, although there are of course other ranges widely available for general-purpose use (such as for car repairs). For artistic purposes, those intended for graphic artists are to be preferred, however, because they tend to show less gloss, and their ranges offer more suitable color selections.

Aerosol sprays may be used on a variety of supports, including paper and board, but only a certain number are suitable for use on expanded polystyrene, and compatibility with that material should always be checked for before using an aerosol spray on it — even within a single range, some colors may be safe to use whereas other may not.

A variety of other useful products are available in aerosol form, including varnishes, glazes, "transparentizers", ultra-violet eliminators and matte-effect lacquers. Among other things matte lacquers are useful for removing unwanted reflections during photography.

LIQUID COLORS/INKS

MANUFACTURER/ DISTRIBUTOR	RANGE	TRANSPARENT COLOR	DRAWING INK	DYE	NUMBER OF COLORS	BOTTLES
Calder (Ocaldo)	Drawing Inks		•		20	28, 600ml, 5 liter
Daler-Rowney	Kandahar Ink	•	•		20	14, 28ml
Faber Castell	Higgins Ink	•	•		19	1oz
	Reform Drafting Ink		•		4	¾ oz
Frisk	Concentrated Dye	•		•	20	1oz, 20oz
Grumbacher	Colored Drawing Ink	•	•		17	30ml
Holbein	Standard Drawing Ink	•	•		28	1oz
Le Franc & Bourgeois	Fluid Line	•			30	50, 250, 1 liter
Lukas	Illucolor	•			20	N/S
Maimeri	Colorin	•			38	30, 250ml
Mecanorma	Creative Color	•			25	25ml
Pebeo	Colorex		•		64	45, 250ml
Pelikan	Artists Drawing Ink	•	•		15	30ml
Rotring	Artists Color	•	•		12	30ml
Royal Sovereign	Magic Color	•	•		24	28, 220ml
Salis International (Dr. P.H. Martin)	Radiant Watercolor	•			56	½, 2oz
	Radiant Watercolor	•			42	½ oz
	Synchromatic Transparent Watercolor	•			38	½ oz
Schmincke	Aero Color	•	•		18	30ml
	Hits Color Dye	•		•	84	N/S
Sennelier	Drawing Ink		•		28	250, 500, 1000ml
Steig Products	Luma Liquid Designers Color	•	•		80	½ oz
	Luma Solar Chromatic Color		•		36	½ oz
	FW Drawing Ink		•		14	1 oz
Talens	Rembrandt Drawing Ink	•	•		18	30, 490ml
Winsor & Newton	Designers Brilliant Watercolor	•		•	36	30ml
	Drawing Inks	•	•	•	26	30, 35, 250ml

PAPERS, BOARDS AND FILMS

Paper and board are the most widely used supports in graphic art. Films have a more specialized application and are perhaps more often used by draftsmen and architects, although they are also used by some designers; film products such as acetate sheet are almost exclusively a graphic designer's material.

Paper and board, of course, are not only used for support; they are also the materials from which many of the end-products of the graphic artist's efforts are constructed. For this reason a designer's interest in paper often goes beyond its use within the studio. As well as being functional, paper and board may be decoratively finished, they may have a special surface texture, or they may possess certain specific properties in use, all of which may be relevant to an artist or designer.

Good performance from a reasonably broad selection of materials is all that is really required for everyday studio use. Many products for graphic artists, however, have primary specialized functions — that is, they are designed for use in a specific way, although they frequently lend themselves to wider applications. For the illustrator, the fine artist and the designer who is selecting a paper or board for finished artwork, other factors may be relevant. A carefully selected paper can contribute to the effect of artwork, or may itself provide a vital part for a finished design.

Many papers are available in the form of pads — indeed, some manufacturers supply their papers only in that format. Among these are a number of products intended specifically for studio use, which are handy and functional. Pad presentation also lends itself to highly specialized uses in which an overprint or an underlay converts the paper into a product with a very definite function.

Films have quite diverse applications; several types fall notionally outside the field of graphic art or design. Even so, it is difficult to exclude many of them from this chapter.

They are discussed in as much depth as seems appropriate, taking into consideration their intended and possible uses, and they are grouped together for convenience. It is possible that film products may form a greater focus of interest for graphic artists and designers in the future, in that the unique properties of some of them are more suited to the modern technology now being introduced in graphic art and in related fields such as printing.

PAPER

Paper was invented by the ancient Chinese, although its English name is derived from papyrus, a writing material used by the ancient Egyptians, which resembles paper outwardly. The Chinese form was most probably invented in around 200–300 BC — samples that can be dated to that time have survived — but its exact origins are uncertain.

Paper-making

Until the very end of the 18th century, paper-making was exclusively a process carried out by hand, each sheet being made individually. The raw material for paper-making was rags, first of linen and later of cotton.

The invention in the 17th century of the Hollander, a machine that helped to pulp rags, did much to improve the paper-making process, and from the time of its introduction the industry expanded.

The first practical paper-making machines were introduced sometime around 1800; modernized versions of the same machines continue to support today's massive paper-making industry. There are two types: the cylinder mold machine and the Foudrinier.

Cylinder mold machines are capable of producing very high-quality papers: they are used, for example, in the manufacture of machine-made watercolor papers.

The Foudrinier machine is faster in production than the cylinder mold machine, although it cannot be used to produce paper quite so high in quality. Its greater speed and efficiency have insured that it has the dominant position in the paper-making industry: most commercially-produced paper is made on a Foudrinier machine.

Hand-made paper continues to be made for artists and can be of use in some graphic applications, such as illustration, but the hand process cannot produce the standardized product that mechanized methods can, and the individual character of each sheet is a disadvantage in several sets of circumstances. Nevertheless, the process is of interest, because it is easier to understand the paper-making process as it is performed by hand on a small scale than it is to understand the workings of the machines. The machines are merely performing scaled-up and continuous versions of the same process. The starting-point is pulp — called "stuff" by paper-makers — which comprises broken-down fibers of vegetable origin suspended in water. To make paper, an operative called a vatman places a wooden frame known as a deckle over a flat screen made of wire; the whole device is then dipped into the pulp and lifted out horizontally. The deckle converts the screen into a sort of shallow tray, and a quantity of pulp is retained. The water drains out through the gaps in the wire screen, and as it does, the fibers in the pulp are deposited as a flat sheet. Fibers trapped against and under the deckle produce the deckle edge. With a deft motion the vatman transfers each wet sheet on to a piece of felt, and after a number of sheets have been sandwiched into a "post," they are pressed to remove water and separated out to dry.

Examples of marbled paper.

Paper surfaces

The wire screens used in paper-making may be "laid" or "wove." In a laid screen, a series of straight wires are laid parallel to each other with a small gap between each wire. The impression of this is left on the resulting paper as a pattern of lines that can be seen when it is held to the light or when a soft drawing instrument such as charcoal is moved over its surface. Paper like this is known as laid paper.

A wove screen is made of finer, interwoven wires with many tiny gaps for the water to pass through at the points at which the wires intersect. Wove screens do leave an impression on the surface of the paper, but it is usually much less distinct than that on laid paper; smooth-surfaced papers are relatively easy to produce on wove molds.

Watermarks are put into the paper as an impression from the screen, and appear on the mold in the form of a slightly raised design in wire or in thin metal sheet. However, the felt sheets between which the wet sheets are stacked are also responsible for the introduction of texture into the paper. When the moisture is pressed out of the paper, the surface pattern of the felt is pressed into it. If the felt is of a fairly uniform texture, with a reasonably flat surface, the result is what is called a CP (cold pressed) surface. This shows a slight texture, the effect is not pronounced; such paper may be used for drawing or painting, for printing or for any of a variety of other end uses. If the felts are more rugged and have a distinct surface pattern, the paper surface will be Rough. This can be pleasantly decorative in effect, and works well with certain paint media, particularly watercolor, but it is too uneven a surface for drawing or for any use involving precise detail.

Another type of surface, called HP (hot pressed) or Smooth, is formed by pressing the paper between heated plates or rollers after it has been made. In effect the paper is being ironed, and its surface texture is substantially flattened during the process. Hot pressed papers are excellent for fine and detailed drawing and for work with pen and ink or line and wash, so they tend to be quite popular with graphic artists.

There are in addition a number of other finishing processes responsible for surface effects in papers. Calendering, for example, involves passing paper between smooth rollers under pressure, and produces a flat surface. The method is often used in combination with surface fillers, which can be pressed into any irregularities on the paper's surface in order to fill them up. Clays, chalks, and even paper dust may be used for this purpose, and the resulting surfaces are exceptionally smooth.

Decorative textures may also deliberately be put into paper surfaces by using engraved rollers, which press a pattern into the paper surface. In this way a linen effect — looking like woven cloth — may be simulated on paper, and more complicated decorative patterns may be embossed too. This can be combined most effectively with printing and with surface laminations of plastic or metal to produce convincing replicas of other materials (such as leather) and highly decorative effects, which find extremely diverse end uses in products specified by designers. Mirror finishes, velvet-like surfaces, soft "flannel" finishes and coarse irregular laid effects also occur on papers in popular use.

Qualities of paper and board

The quality of paper depends on both its raw materials and its method of production. The use of rags as the source of fibers has now been discontinued; in a large proportion of modern cloth cotton is used in combination with synthetic fibers, and produces rags which are unsuitable for paper-making. Natural cotton linters are now used, but the term "rag paper" is still used to describe a paper that is made from cotton or from a mixture of plant fibers of a similar quality and origin — flax, hemp and jute for example.

Some manufacturers prefer to make paper befitting a description such as "100% Cotton" or "Cotton with other fibers." Papers made completely of cotton are of a very high quality — but the raw material is now increasingly expensive, and it is common for papers to be made of mixes based on a reduced cotton content. Papers of anything more than 50% cotton in composition are usually of a fair quality.

Since the 19th century wood pulp has been used as a raw material for paper-making. It can be converted to pulp either mechanically or by chemical breakdown. Wood-pulp paper discolors and disintegrates in a relatively short time. There is now, however, a type of paper known as wood-free. This is, in fact, made of wood, but of grades known as photographic quality wood pulp and alpha cellulose.

Paper's acid content is important, and acid is present in crude wood-pulp papers. In other papers where the paper content is acid-free it can be introduced during sizing or coloring. The importance of using acid-free paper has come to the fore only relatively recently, with the development of the science of paper conservation.

Paper weight

The heavier a paper is, the more stable it is, and the more suitable it is for use with water-based paints. Lighter-weight papers may need to be stretched for such use. Lightweight papers, however, are quite common as graphic artists' materials because transparency, or semi-transparency, may be a required feature in some instances. Paper weights are also relative to their end uses — an imposing letterhead looks better on heavier paper, for instance, and the cover of a pamphlet needs to be thicker and heavier than its pages (see Appendix on Paper weights and sizes.)

Board thicknesses are expressed either in microns or in sheets, the latter descriptions referring to the fact that some board is built up from single-thickness layers.

Graphic designers' papers

The following types of paper are made specifically for graphic artists and designers. Many are sold in pad form for convenience, usually in a range of standard sizes from A1 to A5, although not all ranges include all sizes. The number of sheets in the pads differs considerably between those of one manufacturer and those of another, and also depends on the quality, thickness and use of the paper.

Typo or detail paper

This is a thin and fairly hard paper, usually around 50 gm^2 in weight. It has a fairly smooth — but not perfectly smooth — surface and is a gray-white in color. Typo or detail paper is translucent: any fairly distinct mark may be seen through it quite clearly when it is laid over the top. At first sight it is very like tracing paper, but it is not quite as clear or as smooth. It is commonly used for instruction overlays and for typographic design, but it is also used for layouts, preliminary sketches and working drawings.

Detail paper accepts most drawing media quite well, but is too thin to cope with liquid media. Typo/detail pads often include a sheet with a printed grid that may be placed beneath the detail paper itself as an aid to design, the grid being visible through the paper as it is used.

Layout paper

Layout paper is also occasionally referred to as visualizing paper or detail paper, although the latter description is more frequently used in connection with typo paper. Layout paper is a thin paper with a smooth surface similar to a lightweight typing paper. It is white and comes in weights that are around 50 gm^2, although 45 gm^2 and 60 gm^2 variants are not unusual. Like detail paper it is translucent, but not to the same extent. A definite mark or line shows through it clearly when it is used over the top of an existing piece of work, but the image is less distinct than with detail or tracing paper.

Its main use is for outline sketches of proposed page layouts, and for preliminary working drawings and sketches of all types. Obviously, by laying a new sheet over an existing sketch one can rework and advance an idea without losing sight of the original concept, and a quick and acceptably presentable summary sketch can be transferred onto layout paper from an overworked idea on a previous sheet. Not surprisingly, layout paper is a popular general-purpose studio paper. It accepts most media, but is too thin for paints.

Marker paper

This is a white paper that frequently has a very smooth surface. Typically, it is 70 gm^2 in weight, and has a slight degree of transparency. It is specially designed for use with marker pens and felt-tips containing either water-based or spirit-based inks. These inks are inclined to bleed on ordinary paper, and produce feathery edges rather than crisp edges along lines; they can also bleed through to the next sheet on pads of some lightweight layout papers. Marker paper is bleed-proof. Most marker paper is a very stark white, such that the surface appears to have been coated, making it exceptionally smooth. Single-sided and double-sided marker papers are available.

Although intended specifically for use with markers, marker paper obviously lends itself to use with most types of pen, and serves as a pleasantly cheap sketching paper for use with technical pens.

1 Langford & Hill Studio Economy typo detail paper, 53gm^2
2 Schoellershammer layout paper, 75gm^2
3 Langford & Hill Studio Economy layout paper, blue
4 Letraset marker paper

Tracing paper

Tracing paper is a thin paper that nonetheless feels substantial between finger and thumb; its surface is smooth and sometimes appears to have a minute surface grain. It is pale gray in color and is almost completely transparent. The better qualities are often called Vallum. Two weights are available in most ranges; as a rule these are 60 gm^2 and 90 gm^2. The lighter weight is a general grade for graphic artists, designers, fine artists and students. The heavier is often described as of professional quality, and is preferred by draftsmen. Tracing paper is intended for transferring designs, but it can be used in much the same way as detail and layout paper in some circumstances. Tracing paper accepts most drawing media, and is used most frequently with pencils and technical pens.

Drawing paper

Drawing paper — called cartridge paper in Britain — is a good general-purpose paper used by both graphic artists and fine artists. It is white or creamy white, and is completely opaque.

As a rule, drawing paper is heavier than all the other papers so far considered, usually weighing around 120-150 gm^2, but it also occurs in weights of as much as 200 gm^2. Its surface is smooth, but with a slight texture, and there is some difference between different brands. Some surfaces are very smooth indeed, whereas others exhibit a surface that approaches the rough surface texture of a few watercolor papers. Some drawing paper is, in fact, offered in a choice of rough or hot press finish, and the term "drawing paper" is occasionally used rather flexibly to describe papers that could as easily be called watercolor papers.

Drawing paper works well with pencils, crayons, pastels and markers. A number of drawing papers also work well with pens — but some work better than others. In the heavier weights they may be used with paints, although for that they are still a little light and should be stretched if a really good result is required. Most good drawing papers are for use on one side only — the other shows the texture of wove screen on which it was made — but there are some double-sided drawing papers on the market, some with both sides smooth and others with one side rough and the other hot-pressed.

1 Langford & Hill Studio
  Economy gateway trace, 90gm^2
2 Daler sketch book
3 Schoellershammer 2R, fine
  paper
4 Schoellershammer fine
  line cartridge paper, 150gm^2
5 Schoellershammer fine
  line cartridge paper, 200gm^2
6 Schoellershammer 2G,
  very lightly textured paper
7 Schoellershammer 4G,
  very lightly textured paper
8 Schoellershammer 6G,
  very lightly textured paper

Line papers and surface papers

Line papers appear under a variety of names. They are for high-standard finished artwork, and have an exceptionally smooth surface that accepts technical pens, dry transfer lettering, and a variety of graphic media extremely well. They are white and heavy enough to remain reasonably stable in use, being around 150 gm^2 as a rule.

The superior surface that line papers possess is the result of calendering or hot pressing; in some instances a coating may be applied, although several manufacturers boast that this is not the case with their products. Surface papers with other finishes are also available for line and wash work, and for use with watercolors and other paint media, but they are still rather lightweight for such use.

Line papers and surface papers generally are used to make the working surfaces of illustration boards, in which case they are mounted on a stiff and fairly thick backing piece. They are obviously more stable in this form, and perform better with liquid media such as watercolor or ink, but there are advantages to using them in the unmounted state. Firstly, they are cheaper to use in this form (and a board is in any event not always necessary or appropriate as a support for artwork), but secondly they are also more suitable for use on scanning equipment, which is increasingly being used in the printing industry in preference to flat-bed photographic processes. Designers' boards cannot be used with modern scanning equipment unless their backings are removed to leave only the surface paper.

Quadrille, graph and technical papers

Papers of various qualities are available with overprinted grids, usually in blue. On quadrille paper all the lines are of equal weight; on graph paper (also called cross section paper) the inch lines are darker. Subdivisions of halves, quarters, eights or tenths of an inch are normally available. European papers have metricated grids, typically in units of 1 or 5 millimetres.

These papers are used by technical draftsmen more often than by graphic artists, but they are useful in a number of design applications where exact reference points and precise dimensions are essential. Overprints in non-reproducing blue do not show up with certain copying and photographic processes, so that the grid need not appear in the finished effect.

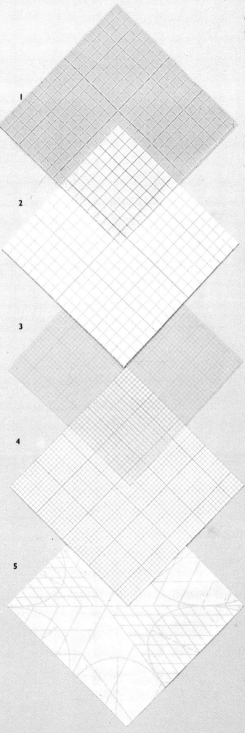

1 Chartwell sectional pad, $\frac{1}{10}$in, $\frac{1}{2}$in and 1 in.
2 Letraset Studio Graph paper, $\frac{1}{10}$in, $\frac{1}{2}$in and 1 in.
3 Schoellershammer millimeter block
4 Chartwell Sectional, 1, 5 and 10mm
5 Frisk Perspecta pad

Cover paper

Cover paper is plain colored paper, which is used for covering pamphlets and books. It is usually quite weighty and fairly stiff, which suits it to its intended use. Strictly speaking, any paper of cover quality — say 150 gm^2 and above — is a cover paper, so the term can apply to a variety of decoratively finished papers, including textured and printed papers, and not only to those that are in solid colors.

The ranges of cover paper aimed at designers, however, are usually selections of plain colored papers, and are used for display backgrounds and for presentation purposes; most may be also used as bases for a variety of graphic media. The surfaces are generally smooth but with a slight rough texture. A typical range might have 40 or 50 colors, many of them rich and bright.

Specialized designers' pads

As mentioned earlier, several types of pads of paper for special applications are produced for graphic artists and designers.

TV layout pads are for planning television, film and video productions, for example; they have pages sectioned off into screen-shaped areas for planning visual images, with accompanying areas for textual copy to indicate the progress of the script or the story. Such pads are often prepared for use with markers, and are constructed on bleed-proof paper.

Page-planning pads are overprinted with the lined text areas of double-page spreads, which may be used to plan the layout of copy and illustrations for publications. These are of use to editors, authors and printers, as well as to graphic artists and book designers.

Perspective pads are for technical-drawing, engineering-drawing and architectural use. Overprinted with perspective grids, or with interlocking cubes with subdivided surfaces showing angled planes, they can also be very useful aids for illustrators. Perspective drawings may be made over them without spending excessive time constructing guidelines. These pads are based on high-grade line papers although they are sometimes additionally available as drafting film. Non-reproducing blue is commonly used for the overprinting.

Pads of quadrille, graph and technical papers are also available for specialized uses.

Three-dimensional grid paper in pads.

Black, white and gray cover paper.

Graphic artists' boards

For a surface with greater stability and strength, or to provide a solid backing to artworks or displays, graphic artists, designers and illustrators use boards. These consist of a central core of backing board faced on the front with a prepared paper, and on the back with a backing paper. There are several varieties to choose from, each intended for a different application, with various surface finishes and differences in construction which affect their performance and cost. The quality of the central core varies considerably, for on some boards it is made of materials far inferior to the facing paper.

Increasingly there is a tendency to offer boards which are acid-free throughout, and which offer additional stability as a result of a specially constructed core. Such high-quality boards are desirable for illustration work, for professional graphics and for technical use, but for many run-of-the-mill studio uses less costly boards with a shorter life are perfectly acceptable.

Bristol board

Bristol board is not a typical designer's board: it is constructed differently and is much lighter than other types of board. Bristol board has a very smooth surface and is very often a brilliant white. Ideal for pen and ink, it is popular for technical illustration and various drawing applications, and is also used in printing. In the lighter weights it is more like a sturdy paper than a board. In fact, Bristol board is not constructed around a core but is built up from single sheets of paper pasted together.

Different thicknesses are available — such as 2-, 3- or 4-sheet thicknesses — and very light versions, perhaps consisting of one sheet only, are sometimes known as Bristol paper. Bristol board is sometimes double-sided and is thin enough to be supplied in pad form. Outwardly it is very similar to a line paper, but is just a little more substantial.

Line board

Line board is constructed around a solid core and is faced with an exceptionally smooth surface paper that has been either hot pressed, calendered or coated. It is designed to accept technical pens and all types of precision drawing instruments, dip pens, ruling pens, technical pencils and fine-pointed marker pens. Many line boards also accept gouache, acrylic and tempera paints, and several are recommended for use with airbrushes. All are suited to use with dry transfer lettering and some take watercolor reasonably well.

The best line boards take repeated use of the surface without loss of quality — so that erasures and scraping back of errors can be done freely. The same area can then be used for redrawing a design with no risk that feathering will occur around the edges of lines. Some boards also resist the effects of masking tapes, which can be peeled back from their surfaces without damage. Line board thicknesses vary between one manufacturer and another, and some suppliers offer a choice of thicknesses. Thicker boards are not necessarily more stable than thinner ones, some of which have very sophisticated core constructions.

1 Chartwell Bristol board, 3 sheet, 220gm²
2 Letraset 2000 line board
3 Daler Superline, silver
4 Daler Superline, gold
5 Frisk CS10 Grafik paper

Line and wash boards

Line and wash boards are designed to combine the qualities of a line board with those of watercolor board. The surface is smooth, but with a very slight texture, and the facing paper is more absorbent in character. Rough and hot pressed surfaced versions may be available in some ranges. Line and wash board performs less well than line board with pen and ink, but it takes pencil very well and accepts pastels and crayons too. Line and wash boards frequently work well with marker pens and also with watercolors and other paints and inks.

Paste-up board

This is usually a cheaper type of board, faced with a plain white paper and intended primarily for use as a support for pasted-up artwork. Paste-up boards frequently make fair general-purpose boards, however, and accept quite finely executed pen and ink work, other drawing media such as colored pencils and charcoal, instant lettering and some paints. Some paste-up boards are said to perform fairly well with an airbrush. It would be wrong to expect too much in the way of performance from such boards, though, and the fact that they are primarily intended for relatively mundane studio use should be kept in mind when they are put to other uses. Most graphic artists' and designers' boards can be used as paste-up boards, but to do so is often more expensive and is a waste of the other specialized functions that they offer.

Some paste-up boards are overprinted with a grid or a series of parallel lines printed in non-reproducing blue, intended to make the accurate positioning of artwork and copy during paste-up a comparatively easy task. Such boards are obviously intended solely for paste-up work.

Watercolor board

This consists of a solid core faced with a good watercolor paper. The extra strength and stability of a board is very useful with watercolor paints; stretching and cockling of the paper is not a problem. Boards are usually faced with rag papers, machine-made on cylinder molds, and a choice of hot pressed and rough surfaces are usually on offer. Not all watercolor board appears to be constructed around an acid-free core — a factor that should be taken into account when selecting a board for a particular use. All watercolor boards give the quality of performance that is required of them, but only those that are acid-free throughout can be regarded suitable as supports for fine art or illustrative work that is intended to last. Watercolor boards are often a natural white, which is less bright and warmer than many of the designers' papers and boards in general use. This is to be preferred, for brilliance is generally achieved by the use of brighteners, of which the effect is only temporary. Watercolor boards may be used with all water-based paint media; they perform well with pastels, crayons, charcoal, pencils and some pens. A number of watercolor boards are said to work well with airbrushes, and the choice of different surfaces means that there is plenty of scope for adaptation of watercolor boards to other uses.

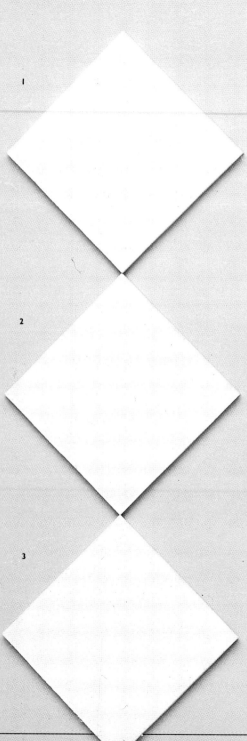

1 Daler line and wash, mounted Hollingsworth paper
2 Daler pasteline board
3 Frisk CS2 watercolor board (also used for brush and airbrush)

Airbrush board and other special application products

Although airbrushes may be used on a number of the boards already described, there is also a surface made especially for this particular use. It is a hard but slightly textured surface sometimes known as abraded board, also suitable for a number of other paint media, and that accepts pastels and crayons. At least one graphic artists' board is specially adapted for use with oil paint and has a non-absorbent, textured surface. Canvas boards intended for the fine-art market are a similar product adaptable to graphic use. Technical boards are printed with a light overlay grid, like graph and technical papers, and are intended for technical draftsmen, designers and architects. The grid patterns are usually in non-reproducing blue.

Strippable board

Of particular interest to graphic artists is a type of board likely to be in increased demand in the future. This is strippable board, on which a comparatively thin facing paper is held to the core of the board by a relatively weak adhesive. The result is that the facing paper, complete with the finished artwork that it carries, can be removed from the board (perhaps in order to fit it around the cylinder of an image scanner, as part of the most up-to-date plate-making techniques). As more and more printing is based on this kind of technology, so the need for this facility is increasing, and it is possible that a greater number of boards will be made strippable.

Some lightweight boards made of a facing paper mounted on Bristol board are also on the market as alternatives; these are flexible enough to mount around the scanning equipment without further modification. Ordinary boards can be stripped, but the process is not without risk.

Illustration board

The term "illustration board" is commonly applied to a range of different boards suitable for different types of artwork. Most of these boards are white, although television illustration board is gray — like a blank television screen — and is used for the presentation of preparatory artwork, showing how an image is intended to appear on television.

The following catagories of illustration board include those of most use to graphic artists and designers.

1 Schoellershammer 4R Dick airbrush board
2 Frisk CS6 abraded board
3 Fredrix USA canvas board
4 Oram & Robinson Academy line board, strippable
5 Letraset 5000 illustration board

Mat, mounting and display board

Ranges of colored boards are available under various names to graphic artists and designers. The boards usually consist of a core faced on one side by a colored paper, and some ranges are matched to ranges of cover paper so that the same selection of shades is available in board and paper form. Sometimes these boards are faced on both sides with co-ordinating colored papers, to make them more versatile.

They are used for mounting and display, and some may be used as a base for artwork, depending on the suitability of the surface. Ranges of mat boards which are intended primarily for use in picture framing frequently include textured and decorative surfaces as well as solid-colored ones. These boards may be particularly useful for display and presentation. The majority of the boards have a pulp core; those offered for very general applications are seldom acid-free.

Conservation- and museum-quality boards

are acid-free and are suitable for applications in which an extensive life is required. They are generally suitable as artwork supports, and are obviously desirable for mounting finished artwork which is valued. Mount board that is not acid-free may damage the artwork it surrounds over a period of time. Unfortunately, conservation board ranges do not always offer a wide choice of finishes.

Art board

is a term applied to at least one range of conservation-quality boards which are faced with fine art papers; these make excellent supports for pastel, gouache, acrylic and for pencil and pen. The same term may, however, also be applied in a much more general way to mean almost any of the boards discussed here, and the manufacturer's specifications should be referred to for verification when products of high quality are being selected.

Solid black mounting boards

are offered by a number of manufacturers. They are black all the way through, so that they show black even when cut, and are popular for mounting transparencies or photographs. They also lend themselves to a variety of display purposes — black being an excellent background against which to show off anything with color.

Laminated foam board

is another very interesting product with a great deal of scope for use in art and design. This consists of a core of polystyrene foam in sheet form, faced on both front and back with a stout sheet of acid-free paper. The resultant sheet is strong, stable, and very light. It may be used as a support for most fine art and graphic media, and can be cut accurately and cleanly for decorative and display purposes.

In addition to plain colors and patterns, conventional boards are also offered in fluorescent and metallic finishes, which are likely to be of interest in some design applications.

1 Mat board
2 Letramax by Letraset
3 Laminated foam board
4 Metallic finish

Fine art papers and boards, decorative papers and other useful products

There is some overlap between the papers used by designers and those used by fine artists — good quality drawing paper, for example, is common to both disciplines. Similarly, the few boards likely to be employed by fine artists — such as watercolor board and art boards — have already been described in the section on graphic artists' boards. What remains are the watercolor papers, specialized drawing papers, print-making papers and calligraphy papers.

There are many print-making papers suitable as drawing papers, of which some take gouache and acrylic quite well too. They are of interest also as papers to use, in that they lend themselves to the production of fine letterheads with engraved, etched or embossed designs.

Watercolor papers and a number of drawing papers are made by hand at the top of the fine-art range of papers. White, off-white, cream, gray and tan papers are produced, and a fair assortment of weights and surfaces is available to choose from. A few hand-made calligraphy papers can also be obtained.

Machine-made watercolor papers are mostly made on cylinder molds. They are produced only in white, but there are considerable differences between one manufacturer's white and another's. Off-whites are generally preferable. Like the hand-made watercolor papers, most machine-made watercolor papers are rag or 100% cotton, but some wood-free papers are also offered as low-cost fine-art papers. Machine-made watercolor papers are more regular in their surfaces and thicknesses than the hand-made products, and rough surfaces in particular can be quite standard on the machine-made products. There are usually three or four weights in a range of watercolor papers, between $190 \, gm^2$ (90 lb) and $640 \, gm^2$ (300 lb); the heaviest of these are extremely stable and sturdy papers, approaching the thickness of a board.

Ingres paper is a hard-surfaced drawing paper with a laid finish. Several ranges are available offering a good selection of colors, and some include flecking, using fibers of different colors, which gives the papers a vibrant and decorative finish. Ingres papers are widely used outside fine art, but they are regarded as especially suitable for pastels and crayons. Other colored drawing papers offered for use by artists do not have the laid effect of Ingres paper, but have instead a slight surface texture which works well with pastels and gouache.

Imitation parchment papers are popular with calligraphers and may be used to give character to printed matter. More decorative still are papers with hide and marble effect.

Japanese papers frequently include exotic materials trapped in the substance of the paper and unusual surface patterns, which make them highly decorative and often works of art in their own right.

A synthetic paper that could be very useful in the future has recently been introduced. It includes unusually long fibers of synthetic materials and is incredibly strong; a thin sheet is almost impossible to tear. The surface accepts print and is suitable for numerous applications.

1 Greens Rough 90lb watercolor paper
2 Cotman 90lb N/P
3 Bockingford 90lb rough
4 Daler tinted Ingres paper
5 Plastic
6,7 Chartwell calligraphy pad

Graphic artists' and designers' films

Plastic film products are used for a number of specialized purposes by graphic artists and designers, and are used more widely by technical draftsmen, architects and printers. The two basic materials in use are acetate sheet — which appears in various forms as acetate, diacetate and triacetate — and polyester.

Acetate is often colorless, although it may sometimes be given a light blue tint. It may have an etched surface, making it translucent rather than transparent, which gives it sufficient tooth to receive pencil or pen. Such film finds use in tracing, in drafting, and in the preparation of color separations for printing.

Alternatively, it may have a gel-coated surface which looks smooth, glossy and perfectly transparent. However, the gel coating enables it to accept most studio media without preparation: paints, inks and dry transfer lettering all sit happily on its surface. This type of acetate is particularly suited to overlays, color separation and use in animation cells. Some gel-coated acetates are coated on both sides.

Finally, clear acetate sheeting is also available. This is uncoated and has a super-smooth finish which accepts only specialized marker pens, film colors, and waxy media such as all-surface pencils. It is used for overhead projection, for animation, and for some overlay applications. Self-adhesive acetate can be used to cover mock-ups or one-off pieces where a simulated gloss finish is required.

Polyester is used mainly for drafting film, and is either an opalescent gray-white or a solid but translucent white. The surface has a matte finish and the minute grain enables it to accept pencil or pen, although film leads and inks are applicable in many instances. Some drafting films are prepared on one side only; others have both sides prepared. The tooth of drafting films varies between one supplier's and another's.

The beauty of polyester film is that it is incredibly stable — it does not alter with humidity changes, does not stretch or shrink, does not degrade with age, and does not yellow or become brittle under the effects of ultra-violet light (which is used in some reproduction processes as well as being present in daylight). These properties are useful in any event, but are of particular importance in technical drawing. Polyester drafting films work exceptionally well on light-boxes because of their translucence.

Other film products of interest to graphic artists include self-adhesive, colored, transparent acetate sheet, grid-printed sheets and drafting films, and red and orange masking films. Red and orange films are used to mask out sensitizing light during plate-making and screen-making parts of the printing process. They are available in self-adhesive, low-tack and non-adhesive versions.

Finally, there are the so-called frisket films. These are generally low-tack products used to mask off areas during airbrush work, as alternatives to stopping-out media.

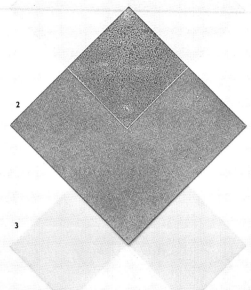

1 Acetate film sales, 0.0125mm
2 Red film, Mecanorma Normapaque
3 Polyester Mecanorma
4 Frisk film, gloss
5 Frisk film, matte

PAPER, BOARD AND FILM SUPPLIERS

SUPPLIER	MANUFACTURER	DISTRIBUTOR	WHOLESALER	RETAILER	Areas where products are available	Local variations in product range	Line Board Cartridge	Graph	Tracing	Layout	Detail	Marker	Colored	Bristol Board	Line Board	Line and Wash Board	Airbrush Paper/Board	Paste-up Board	Foam Board	Designers Pads	TV Layout Pads	Strippable Board	Watercolor Paper/Board	Acetate	Draft	Draw	Trace	Photolith	Self-Adhesive	Soft-Tack
Abelscot-Marchant	•	•	•		W	No			•	•		•	•	•						•					•	•	•		•	
Alvin	•	•	•		W	No			•	•			•											•						
Arjomari	•				W	No							•										•							
The Art Factory	•	•			W	No			•	•		•	•		•	•			•						•	•				
Art Material International	•	•	•		W	N/S				•		•	•			•			•				•	•				•	•	•
Atlantis			•	•	N/S	No			•	•			•		•			•	•				•							
Badger	•				W	No										•												•		
Charles T. Bainbridge	•				US	No									•	•	•													
Barcham Green	•				W	No																	•							
Berrick Brothers	•	•	•		E	N/S							•										•							
R.K. Burt	•	•	•	•	UK	No	•						•	•	•								•							
Canson et Montgolfier	•				W	No			•	•			•	•									•							
Columbia	•				US	No									•	•														
Cotech Sensitising	•				W	No																		•						
Conté	•				W	Yes																							•	
Crescent	•				W	N/S							•	•	•	•	•	•	•				•							
Daler-Rowney	•	•			W	No		•	•	•		•	•	•	•	•	•	•	•			•		•		•				
De Visu (Roger Jullian)	•				E UK US	No		•	•	•			•	•	•		•			•	•	•	•		•	•				
Fabriano	•				E UK US	N/S							•										•							
Falkiner Fine Papers		•	•	•	UK	No	•			•			•	•									•							
Film Sales		•	•		W	No																			•	•	•			•
Sam Flax	•			•	W	No							•						•											
Frisk	•	•	•		UK	No		•	•			•		•	•	•	•		•	•			•	•	•	•	•		•	•
GB Papers	•				E UK	N/S							•																	
John Heyer Paper		•			UK	N/A					•		•										•							
Holbein	•			•	W	No				•		•	•					•												
Inveresk	•				W	N/S	•																•							

KEY: A – Australia **C** – Canada **E** – Europe (excluding UK) **S** – Scandinavia **UK** – United Kingdom **US** – United States **W** – Worldwide **N/S** – Not Stated

Continued

Continued

PAPERS AND BOARDS   **FILMS**

SUPPLIER	Manufacturer	Distributor	Wholesaler	Retailer	Areas where products are available	Local variations in product range	Line Board Cartridge	Graph	Tracing	Layout	Detail	Marker	Colored	Bristol Board	Line Board	Line and Wash Board	Airbrush Paper/Board	Paste-up Board	Foam Board	Designers Pads	TV Layout Pads	Strippable Board	Watercolor Paper/Board	Acetate	Draft	Draw	Trace	Photolith	Self-Adhesive	Soft-Tack
KIN Rapidograph	•	•			C US	No		•		•															•					
Langford & Hill		•	•	•	W	No		•	•	•	•	•	•		•	•	•	•	•	•	•	•	•	•	•	•	•	•	•	•	•
T.N. Lawrence		•	•	•	UK	No	•		•					•	•									•						
Letraset	•				W	N/S							•							•										
Mecanorma	•				UK	N/A				•			•	•			•			•				•					•	
MET Graphic Supplies		•			UK	N/A		•	•	•	•	•		•	•	•	•			•	•	•	•							
Omnicrom Systems	•				W	No							•										•						•	
Oram & Robinson	•				A E UK	No		•	•	•	•	•	•	•	•	•	•						•							
Osmiroid	•				W	Yes				•																				
H.W. Peel & Co	•	•			W	No		•	•	•				•	•	•				•			•	•	•					
Plastic Suppliers	•	•			W	N/S																	•	•			•			
Rexel (Derwent Cumberland)	•				W	Yes																	•	•						
Salis International (Dr. P.H. Martin's)	•				W	No																							•	•
Schleicher & Schuell (Selecta)	•				W	No		•	•	•		•	•	•			•			•			•							
Schmincke	•				W	No		•		•			•										•							
Schoellershammer	•				W	No		•	•	•			•	•	•		•			•			•	•						
Sennelier	•				N/S	N/S																	•							
Skycopy	•	•			UK	N/A																	•	•	•	•		•		
Sommerville	•				W	Yes							•						•				•							
Strathmore	•				W	N/S	•						•	•	•	•							•							
Tumba	•				E UK	N/S							•										•							
Two Rivers	•			•	N/S	No							•										•							
A. West & Partners	•	•			A E S UK	No		•	•	•	•	•	•	•	•	•	•		•		•	•	•	•	•	•			•	•
Whatman	•				W	No																	•	•						
Wiggins Teape	•	•	•		UK	N/S	•		•																					
Winsor & Newton	•	•		•	W	No		•	•	•	•	•	•				•			•			•							
Zanders	•				E UK	N/S			•					•	•	•			•				•							

KEY: A = Australia **C** = Canada **E** = Europe (excluding UK) **S** = Scandinavia **UK** = United Kingdom **US** = United States **W** = Worldwide **N/S** = Not Stated

PAPER AND BOARD APPLICATIONS

Applications

MANUFACTURER SUPPLIER	PRODUCT	Drawing (Cartridge)	Graph	Tracing	Layout	Detail	Marker	Bristol Board	Illustrators' Board	Paste-up Board	Watercolor Paper/Board	Fine Art Paper	Graphic Designers' Paper	Pen	Pencil	Crayon	Watercolor	Gouache	Acrylic	Marker Pens	Airbrush	Print	Illustration	Wash & Wipe	Paste-up
Abelscot Marchant	Sketching Detail Paper				•								•	•	•										
	Supreme Rag Detail Paper				•								•	•	•										
	Transbond Detail Paper				•								•	•	•				•						
	Transbond Glazed Detail Paper				•								•	•	•				•						
	Premier Fluorescent Drawing Cartridge	•																							
	Layout 60 Marker Pen						•						•	•						•					
Alvin	Alva-Line Tracing Paper			•									•	•	•	•	•	•	•		•				
	Alva-Blue Line Non-Repro Drawing Paper			•									•	•											
	Draft Art Illustration Board								•				•	•	•	•	•	•	•			•	•	•	
	Graphic Art Illustration Board								•				•	•	•	•	•	•	•	•	•	•	•	•	
	School Art Illustration Board								•				•	•	•	•	•	•	•			•	•	•	
APT	Aptline Board								•				•	•	•	•	•	•	•				•	•	
	Aptline Paper										•		•	•	•	•	•								
	Apt Layout Pads				•								•	•	•										
Atlantis	Indian Handmade Paper										•		•	•	•	•	•	•							
	Atlantis Drawing and Watercolor Paper										•		•	•	•	•	•	•		•		•			
	Heritage Wood-Free Paper										•		•	•	•							•	•		
	Heritage Rag Paper										•		•	•	•							•	•		
Barcham Green	RWS (Royal Watercolour Society)										•		•	•	•	•	•	•				•	•	•	
	De Wint										•			•	•	•	•							•	
	Turner Grey										•		•	•	•	•	•	•				•	•	•	
	Cambersand Tan Wove										•		•	•	•	•	•	•				•	•	•	
	Greens' Pasteless Board										•						•	•	•				•		
	Mediterranean Badger											•	•	•	•	•	•	•	•		•				
R. K. Burt	R.K.B. Wana										•		•	•	•	•	•	•							
	Aquarelle																								
	R.K.B. Arches										•		•	•	•	•	•	•	•			•	•		
	R.K.B. Rives Offset											•	•	•							•		•		
Charles T. Bainbridge & Sons	Bainbridge No. 80 Illustration Board								•				•	•	•	•	•	•	•	•	•	•	•	•	•
	Bainbridge No. 172 Illustration Board								•				•	•			•	•	•	•	•	•	•		•
	Bainbridge No. 99 Presentation Board									•															•
	Bainbridge Mat Board									•															•

Continued

Continued

Applications

Manufacturer/Supplier	Product	Drawing (Cartridge)	Graph	Tracing	Layout	Detail	Marker	Bristol Board	Illustrators Board	Paste-up Board	Watercolor Paper/Board	Fine Art Paper	Graphic Designers' Paper	Pen	Pencil	Crayon	Watercolor	Gouache	Acrylic	Marker Pens	Airbrush	Print	Illustration	Wash & Wipe	Paste-up
Canson et Montgolfier	Mi-Teintes Paper											●		●	●	●	●	●					●		
	Ingres Vidalon Paper											●		●	●	●	●	●					●		
	Verge Gallery Paper											●		●	●	●	●	●					●		
	Fine Art Board								●					●	●	●	●	●	●			●	●		
	C A Grain											●		●	●	●	●	●					●		
	White Paper																								
	Bristol Paper												●	●		●	●	●	●			●	●	●	
Chartwell	Bristol Board Pads						●						●	●		●	●	●	●			●	●	●	
	Typo/Detail pads				●								●	●	●	●									
	Professional Cartridge	●											●	●	●	●	●	●					●		
	Layout Pads			●									●	●	●	●									
	Professional Tracing			●									●	●	●	●	●	●		●					
	Aquarelle									●			●	●	●	●	●	●	●						
	Ingres											●		●	●	●	●	●					●		
	Bleed Proof Marker					●							●	●						●					
	Graph		●										●	●											
Columbia	1776 Presentation Board							●					●	●	●	●	●	●	●			●	●	●	
	1812 Illustration Board							●							●	●	●	●				●	●	●	
Crescent	Art Poster Board								●				●	●			●	●	●			●	●	●	
	Display Blanks								●				●	●			●	●	●			●	●	●	
	Melton Mounting Board								●				●	●			●	●				●	●	●	
	Regular Mat Board								●				●	●	●	●	●	●				●	●	●	
	Illustration Board No. 201						●						●	●	●	●	●	●	●		●	●	●	●	
	Illustration Board No. 200						●						●	●	●	●	●	●	●		●	●	●	●	
	Illustration Board No. 300						●						●	●	●	●	●	●	●	●	●	●	●	●	
	Illustration Board No. 100						●						●	●	●	●	●	●	●	●	●	●	●	●	
	Illustration Board No. 99						●						●	●	●	●	●	●				●	●	●	
	Illustration Board No. 1						●						●	●	●	●	●	●				●	●	●	
	Illustration Board No. 215						●						●	●	●	●	●	●				●	●	●	
	Line-Kote No. 220						●						●										●		
	Line-Kote No. 210						●						●										●		
Daler-Rowney	Designer Series Typo Pads				●								●	●	●	●									

MANUFACTURER/SUPPLIER	PRODUCT	Drawing (Cartridge)	Graph	Tracing	Layout	Detail	Marker	Bristol Board	Illustrators' Board	Paste-up Board	Watercolor Paper/Board	Fine Art Paper	Graphic Designers' Paper	Pen	Pencil	Crayon	Watercolor	Gouache	Acrylic	Marker Pens	Airbrush	Print	Illustration	Wash & Wipe	Paste-up
Daler-Rowney	Designer Series Cartridge Pads	•												•	•	•	•	•	•				•		
	Designer Series Layout Pads				•									•	•	•									
	Designer Series Marker Pads						•							•	•					•					
	Designer Series Tracing Pads			•										•	•	•	•	•					•		
	Designer Series Graph Pads		•											•	•										
	Daler Superline Pads											•		•	•								•		
	Series 'A' Layout Pads				•									•	•	•									
	Series 'A' Tracing Pads			•										•	•	•									
	Superline Board							•						•	•	•	•	•	•		•	•	•	•	•
	Truline Board							•						•	•	•	•	•	•		•	•	•	•	•
	Pasteline Board							•						•	•	•	•	•	•		•	•	•	•	•
	Line and Wash Board							•						•	•	•	•	•	•	•	•	•	•	•	•
	Watercolour Board										•			•	•	•	•	•	•		•		•		
	Canford Cover Paper										•			•	•	•							•		•
	Ingres Paper											•		•	•	•	•	•	•				•		
Dramant	Tracing Paper			•										•	•	•									
Sam Flax	Flax No. 38 Tracing			•										•	•	•									
	Flax No. 514																								
	'Heavyweight' Tracing			•										•	•	•	•	•	•						
	Flax No. 1 Vellum Pads			•										•	•	•									
	Flax Ledger Pads										•			•	•	•	•	•	•						
	Flax Layout Pads				•									•	•	•				•					
	Flax Marker Pads						•							•	•					•					
	Flax Bond Pads				•									•	•	•									
	Technaflax Pads										•			•	•					•					
	Flax Bristol Pads and Sheets						•							•	•	•	•	•	•	•	•	•	•	•	•
	Flax Ultra Bristol Pads						•							•	•	•	•	•	•	•	•	•	•	•	•
	Ultra Flax Illustration Board								•					•	•		•	•	•	•	•		•	•	
Frisk	CS10 Line Board							•						•	•		•	•	•	•			•	•	•
	CS10 Paper										•			•	•		•	•	•				•		
	CS10 Bristol 4						•							•	•		•	•	•		•	•	•	•	•
	CS10 Media 6							•						•	•		•	•	•				•	•	
	CS10 Grafik 8							•						•	•		•	•	•				•	•	
	CS10 Display 12							•						•	•		•	•	•	•			•	•	•

Continued

Applications

Manufacturer/Supplier	Product	Drawing (Cartridge)	Graph	Tracing	Layout	Detail	Marker	Bristol Board	Illustrators Board	Paste-up Board	Watercolor Paper/Board	Fine Art Paper	Graphic Designers' Paper	Pen	Pencil	Crayon	Watercolor	Gouache	Acrylic	Marker Pens	Airbrush	Print	Illustration	Wash & Wipe	Paste-up
Frisk	CS4 Keyline						●						●	●		●	●	●	●				●	●	●
	CS2 Not Watercolor										●		●	●	●	●	●	●		●			●		
	CS2 HP Watercolor										●		●	●	●	●	●	●		●			●		
	CS6 Abraded Board						●						●	●	●	●	●	●		●			●		
	CS8 Technik Board						●						●	●		●	●	●					●		
	Bristol Board					●							●	●		●	●	●	●				●		
	Doodle Block Pads				●								●	●	●										
	Video Visual Pads												●	●	●					●					
	Page Planner Pads												●	●	●					●					
	Perspecta												●	●	●										
	Colorscope Pads												●	●	●	●									
	Calligraphers Pads												●	●									●		
	Sectional Pads				●								●	●											
	Studio 60 Pads												●	●	●	●				●					
	Studio 45 Pads												●	●	●	●				●					
	Layout Pads				●								●	●	●					●					
	Marker Pads												●	●	●	●				●					
	C-Trace 60 Pads			●									●	●	●										
	C-Trace 90 Pads			●									●	●	●										
	Typo Detail Pads					●							●	●	●					●					
Guarro	Acuarela Paper										●		●	●	●	●	●	●					●		
	Acuarela Board										●		●	●	●	●	●	●					●		
Hahnemuhle	Aquarelle Paper										●		●	●	●	●	●	●					●		
	Ingres Paper											●	●	●	●	●	●	●					●		
	Burga Butten Paper											●	●	●	●								●		
Herga	Pastel Paper											●		●	●								●		
Hollingworth	Kent Drawing Paper											●	●	●	●	●	●	●	●				●		
Inveresk	Bockingford Watercolour										●		●	●	●	●	●	●			●	●			
	Saunders Watercolour										●		●	●	●	●	●	●			●	●			
Keuffel & Esser	Albanene Tracing Paper			●									●	●	●										
	Crystalene Tracing Paper			●									●	●	●										
Melrat	Velasquez Aquarelle Paper										●		●	●	●	●	●	●					●		

MANUFACTURER/ SUPPLIER	PRODUCT	Drawing (Cartridge)	Graph	Tracing	Layout	Detail	Marker	Bristol Board	Illustrators Board	Paste-up Board	Watercolor Paper/Board	Fine Art Paper	Graphic Designers' Paper	Pen	Pencil	Crayon	Watercolor	Gouache	Acrylic	Marker Pens	Airbrush	Print	Illustration	Wash & Wipe	Paste-up
Oram & Robinson	Fine Pen Board							•						•	•		•	•	•				•		
	Academy Line Board							•						•	•		•	•	•				•		
	Tracing Paper			•										•	•	•									
	Tolmers Wash Paper											•		•	•		•	•	•				•	•	
	Academy Line Paper											•		•	•								•		
Papeterie Arjomari Paioux	Arches Aquarelle Paper										•			•	•	•	•	•	•				•		
	Arches Lavis										•			•	•								•		
	Fidelis Paper																								
	Arches MBM										•			•	•	•	•	•	•				•		
	Ingres Paper																								
Rising Paper	Photolene Bristol Board						•							•	•		•	•	•				•		
	Mirage Paper											•		•									•		
Schoellershammer	Fine Line Illustration Board								•					•	•								•		
	Laminated Drawing Board								•					•	•								•		
	Trifolda Tracing Paper			•										•	•	•									
Strathmore	400 Series Watercolor Paper										•			•	•	•	•	•	•						
	500 Series Watercolor Paper										•			•	•	•	•	•	•						
	Aquarius II Watercolor Paper										•			•	•	•	•	•	•						
	Gemini Watercolor Paper										•			•	•	•	•	•	•						
	300 Series Bristol Paper						•							•	•	•	•	•	•	•			•		
	400 Series Bristol Paper						•							•	•					•			•		
	500 Series Bristol Paper						•							•	•	•	•	•	•	•			•		
	500 Series Illustration Board								•					•	•	•	•	•	•	•			•		
Tumba	Ingres Paper											•		•	•	•	•	•	•				•		
Two Rivers	Watercolour Paper										•			•	•	•	•								
Utrecht	Watercolor Paper										•			•	•	•	•	•							
	Bristol Board						•							•	•	•	•	•	•	•			•		
J. & R. Walker	Bemboka Handmade Artist's Paper											•		•	•	•	•	•	•				•		
Wiggins Teape	Gateway Tracing Paper			•										•	•	•									
	British Drawing Cartridge Paper	•												•	•	•	•								
Zanders	Parole										•			•	•	•	•	•	•						
	Parole Grafikkarton								•					•	•		•	•	•	•	•	•	•	•	•
	Parole Artnorm		•											•	•		•	•	•	•			•		
	Parole Zeichenplatten								•					•	•	•	•	•	•	•	•	•	•	•	•

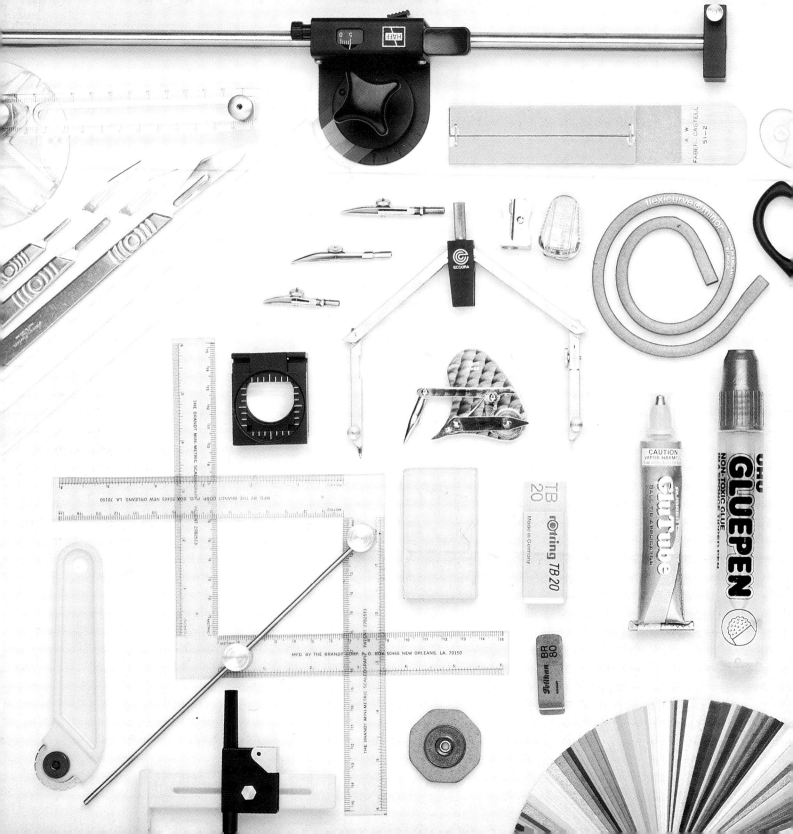

DESK EQUIPMENT

Rulers • Drawing Aids
Compasses • Erasers
Sharpeners • Cutting
Instruments • Tapes
Adhesives • Instant Lettering
Color Specifiers

DRAWING AIDS

Illustration and much of graphic design is more concerned — in its initial stages, at least — with the relatively free use of materials, and with composition that is more dependent on flair, than on accurate construction. There comes a time, however, when the imagination of a designer or the work of an illustrator has to be fitted into a professional and workable form for its end use. At this stage designers become technicians and must exercise draftsmanship of a higher order. In advertising or publishing, for example, a rough layout eventually has to be made into a real page; an industrial designer or an interior designer has to produce an accurate working drawing that others can follow; a technical illustrator has to produce illustrations that are both decorative and precise; and a general illustrator may need to translate an original sketch into a more finished painting or drawing on a different scale.

A fairly broad selection of drawing aids and instruments is surveyed here. Many of these are in everyday studio use, but others are perhaps more specialized in their applications, and may be products more familiar to technical draftsmen, industrial designers and architects. Graphic artists should find all these products potentially useful, and may find that several are adaptable to practical applications within the studio which may not in fact be the primary function for which they are intended. For example, a professional-quality straightedge, or an engineer's rule, both of which are frequently made of metal, make excellent edges to cut against during pasting-up operations.

Rulers, straightedges and scales

A ruler is a combination of a straightedge and a scale. For many years 12 inches (one foot) has been the standard length for a ruler, although they are available in both shorter and longer lengths. The wider adoption of the metric system has lead to the common use of a hybrid ruler measuring 300 mm, which is the nearest neat metric equivalent of a foot. These carry gradations in both millimeters and inches, and maintain the traditional format of a 12-inch ruler; 6-inch and 18-inch are also standard sizes. The 6-inch converts to a 150 mm ruler, but the 18-inch is gradually being supplanted by 24-inch rulers, equating to 600 mm, and by metric sizes such as 500 mm, which do not translate neatly into a standard equivalent. All-metric rulers and scales are also available.

A typical studio or office ruler is flat on one side, and on the other — which is the top side of the ruler — both the long edges are normally beveled. Used with the top side uppermost, the ruling edge is flat against the drawing surface. Used with the top side down, the edge is lifted clear of the drawing surface by means of the bevel, and lines may be drawn along it with a pen. If the rule is not used this way around with a pen, ink tends to flow under the edge of the ruler as the pen is drawn along, and a blotted, smudged and inaccurate line results. With a dip or a ruling pen this technique is essential, although most technical pens have a shouldered tip which makes blotting on a ruling edge less likely.

Wooden rulers are now used mostly as an educational product, but a few high-quality ones are still made. Some of these have an inset metal edge to insure accurate straightedge ruling.

Plastic rulers are now most popular, and clear plastic rulers are probably the most useful for graphic artists. White plastic rulers make the reading of measurements very clear and are sometimes beveled in section, which allows the edge to be placed right up against a flat surface for very accurate measurements. Flat scale rulers are often in this form. Clear plastic rulers have the advantage of transparence, which can be very useful when working on partly completed artwork or when pasting-up, or in any other situation when the position of other elements in the design is relevant.

Particularly useful are clear plastic rulers with a series of evenly-spaced parallel lines scored lengthwise along the center of the ruler. These may be positioned against an existing line or a line of text, for example, and a reasonably accurate line can be constructed at a set distance parallel to it.

Metal rulers are flat, thin, and without a bevel. The edges of a metal ruler are not easily damaged nor are the ends, which means that most use one end as the zero calibration, instead of having a protective shoulder like other rulers. They can thus be placed dead against the edge of a surface so that a measurement can be taken to a point from it.

RULERS

Clear plastic rulers are included in the ranges of Helix, Jakar International, Linex, Faber-Castell, Staedtler, and Blundell Harling. The Helix series "L" Officer Ruler and the Blundell Harling Graphics Model Acrylic rules have parallel line grids down the center for lining up operations. The Blundell Harling range also includes professional-quality designers' rules in clear plastic with 6- and 12-point type-scales running along one edge. The Jakar International range has steel rules in three sizes (15cm [6"], 30cm [12"], and 50cm [20"]) and Faber-Castell in sizes up to a full meter. They also offer stainless steel straightedges in 500-mm (20") and 800-mm (31½") lengths.

Maun produces non-graduated stainless steel straightedges, and Rabone-Chesterman chrome-finish rules and typescales. Fairgate, Vari-Line and General manufacture steel and aluminum rulers of a professional quality.

Transparent plastic rulers, two metal rulers with and without a beveled edge.

A straightedge in many instances is not noticeably different from a ruler. It is a reinforced or specially fitted edge that guarantees an accurate and unwavering line. A metal strip fitted into a wooden or plastic rule, or a steel strip set into an aluminum rule, is a most reliable form of straightedge. A professional draftsman's rule typically has a beveled edge, marked for measurement along its top, and an unmarked straightedge along its bottom edge. A straightedge in the form of an inserted metal strip frequently projects slightly so that the ruling edge is lifted cleanly from the paper, making it suitable for use with pens. A professional draftsman's straightedge and rule is usually one-sided, with a cork- or rubber-faced back to prevent it from sliding from its position during use.

A T-square is one form of straightedge with which most graphic designers are familiar. This consists of a broad tapering length of wood or plastic, with a straight drawing edge running along its top. At right-angles to the drawing edge this is attached at the thicker end to a shorter cross-piece of more substantial wood, which in use is kept tight up against the edge of the drawing board. This means that the straightedge is permanently at right-angles to the edge of the board, so that if moved up and down the T-square allows lines parallel to each other to be constructed.

In addition to straightedges and rulers there are several rules with special applications.

Parallel rulers are really a navigation instrument consisting of two ruling edges which are on hinged joints so that they remain parallel to each other as they are opened out. They can be quite useful as drawing instruments. Of definite interest to graphic artists and designers are cutting rulers. These have a shaped section designed to protect the fingers of the hand steadying the ruler while a knife is drawn along its edge.

The term "scale" refers to the measuring facility of a straight edge marked in divisions;

T-SQUARES

T-squares in wood, plastic and steel from Langford & Hill, Alvin, Sam Flax, Faber-Castell, Fairgate and Hellerman. The C-Thru T-square by Alvin has an adjustable head. Langford & Hill offers a stainless steel model recommended for use in cutting or with a pen. Parallel rules are included in the ranges of Linex, Jakar International, Blundell Harling, Sam Flax and Hellerman. Triangular scales, reduction scales and conversion scales are offered in professional and student versions. High-grade products are frequently constructed in white plastic over a core of boxwood or pear wood; Linex, Alvin and Faber-Castell are respected makes. Blundell Harding offers a particularly good selection of scale rules, conversion scales and triangular scales in their Verulam, Centex and Academy series.

1 Type gauge
2 Cutting rule
3 Rule with non-slip backing
4 T-square with reinforced straight edge
5 T-square
6 T-square with plastic blade
7 Adjustable T-square

SCALES

The Gaebel range includes precision-engineered rules and scales, specialized selections for graphic artists, advertising agency rules, printers' line and type gauges, and high-quality drawing office rulers and straightedges. Gaebel, Hellerman, Linex and Fairgate all include cork- or rubber-backed non-slip rules and straightedges, and Hellerman offers a particularly versatile aluminum rule of this type, with an inset stainless steel straightedge and a non-slip rubber backing. The Faber-Castell Typometer is a useful multi-purpose type gauge. Geliot Whitman depth-scales are also popular.

Printers' scales and type gauges.

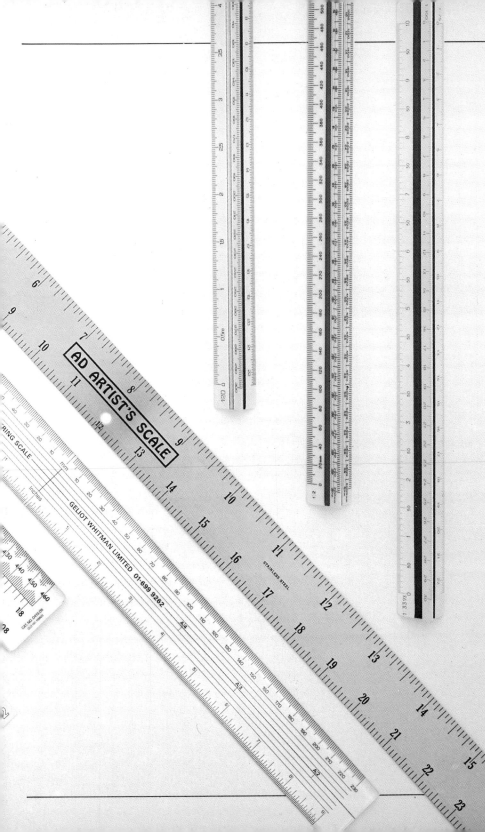

it is applied specifically to items intended either solely or primarily for measuring, rather than for drawing or ruling. Scales are often made with considerable accuracy. In some cases the divisions are cut individually by a process known as engine-dividing, which insures that each division is absolutely equal to the next. Other processes, such as photo-engraving, are also used to make certain that all the measurements are the same.

As well as standard units of length, scales are made to measure other divisions. Graphic artists' and printers' scales are made for measuring copy and type sizes. Graphic artists' scales measure in picas (twelve points or one-sixth of an inch in the standard system of measuring type) and in inches or millimeters as well.

A printer's or compositor's typegauge is similar to a graphic artist's scale. A type gauge has a series of edges pierced into an oblong format, along which are marked off various type-sizes and type-measuring scales. These can be used to calculate the space to be occupied by text when set to a specific type-size or line-spacing, or, conversely, can be used to calculate the amount of text that can be set into a given area. Printers' gauges are also made as individual line gauges, with only two edges, instead of the all-purpose oblong gauges.

Triangular scales are used by draftsmen and engineers. These have a total of six measuring edges which may be placed accurately in turn against a flat surface. Each of the six faces carries a different scale. Triangular scales are often constructed for great dimensional stability so that their accuracy is not impaired by temperature or atmospheric changes. The scale markings on triangular scales are usually related to standard reduction scales used in technical drawing, and a choice of scale combinations across the six faces is available. Triangular and flat reduction scales allow the user to enlarge or reduce the scale of a drawing easily and accurately.

There are many devices that have been designed to improve, or speed up, the drawing process. Several are concerned with accuracy, but others are intended just to make drawing easier, or to simplify some otherwise difficult operation.

Triangles are drawing aids for quick and accurate drawing of angles. The two common forms of triangle are a 90°-45°-45° and a 90°-60°-30° triangle. There is also an adjustable form of triangle that has a pivoted side facing the right-angle (the hypotenuse). This is attached to a sliding scale and can be moved and set to almost any combination of angles, given that the fixed third angle is always a right-angle. An equilateral triangle with equal sides and angles can easily be constructed using a 90°-60°-30° triangle. However, in terms of graphics generally, the most useful angle is the right-angle, which is essential to any work being constructed on a rectangular format.

Parallel lines may be constructed quickly using a triangle and a ruler, each line being constructed at a right-angle to a horizontal or vertical guideline. Some triangles are plain; others are marked on one or more edges with measuring scales. The edges may be plain or beveled, and some models have a metal-covered edge, making them suitable for cutting against. The 45° and 30° angles which are a feature of the two common triangles are essential for certain approaches to technical drawing.

Protractors are used for measuring or constructing angles, and are in the form either of a semi-circle or of a full circle, marked off around the edge in degrees, thus representing either 180° or a full 360°. They are generally made in clear plastic, and often have guidelines scored at every 10°. A base or center line showing the central point of the circle is an essential feature. Obtuse angles may be measured only with a circular protractor, or by calculating back from its complementary acute angle. Angles can be measured to an accuracy of a fraction of a degree using a large protractor. Most,

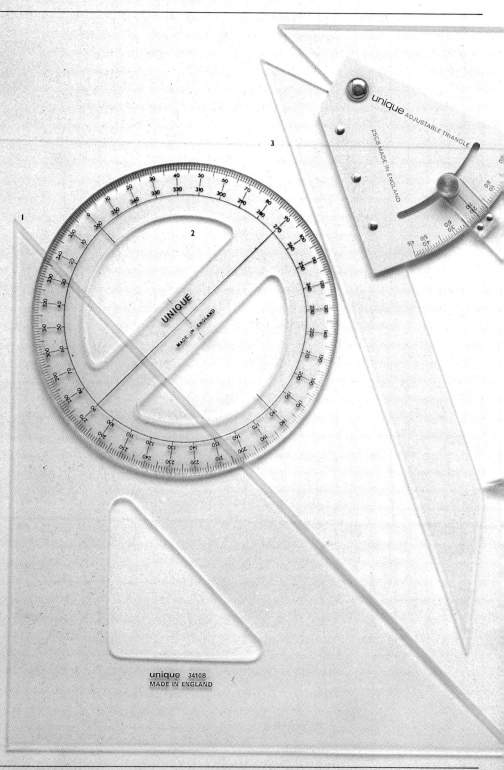

however, are marked in single degrees, which offers sufficient accuracy for most purposes.

Protractors are sometimes combined with triangles and other drawing aids in a single multipurpose unit. A special elliptical protractor is used for isometric drawing (a system of technical drawing) and can be used to measure angles in the three isometric planes. Protractors and triangles are generally made of transparent plastic, with or without a light tint. They are occasionally available in metal.

A pantograph is used for copying a drawing to a larger or smaller scale. It consists of four rods pivoted at their intersections to form a folding, extending lattice. For use, one end of the pantograph is fixed; a pen or pencil is placed at the end of one of the extending arms; and another is placed at the junction of

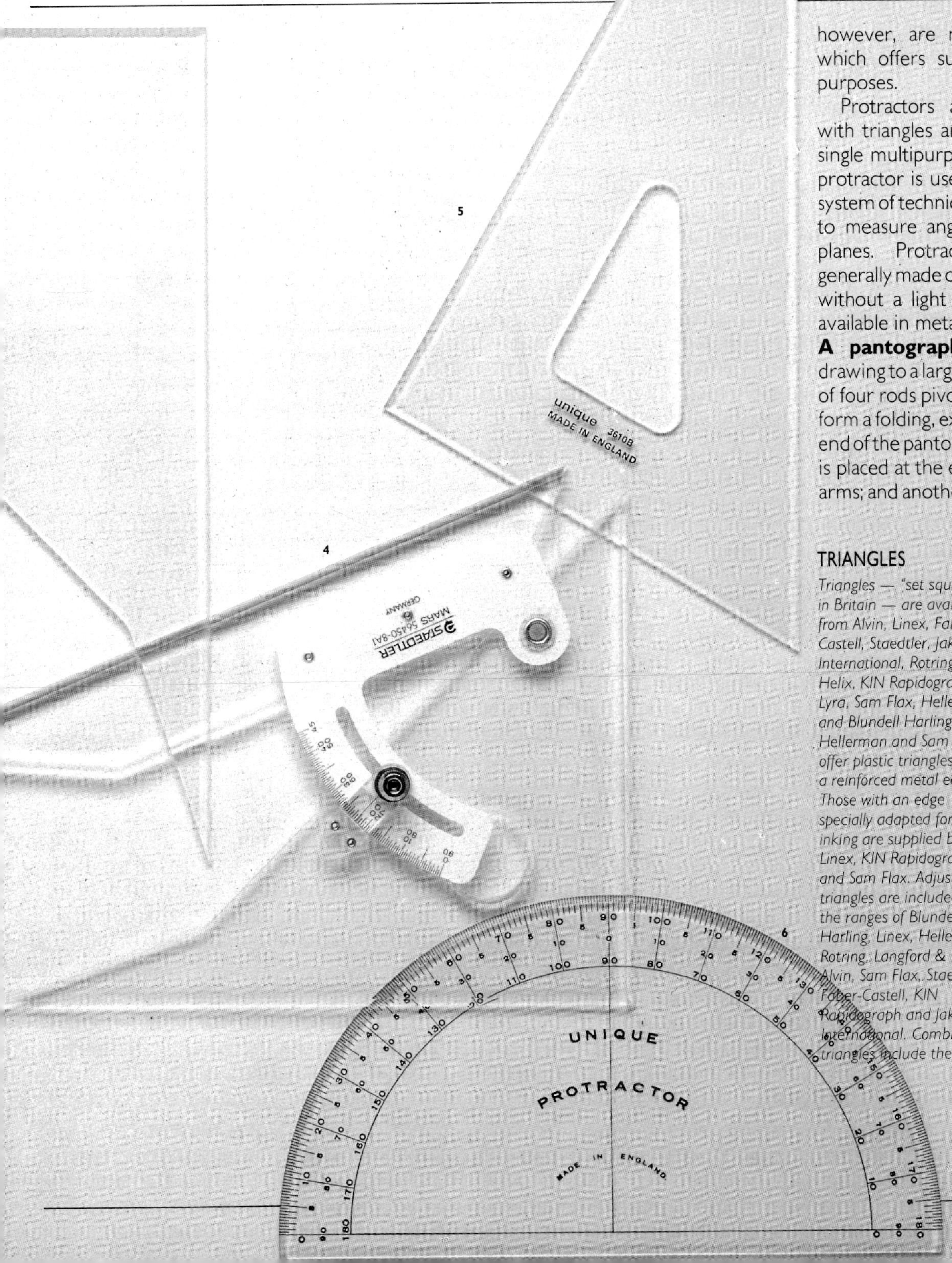

TRIANGLES

Triangles — "set squares" in Britain — are available from Alvin, Linex, Faber-Castell, Staedtler, Jakar International, Rotring, Helix, KIN Rapidograph, Lyra, Sam Flax, Hellerman, and Blundell Harling. Hellerman and Sam Flax offer plastic triangles with a reinforced metal edge. Those with an edge specially adapted for inking are supplied by Linex, KIN Rapidograph and Sam Flax. Adjustable triangles are included in the ranges of Blundell Harling, Linex, Hellerman, Rotring, Langford & Hill, Alvin, Sam Flax, Staedtler, Faber-Castell, KIN Rapidograph and Jakar International. Combination triangles include the Linex Geometry triangle, the Faver-Castell Combi triangle or the Lyra Rembrandt 3130 and 4130, and large triangles are offered by Linex and Hellerman.

PROTRACTORS

Both semi-circular and fully-circular protractors in clear or tinted plastic are supplied by Linex, Lyra, KIN Rapidograph, Jakar International, Rotring, Faber-Castell, Staedtler, Helex, Hellerman, Alvin, Langford & Hill, Blundell Harling, and Sam Flax. Protractors attached to a short ruler feature in several ranges, including those of Staedtler, Lyra, Rotring and Linex.

1 45° triangle
2 Circular protractor
3,4 Adjustable triangles
5 60°, 70°, triangle
6 Semi-circular protractor

the other two. When one of the pens or pencils is moved, the other repeats the movements, but on a different scale. The rods of a pantograph are fitted with a choice of pivot points, and depending on how these are set, different proportional movements can be achieved. In practice, one pen position is occupied by a stylus which is used to trace around the original drawing, while the pen or pencil in the other position redraws the same subject. Pantographs are extremely useful items of equipment for both illustrators and fine artists, and have further applications in more specialized areas of design.

A scaleograph is a device vaguely similar to the pantograph. Although this is not actually a drawing aid, this is an appropriate place to mention it. It consists of two L-shaped scales, often marked in picas as well as in inches or centimeters, which may be moved against each other to enlarge or reduce the rectangular area that they enclose. Once set to a particular proportion the scale may be moved outward or inward in such a way that the proportions of the space remain the same.

In graphic design a scaleograph is particularly useful for cropping (proportioned cutting) and scaling up or down to make photographs and illustrations fit into a specified area. Proportional scales or calculators perform a similar function, but are in the form of a disk calculator from which the appropriate reduction is read off, rather than in the form of a device which is actually laid over the drawing or photograph in question.

Drawing an ellipse is a particular problem, and an important one, since so many shapes when seen in perspective are built around a series of ellipses. There are several drawing aids which seek to help out on this.

An ellipsograph consists of two plastic disks within a rectangular frame; two sliding scales allow the dimensions of the ellipse to be set, and a pen or pencil is fitted into a holder in a slot down the middle of the disks.

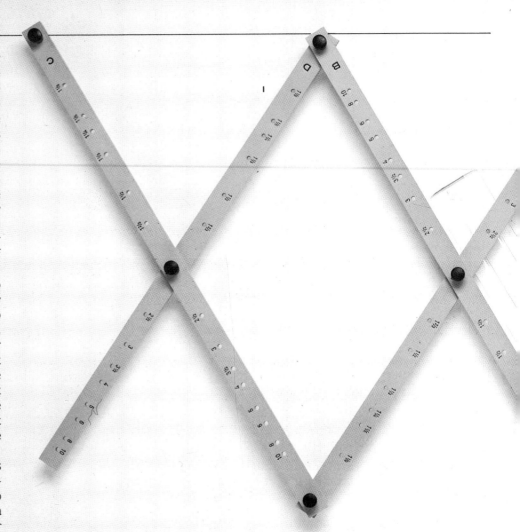

When the outer disk is rotated, a combination of the circular motion with the straight line motion of the pen in the slot, accurately describes an ellipse.

An ellipse machine consists of a base with a swinging arm. The drawing instrument is fitted to the end of the arm and the machine is set to produce the desired dimensions. The arm in fact pivots in two places and is guided, as with the ellipsograph, by a combination of sliding and circular motions. An ellipse machine draws only half an ellipse at one stroke and must be reversed to complete the drawing; it can, however, cope with much larger ellipses than an ellipsograph. Less complicated than either of

these methods is the use of templates. Ellipse templates are available in an extensive selection of sizes and proportions. An ellipse wheel or angle calculator may be used with ellipse templates to determine which template is appropriate for a specific angle of perspective.

Speedliners or rolling rulers are a form of parallel ruler which can be moved systematically to produce a series of parallel lines. The base is in the form of a roller which shows readings that indicate how far the ruler has been moved.

A cross-hatching machine is not dissimilar. This is used to produce quick, neat cross-hatching in the form of parallel lines.

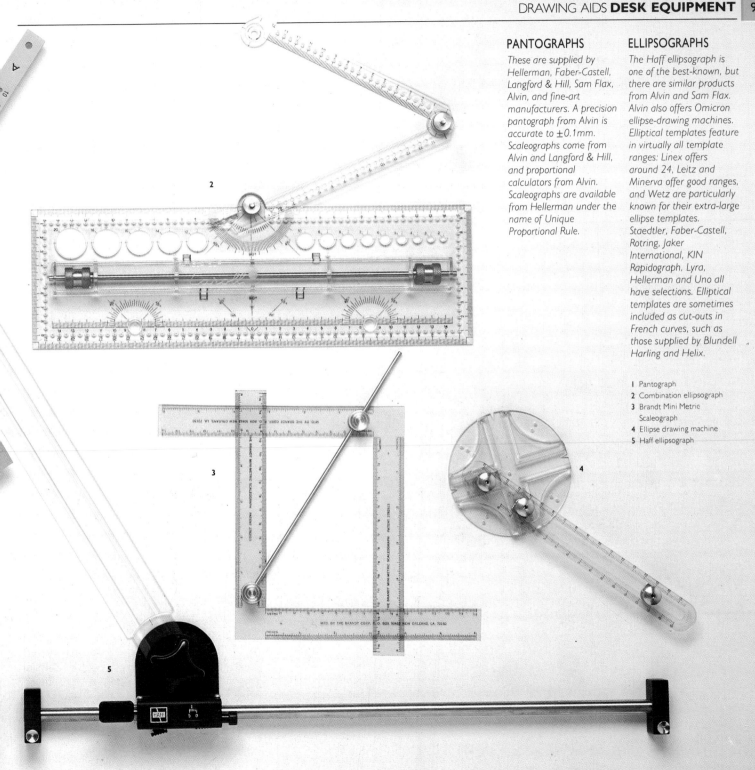

PANTOGRAPHS

These are supplied by Hellerman, Faber-Castell, Langford & Hill, Sam Flax, Alvin, and fine-art manufacturers. A precision pantograph from Alvin is accurate to ±0.1mm. Scaleographs come from Alvin and Langford & Hill, and proportional calculators from Alvin. Scaleographs are available from Hellerman under the name of Unique Proportional Rule.

ELLIPSOGRAPHS

The Haff ellipsograph is one of the best-known, but there are similar products from Alvin and Sam Flax. Alvin also offers Omicron ellipse-drawing machines. Elliptical templates feature in virtually all template ranges: Linex offers around 24, Leitz and Minerva offer good ranges, and Wetz are particularly known for their extra-large ellipse templates. Staedtler, Faber-Castell, Rotring, Jaker International, KIN Rapidograph, Lyra, Hellerman and Uno all have selections. Elliptical templates are sometimes included as cut-outs in French curves, such as those supplied by Blundell Harling and Helix.

1 Pantograph
2 Combination ellipsograph
3 Brandt Mini Metric Scaleograph
4 Ellipse drawing machine
5 Haff ellipsograph

The desired spacing is set prior to use — these machines usually have the benefit of a vernier scale, so that the setting is extremely accurate. The base of the machine rests under the operator's free hand, and is held steady. The straight edge protrudes from it and, at the touch of a button, moves a fraction nearer the base. A line is drawn, the button is touched, and the process is repeated until the desired area of hatching is complete. Of particular value is the fact that most cross-hatching machines may be fitted with a template holder, so that any shape — not just straight lines — can be repeated to form a hatched pattern.

Templates and curves offer a very wide range of shapes and sizes intended to assist drawing in both specific and general applications. They are in effect shapes that you draw around, and are usually in the form of a thin plastic sheet with cut-out shapes in a variety of sizes. Arrows, circles, ellipses and lettering templates have general uses and may be of interest to many graphic artists and illustrators; templates for house-furnishing plans and office-planning may be useful for interior designers. Some stencils and templates are for figure drawing.

Curves, generally known as French curves, are templates composed of several changing and graceful curves which offer fixed shapes that can be repeated, or at least rendered accurately, without the need for any elaborate construction. Special curves are available for applications such as shipbuilding and railway planning, but the majority are for general studio use. Flexible curves are particularly useful for graphic artists who may not wish to use the rigid and formal lines offered by set curves and templates. A flexible curve is in the form of a strip that can be bent to virtually any desired shape; it holds its shape while being drawn around, but can then be reformed to another shape if wished.

Perspective grids are useful drawing aids for technical illustrators, technical draftsmen, architects, and any artist or

TEMPLATES

Linex offers a good range; many are for specialized use, but a few (like the 1147 and 1148) can be adapted for general use. Hellerman offers products which include human-figure templates, both in set positions and as jointed mannikins. Templates and curves are also found in the ranges of Faber-Castell, Lyra, Blundell Harling, KIN Rapidograph, Staedtler, Rotring, Jakar International, Helix, Alvin and Sam Flax.

1,2 Templates
3,4 Flexible curves
5,6,7,8 French curves
9,10,11,12 Templates

designer wishing to construct a perspective drawing with speed. These are already marked with a detailed grid that follows the lines of perspective. They may be placed beneath the drawing, if the latter is on semi-transparent material.

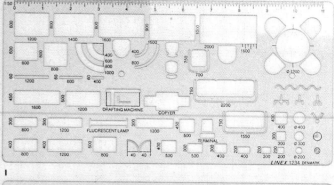

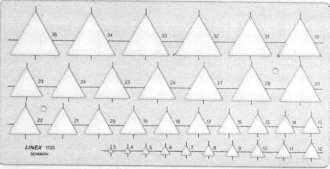

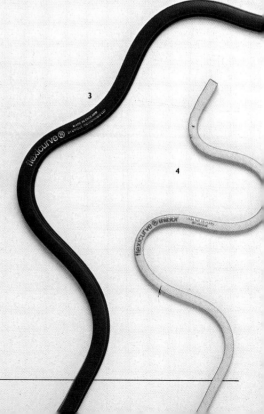

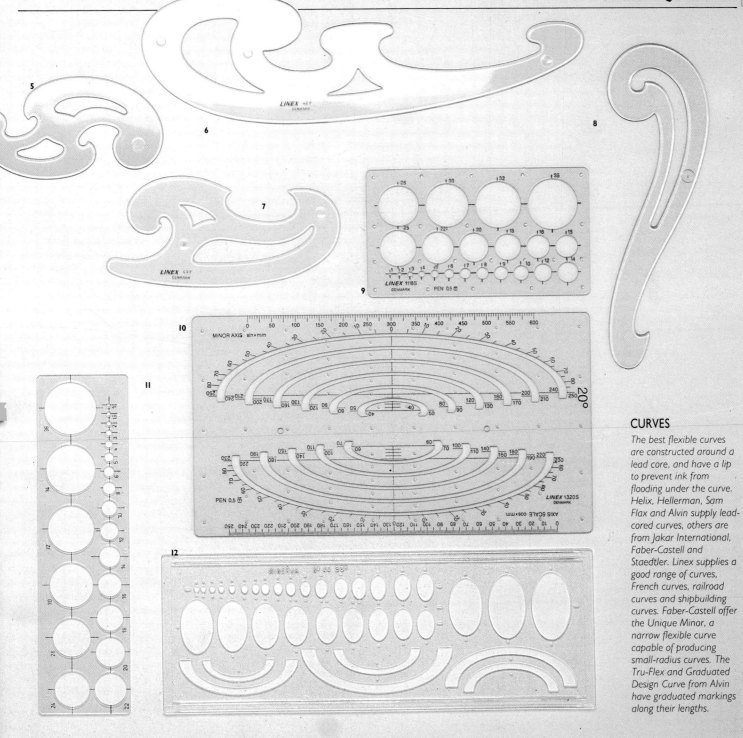

CURVES

The best flexible curves are constructed around a lead core, and have a lip to prevent ink from flooding under the curve. Helix, Hellerman, Sam Flax and Alvin supply lead-cored curves, others are from Jakar International, Faber-Castell and Staedtler. Linex supplies a good range of curves, French curves, railroad curves and shipbuilding curves. Faber-Castell offer the Unique Minor, a narrow flexible curve capable of producing small-radius curves. The Tru-Flex and Graduated Design Curve from Alvin have graduated markings along their lengths.

DRAWING AIDS

SUPPLIER	Manufacturer	Distributor	Wholesaler	Retailer	Areas where products are available	Local variations in product range	Rulers	T-Squares	Parallel Rules	Scales	Type gauges	Triangles	Ellipse Aids	Angle Calculators	Perspective Grids	Pantographs	Scaleographs	Protractors	Compasses/Beam	Dividers	Templates	French	Flexible	Elliptical	Manual	Computer	Electronic	Plastic Rubber	Kneaded	Putty	Battery	Clutch	Wrap-around	Ink	Pencil
Abelscot-Marchant	•	•	•		W	No	•			•	•				•	•	•	•	•	•	•	•			•	•	•	•	•	•	•	•	•	•	•
Alvin	•	•	•		W	No	•	•	•		•	•	•	•	•	•	•	•	•	•	•	•			•	•	•	•	•	•	•	•	•	•	•
Art Material International	•	•	•		W	N/S					•																								
Atlantis		•	•	•	N/S	N/A				•																									
BFE/Drafton		•	•		E UK US	No	•																	•											
Cannon & Wrin	•	•			A C E S UK	No		•				•		•				•	•	•	•	•	•												
Caran d'Ache	•				W	N/S																			•	•			•			•	•	•	
Conté	•				W	N/A																			•		•			•				•	
Daler-Rowney	•	•			W	No							•												•	•	•			•					•
De Visu (Roger Jullian)	•				E S UK US	No	•	•	•	•					•							•	•	•											
Eberhard-Faber	•				C US	No																			•	•			•			•	•	•	
Edding	•				W	No																			•		•						•	•	•
Educaid		•			UK	N/A	•																		•	•	•								
Sam Flax	•	•			W	No	•	•	•		•		•	•	•	•	•	•	•	•	•			•	•	•			•	•	•	•	•		
Gaebel (Stazput)	•				S US	Yes	•	•	•	•	•			•		•	•																		
Graphic Products International		•			S UK	N/S	•			•																									
Griffin (Grifhold)	•	•			W	No									•																				
Helix	•				N/S	N/A	•		•		•				•	•	•	•	•	•						•							•	•	
Holbein	•		•		W	No	•			•															•								•	•	
Jakar International		•			UK	No		•	•	•				•	•	•	•	•	•	•	•	•	•	•	•	•			•	•	•			•	•

SUPPLIER	MANUFACTURER	DISTRIBUTOR	WHOLESALER	RETAILER	Areas where products are available	Local variations in product range	Rulers	T-Squares	Parallel Rules	Scales	Type gauges	Triangles	Ellipse Aids	Angle Calculators	Perspective Grids	Pantographs	Scaleographs	Protractors	Compasses/Beam	Dividers	Templates	French	Flexible	Elliptical	Manual	Computer	Electronic	Plastic Rubber	Kneaded	Putty	Battery	Clutch	Wrap-around	Ink	Pencil
KIN Rapidograph	●	●			C US	No	●		●							●	●	●	●	●	●	●			●		●					●		●		
Langford & Hill		●	●	●	W	No	●	●	●	●	●	●	●	●	●	●	●	●	●	●	●	●			●	●	●	●			●	●	●	●		●
Letraset	●				W	N/S											●																			
Lyra	●				N/S	N/S											●		●								●	●						●		●
Marabu	●				W	No	●			●				●			●		●	●	●	●			●	●	●	●	●	●	●	●	●	●	●	●
Mecanorma	●				W	N/A	●		●		●						●		●																●	●
Microflame			●		N/S	N/A	●	●	●		●						●		●	●	●	●			●	●	●	●	●	●	●	●	●	●	●	●
Pelltech		●			UK	No	●	●	●		●		●	●			●	●	●	●	●	●	●													
Pentel	●				W	No																					●									
Pilot	●	●			W	No																					●									
Reprodraft		●	●		UK	N/A																		●	●	●										
Rexel (Derwent Cumberland)	●				W	Yes				●																	●	●								
Rotobord	●	●	●	●	A E UK US	No																		●	●	●										
Rotring		●			W	No	●		●			●	●	●			●	●	●	●	●				●	●	●								●	●
Schleicher & Schuell (Selecta)	●				N/S	N/A								●		●																				
D. & J. Simons			●		W	No								●																						
Staedtler	●				W	No	●	●	●		●						●	●	●	●	●	●					●			●						●
A. West & Partners	●	●			A E S UK	No		●	●								●	●	●					●	●											
Winsor & Newton	●	●		●	W	No								●										●	●											

KEY: A – Australia **C** – Canada **E** – Europe (excluding UK) **S** – Scandinavia **UK** – United Kingdom **US** – United States **W** – Worldwide **N/S** – Not Stated

Dividers and ruling pens

Ordinary dividers resemble a compass, except there is no drawing-tip: both legs end in a needle point. There are, in addition, specialized dividers called proportional dividers and spacing dividers.

Proportional dividers are for scaling measurements up or down, and may also be used to divide lines or circles into equal parts. The legs of proportional dividers are blade-like and carry points at both ends. Each arm carries a central slot along which a locking nut is free to move, and the legs are calibrated with either a proportional scale or a universal scale which can be used in conjunction with a chart to set ratios. Moving the central locking nut changes the point at which the legs pivot, so altering the ratio of the movement between each of the divider legs when they are set.

Spacing dividers are for making a series of equal divisions. They have a series of points attached to a trellis of rods which reaches from one leg of the divider to the other. As the legs of the divider are opened the trelliswork opens too, and the points move apart to create a series of equal divisions.

Ruling pens have already been described in the section on pens, as a type of reservoir pen. The drawing part consists of a pair of sprung jaws; the gap between them can be adjusted by means of a screw, and opening or closing the gap thus sets the width of the line. There are ruling pens for thin lines, for thick lines, and for curved lines; there are also easy-to-clean versions which open out, and double-headed versions which draw two lines at once. A dotting pen is a highly specialized type of ruling pen which lays down a dotted line, or a line of dashes, or even dots and dashes. Ruling pen attachments feature frequently as fittings for compasses, and many versions of dropbow compasses are fitted with a ruling pen drawing-tip.

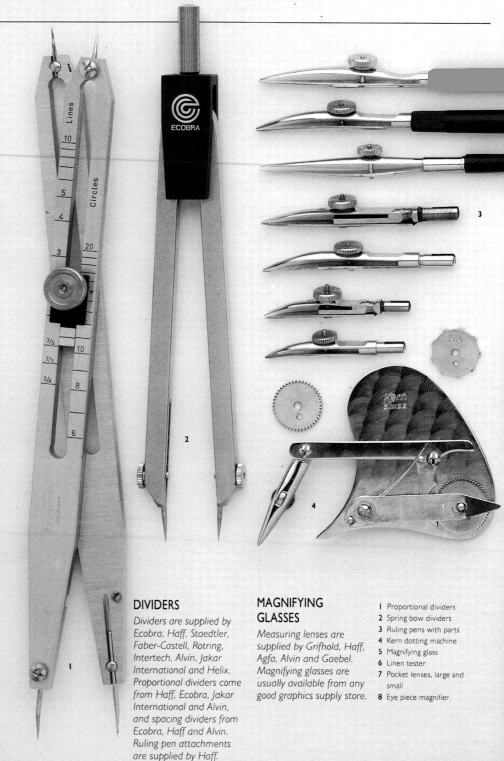

DIVIDERS

Dividers are supplied by Ecobra, Haff, Staedtler, Faber-Castell, Rotring, Intertech, Alvin, Jakar International and Helix. Proportional dividers come from Haff, Ecobra, Jakar International and Alvin, and spacing dividers from Ecobra, Haff and Alvin. Ruling pen attachments are supplied by Haff.

MAGNIFYING GLASSES

Measuring lenses are supplied by Grifhold, Haff, Agfa, Alvin and Gaebel. Magnifying glasses are usually available from any good graphics supply store.

1 Proportional dividers
2 Spring bow dividers
3 Ruling pens with parts
4 Kern dotting machine
5 Magnifying glass
6 Linen tester
7 Pocket lenses, large and small
8 Eye piece magnifier

Measuring lenses and magnifying glasses

When working on a small scale, or when absolute accuracy is required, a magnifying glass can be very useful. Mounted on a stand or on a flexible arm, they are suitable for continual working. However, for checking detail and for making small measurements, measuring lenses are more practical. These consist of a small lens mounted above a measuring scale, which can be laid flat against a work surface. Such devices are sometimes called thread counters, or linen testers, because they are used to examine textiles, although some measuring lenses are made more specifically for engineers and draftsmen. At least one model exists which is made for measuring type-sizes. They can be quite useful items for graphic artists, and are particularly useful in applications such as photo-retouching and technical illustration.

Drafting machines

A drafting machine is a drawing-board which has two straightedges set at right-angles to each other on an adjustable arm so that they can be moved about the surface of the board. This combines the function of a drawing-board with those of a ruler and a straightedge, and of a protractor and a set square. Drafting machines are mostly used for precision drafting by designers, architects and engineers, but they may be put to more general applications. With them it is easy to produce parallel lines in either a vertical or horizontal direction, and they can also be tilted to operate at an angle during use. The original design makes use of a hinged arm, but many modern drafting machines have a movable bar instead, which is said to be more accurate.

Computer-controlled drafting machines and electronically-assisted versions of the manual machines are now increasingly being employed, and such equipment will probably become even more widely available in future.

Erasers

When a drawing goes wrong, the right eraser can make it right. They are not, of course, solely for correcting errors — an eraser can be used to remove guidelines from a piece of artwork, and some illustrators actually use them as a tool for achieving certain effects in drawing (rather than for corrections). Erasers are made of either soft rubber or plastic, for use on pencil. A kneaded eraser is also made for use on pencil: soft enough to mold into shape, it can be pointed up for delicate erasures. A kneaded eraser has another useful feature — it picks up its own rubbings as it is used.

Special erasers are made for removing ink, although these are not always completely successful. Other erasers are also specifically made for use on drafting films, and give much better results than ordinary erasers for that particular application.

For accurate erasure of small areas, many graphic designers find pencil-shaped erasers very practical; some wooden-cased ones resembling an ordinary pencil are made. There are also ones in which the case is made of rolled paper which is peeled back as more of the eraser point is required. A clutch eraser holds a small eraser in a holder on a pencil-like shaft. These have the advantage of being rechargeable. Finally, there are electric erasers. These usually have a small erasing point, making them suitable for accurate work, and are power-driven to make them quick and efficient. The erasing point is (needless to say) rechargeable.

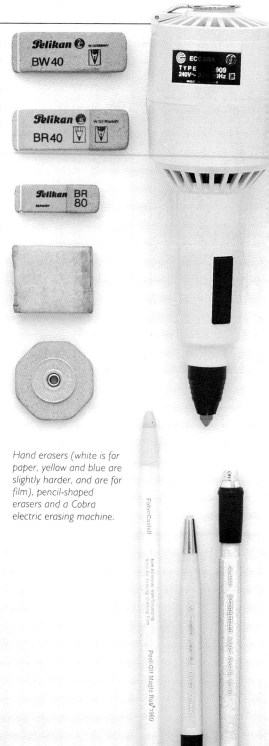

Hand erasers (white is for paper, yellow and blue are slightly harder, and are for film), pencil-shaped erasers and a Cobra electric erasing machine.

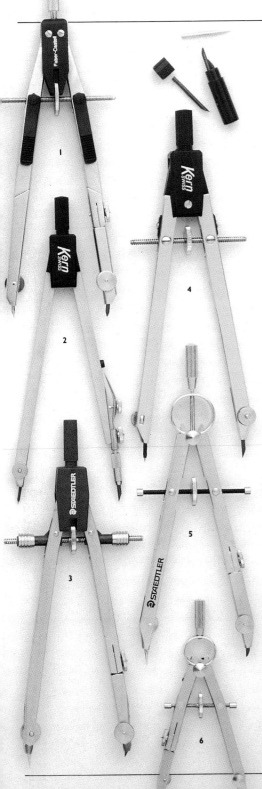

Compasses

Compasses not only describe circles, but may be used also to construct shapes or divide lines or angles. The basic format consists of two legs, one of which ends in a pivotal point and the other in a drawing-point. Around this simple structure there exist numerous variations.

Bow compasses, for example, are topped by a circular spring which holds the legs of the compass together under tension and equalizes the movements of each leg against the other. Bow compasses have to be set against the action of the spring, and therefore always have a cross-bar or swinging arm on a thread mechanism to position the arms exactly and to keep them in place.

Bow compasses tend to be high-quality products, although the term "bow" is used in a rather indiscriminate fashion by some manufacturers to describe in effect just ordinary, simple compasses. In several better-quality ranges the term "bow" is definitely used to refer to good precision instruments, although again they may not in fact be true spring bow compasses. The point is, however, that a correct or meaningful use of the term cannot always be relied upon.

An alternative to the spring bow, which also occurs on many better-quality compasses, is to have interlocking gears at the junction of the compass legs: once again these create a correspondence between the movements of the legs in relation to each other. Such compasses usually include a threaded cross-bar for accurate setting in the same manner as a spring bow. Less sophisticated compasses may have a simple pivot joint at the junction of the legs, and may not have a cross-bar or similar device to adjust and hold the setting.

General-purpose compasses are perfectly acceptable for many drawing applications, and the average graphic artist or designer may not need the precision offered by the bow or spring bow compasses.

Quick-acting compasses are a variation of the bow or spring bow type. They may also be called quick-set compasses because the facility can work in either direction. Like the ordinary bow, these compasses have a threaded cross-bar or swinging arm by which they are set. However, by depressing a button or lever on each of the legs the hold on the thread can be temporarily released, and the position of the legs can be altered quickly by pulling or pushing with the hands. When the buttons or levers are released, the grip on the thread of the cross-bar returns and fine adjustment can be made in the usual way by turning the thumb-wheel on the cross-bar. On compasses that have a swinging arm rather than a threaded cross-bar a slightly different mechanism may be employed, but the principle is essentially the same: the screw device for adjustment may be temporarily disengaged.

Quick acting or quick setting is obviously an advantage where compasses are being used extensively and where large and continual variations in the settings have to be made.

COMPASSES

Bow compasses, spring bows and professional-quality compasses all come from Ecobra, Haff, Rotring, Hellerman, Staedtler, Kern, Faber-Castell, Alvin and Intertech. Helix, Grifhold and Sam Flax also include a bow compass in their ranges. Jakar International offers both professional and student compasses. Quick-release compasses are supplied by Kern, Intertech, Faber-Castell,

Rotring, Haff, Ecobra and Hellerman. Compasses that will accept technical pens are made by Faber-Castell, Staedtler and Rotring, although most ranges include a technical pen adapter fitting.

1 Quick release compass with ruling pen attachment
2,3 Large spring bow compass
4 Quick release compass
5 Large spring bow compass
6 Small spring bow compass with ruling pen attachment

Jointed compasses have a joint about half-way down one or both legs, or just back from the leg's end, which allows the point and the drawing-tip to be tilted inward to correct the angle of presentation. As a compass is extended, the angle between the legs and the drawing surface becomes smaller and smaller, and it becomes increasingly likely that the point or drawing-tip will slip, or that it will actually waver slightly in position. By jointing the legs this hazard can be overcome: the point and the drawing-tip can be kept at right-angles to the drawing surface, no matter how wide the compass is set. A yet more sophisticated form of this mechanism occurs on parallel compasses, in which an integrated system of rods automatically tilts the tips of the legs as they are opened or closed, and insures that the point and the drawing-tip are always presented vertically to the drawing surface.

In addition to joints, compasses may have legs to which different fittings may be attached. By releasing a screw, sliding out one socketed attachment and replacing it with another, a compass may thus be extended, for example, or converted into a divider, or fitted with a ruling pen attachment or some other specialized attachment. An extension bar is a particularly useful fitting, and increases the reach of compasses significantly, so that large-diameter circles can be drawn. Additional points (needles), lead-holding drawing-tips, sockets which accept technical pens, and ruling-pen attachments are all typical fittings available for these compasses.

Although it is still common to find compasses with the universal holding device that screws in to clamp on a pencil, a technical pencil, a technical pen, or a similar drawing-point such as fine-pointed fiber-tip, compasses that have their own integrated leadholder or a special technical pen attachment are now fairly standard.

Leads for compasses are often purchased pre-sharpened at an angle; because they move against the drawing surface in one direction only, a point as such is not essential. Special sharpening devices are available from some manufacturers to keep the lead tips trimmed in the appropriate fashion.

A dropbow compass may be used for drawing small circles. This consists of a central, vertical shaft with a needle point at one end; from the shaft a drawing-point hangs on a piece of steel. The central shaft is topped by a flat button which is held under the fingertip to keep the instrument in place while being rotated. Rotation causes the drawing-point to move around the central shaft and describe a tiny circle. A screw can be adjusted to alter the distance between the central shaft and the drawing-point to set the compass, and it is possible to draw a circle as small as $\frac{1}{32}$ of an inch in diameter with such an instrument. A dropbow compass does not normally accommodate circles of much more than $\frac{1}{2}$ inch in diameter, and is primarily intended for use on a very small setting. Various models are available, either with

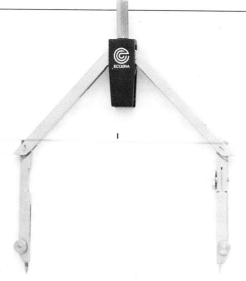

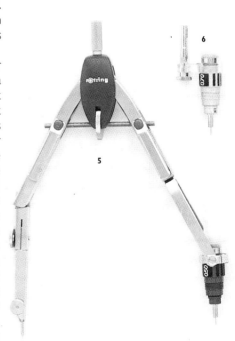

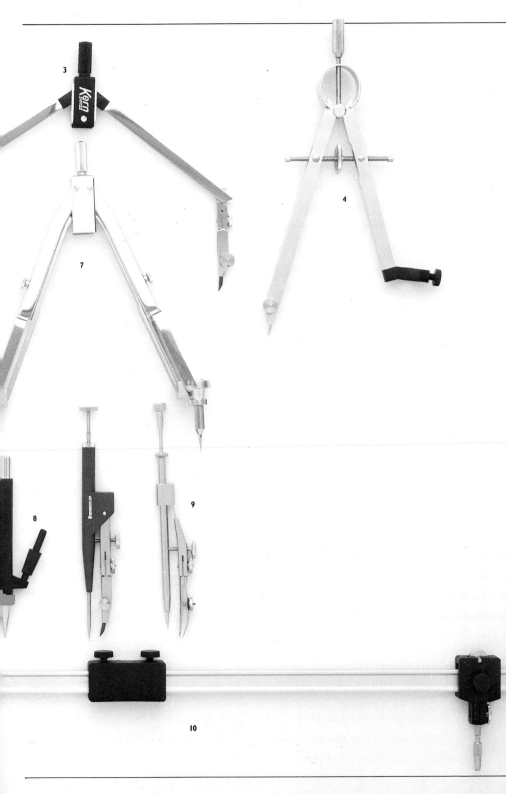

leadholders or with fittings for technical pens.

There is another system for drawing small circles. This consists of an ordinary bow compass fitted with a special needle that features two right-angled bends so that the point actually sets down at a short distance from the end of the compass's leg. This brings the point much nearer the drawing-tip, so that the compasses actually pivots off center, and the drawing-point moves immediately around the displaced needle tip. **A beam compass** can be used to draw very large-diameter circles. It consists of a straight and sturdy metal rod with two movable attachments in the same plane along its length at right-angles to it. One carries the pivotal point, and the other the drawing-tip. The chosen diameter can be set by moving these along the rod or beam, and then securing them with a locking screw. Some beam compasses have an additional knob that can be positioned part way along the beam to make handling easier. One type is in the form of a metal tape measure with a pen or leadholder fitting and can be extended to a radius of up to 72 inches.

DROPBOW COMPASSES

Dropbow compasses are offered by Ecobra, Haff, Rotring, Staedtler, Faber-Castell, Kern, Hellerman and Alvin. Haff also supplies compasses with formed needles as an alternative for drawing small circles.

BEAM COMPASSES

Beam compasses are supplied by Ecobra, Haff, Grifhold, Jakar International, Alvin, Intertech and Blundell Harling. Alvin, Blundell Harling, Haff and Ecobra
all produce long-reach beam compasses which can be extended by the addition of extra compass bars. The longest reach is offered by the Haff Beam Compasses, which can give a radius length of up to 6½ feet.

1,3 & 5 Large spring bow
    compasses
2,4 Spring bow compass
    with universal attachment
6 Technical pen compass
    attachment
7 Quick acting compass
8 Compass attachment
9 Dropbow compass
10 Beam compass
11 Extension bar for spring
    bow compass

ADHESIVES AND CUTTING EQUIPMENT

Among the sundry items that find regular use in the graphic design studio are adhesives, sharpeners and cutting equipment. Adhesives and cutting equipment are obviously linked by their common use in pasting up artwork and in the preparation of display materials. Sharpening equipment insures that drawing points on pencils and lead-holders are kept in trim. Some cutting equipment may also double as sharpening equipment — for example an x-acto knife may be used both to cut and to sharpen.

Tapes

Tapes are common office and studio materials. There are clear plastic tapes, colored or printed tapes, paper-backed tapes, gummed tapes, insulating tapes and double-sided tapes. With the exception of double-sided tapes, none of these is suitable for discreet final mounting. They do, however, have other practical applications.

General-purpose clear tapes can be used for holding down sheet materials such as paper and drafting film, and for repair to items that need only short-term mending. Taping the back of a tear on artwork, for example, often makes a satisfactory repair, but the shiny-finish transparent tapes age badly, eventually coming free of their adhesive, which hardens and darkens and frequently eats into the paper. So they should not be used on anything that has value and is intended to last.

The better-quality transparent tapes have a matte finish and are supposedly near-invisible on most surfaces. In practice, the matte-surface tapes are more noticeable than the manufacturers tend to suggest, but they do not show up on camera and can be used on mock-up pieces with good results. They have the additional advantage that they accept drawing and writing instruments because of their minutely-toothed surface.

Removable tapes also usually have a matte surface. Their adhesive produces a good bond, but the tape can be peeled off and repositioned if required without damage to the artwork surface. Some brands claim that they can be removed and repositioned many times over, thus allowing minute and repeated changes in positioning to be carried out. These matte-surface tapes usually also accept dry transfer lettering as well as pen and pencil, so that they may be used as a carrier for elements of artwork as well as for sticking things down.

White tape is another product specifically made for graphic artists; it is usually a removable tape also, so that it can be applied and removed from artwork without damage. The pure, opaque, white color means it can be used to cover small errors in artwork, to attach pieces of copy or illustrations, to paste up board, and to crop or block out areas on artwork or transparencies. White tapes are also suitable for attaching overlays and for joining white surfaces to other white surfaces in displays and mock-ups where such joints need to be disguised. Matte-surfaced white tape can be a useful carrier for dry transfer lettering.

Red blockout tapes, also called lithographers' tape, should also be mentioned briefly, along with transfer tapes. Red tapes block light, and are used to secure and trim negatives during photographic processing. Transfer tapes themselves are, of course, adhesive tapes, but they are used for the designs they carry and not for their adhesive properties — hence their inclusion in the following chapter rather than here.

Colored and metallic tapes are also available for direct application to artwork, and are similarly referred to in the next chapter.

1

2

TAPE

*The Sellotape range
(available in Britain)
includes general-purpose
transparent tapes, colored
tapes, double-sided
mounting tapes, masking
tapes and drafting tapes,
an invisible tape and a red
lithographic masking tape.
The 3M standard product
is Scotch clear tape. 3M
produces the 281
Removable Transparent
Tape, and their range also
includes the translucent
Scotch Magic Tape, and
their range also includes
the translucent Scotch
Magic Tape, Scotch Black
Photographic Tape and
Scotch Silver Photographic
Tape. Scotch White Artists'
Tape can be used for
blocking and correcting
artwork.*

1 Red gummed tape
2 Sellotape's double-sided
  tape
3 Gold metallic tape, also
  available in silver
4 Clear touch-sensitive
  Scotch Magic tape
5 Red blockout tape
6 Large clear touch-sensitive
  Scotch tape
7 Plain Sellotape
8 Green gummed tape

Black photo tape is also available in colors. These tapes have little or no direct use in artwork, but they may make very sturdy bonds for a variety of studio uses. Photo tape is very often useful, for example, during a photographic session, for holding things in place, even for steadying cameras or lights — but since it is most definitely not invisible, it must be kept out of shot.

Masking tape is a brown tape backed with a waxy paper which is quite tough. It has a strong adhesive that is nevertheless easy to remove. As its name suggests, it is for masking off areas, but it is intended primarily for use in decoration for keeping paint off surfaces such as glass, wood or metal. On some paper or board surfaces it is difficult to remove without damaging them, so it should be used with caution. It is a favorite with graphic artists, illustrators, and a variety of technical draftsmen for securing materials to drawing-boards. Professional versions of this tape (called drafting tape) are made for designers and draftsmen; these may perform better than the general product although they do tend to be more expensive.

Brown paper tape with a gummed backing that has to be moistened for use is now considered old-fashioned. Its use has been supplanted by more modern tapes for most applications, but it is still the most suitable tape for use when stretching paper. As it carries waterbased gum it can be used to stick down wet paper, something that other tapes cannot do. However, its need of moisture is a disadvantage in circumstances in which it can cause cockling, to the detriment of the finished artwork.

1,2 Masking tape
3 Gum-backed tape
4 Double-coated tape
5 Fixing pads

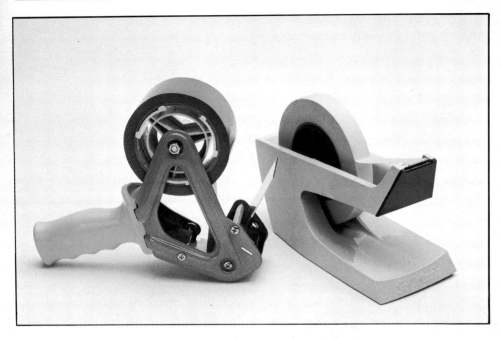

Tape dispensers

Tape dispensers make the use of tapes a little more convenient. There are both static desk-top models and hand-held rolling dispensers which place the tape directly onto the artwork. The latter are useful when tape is in constant use or when a large volume of work is undertaken. Hand-held rolling dispensers of this type are also available to go with double-coated tapes. Clamp-on bench dispensers can be quite practical in studio conditions.

*Two tape dispensers, hand-held (**left**) and Sellotape's desk dispenser.*

Double-coated tapes

Double-coated tape, as its name suggests, carries an adhesive on both surfaces. Typically it might be used to mount photographs or elements of artwork flat on a backing board. It might also be used, for example, to hold mock-up labeling on packages. Its advantages are that it is quick, clean and unseen — but there are some mounting jobs for which it is inappropriate. It can be recommended for small corrections to artwork, and for attaching overlays, but it is not generally used for pasting-up operations because materials mounted with

it are inclined to cast a slight shadow. For applications that require stronger bond, or that have to carry weight, there is also double-coated foam tape. This is a thin strip of foam with a powerful adhesive on each side. Double-coated foam also comes in the form of individual mounting squares. For use, an appropriate length of the tape is cut, positioned and stuck down on the adhesive lower side; then the top adhesive surface is revealed by peeling back the protective coating.

Foam tape usually takes a very firm grip as soon as its surface touches an object, so there is little scope for repositioning. It is excellent for mounting quite large display items on hevyweight board and is consequently popular in advertising and marketing applications. Foam tape may also be used to secure the positions of objects during photographic sessions.

Scotch produces a double-coated tape, a lithographic tape, and a drafting tape, as well as Scotch Fixing Pads, which are double-sided pads on a roll. Alvin's range of tapes includes masking tape, graphic tape, double-sided tape, invisible-mending tape, plain cellophane tape, and lithographers' tape. Alvin also produces Alvin

Drafting Dots. Letraset UK produce Tape Set, which is a double-side tape for mounting and general-purpose studio use. Plain gummed-paper tapes are also available, and feature in the Sericol range of products, along with crêpe paper masking tape.

4

5

Aerosol adhesives

Aerosol adhesives are well suited to pasting-up work because they can lay an even coat of glue over large areas — such as the whole of the reverse side of the artwork to be pasted up — very efficiently. This insures a good, flat bond. A spray is perfect for administering just the right amount of adhesive to the edges of the artwork so that they are held firmly and flat without the use of such a quantity of glue as would ooze during mounting, and would require a further cleaning operation. Occasionally, problems can arise with very lightweight artwork, when the power of the spray causes a slight movement that pushes the artwork onto an area of excess glue which has accumulated on the protective sheet.

Most aerosol glues allow for repositioning and are either permanently removable or have a prolonged setting time during which the work can be lifted and repositioned. For temporary bonding the glue is applied to one surface only, but if a more permanent and secure bond is required, both surfaces must be coated. When both surfaces are coated, repositioning is difficult.

Aerosol adhesives are generally available in three different grades: a plain mounting quality intended for paste-up work and general light-duty mounting jobs; a photomounting quality, which is a heavier-duty adhesive capable of a more permanent bond; and a heavier quality still for display mounting when the objects to be stuck down are of a large size or are made of a heavy material such as illustration board. These display-mounting products generally mount fabric, polystyrene and light sheet wood as well.

Aerosol sprays can be used for very accurate application if the can is fitted with a special nozzle that has a straw-like protuberance which can deliver a spot of glue exactly where desired. Some manufacturers supply such nozzles with each can of glue, to be fitted if and when required.

The nozzles of aerosol glues are easily blocked by a build-up of adhesive during spraying. This affects the spray pattern of the glue, and ordinarily results in a less even coverage and a spluttering spray. It is advisable to clean the nozzle periodically, or — where the manufacturer supplies a replacement nozzle, as many do, taped to the inside of the aerosol cap — to change the nozzle when the original becomes fouled. It is recommended that aerosol adhesives in regular use be turned upside down and sprayed for a few seconds at the end of each day to clear the nozzle of traces of glue.

Nozzles that give a choice of spray patterns are occasionally supplied by some manufacturers. Excess applications of aerosol glue can be cleaned away with appropriate cleaning fluid.

Some of the basic mounting glues supplied in aerosol form actually lose their adhesive qualities over a period of time: pasted-up work may well peel off some time after its original preparation. The time limit is sufficiently long for this not to be relevant to most graphic applications, but where the work has to be intact at a later date, the possibility should be borne in mind, and if need be a photomounting or a more permanent type of mounting glue should be used. Some aerosol adhesives can stain or discolor artwork, although many products claim to be free of this defect.

Several other useful products for the graphic artist and designer are also offered in the form of aerosol sprays. Some of these are discussed briefly at the end of the chapter on paints.

Scotch Spray Mount is a general-purpose aerosol glue for paste-up and light mounting operations. For mounting photographic prints and illustrations 3M offers Scotch Photo Mount and Scotch Display Mount, which will mount fabrics, cardboard, wood and polystyrene. Haftspray from Marabu is for paste-up work and temporary mounting of artwork, and Letraset offers Spray Set for the same. Mecanorma offers Artwork Spray, a repositionable mounting adhesive for general studio use and Zipatone supplies Sipatone Spray Adhesive and Zipatone Spray Cement. A-Der is from Alfack and is non-flammable. T-Fix and T-Fix Extra are unusual aerosol glues from Sericol. T-Fix produces a medium tack which holds fabrics firmly.

Aerosol mounts and repositionable adhesives, Kleerpak rubbere cement and gum arabic from Winsor & Newton.

Rubber and latex cements are still favorites in some studios. A well-known product in Britain is Cow Gum, a colorless rubber solution from Royal Sovereign Graphics. Cow Gum is available in cans or tubes. Special spreading spatulas are supplied with it, to insure thin, even applications of gum. Fixogum is a product from Marabu; a rubber cement, it is available in large or small tubes and in cans. There is also a special version of Fixogum called Fixogum One Coat, intended to give a strong adhesion from only one coat of glue. Fixogum Thinner is available in cans of various sizes and can be used for thinning, correcting or cleaning gum traces. Kleer Tak is a pure latex adhesive from Mecanorma that can be used for general studio mounting. At any time the glue bond can be separated; a special Kleer Tak Eraser is available for removing excess glue once it has dried.

Rubber cements and glues

A more traditional approach to sticking things down, particularly in paste-up and mounting operations, is the use of rubber cement or glue. In graphic art, rubber-based or latex cements are widely used, in the form of syrupy and virtually colorless liquids. Other paper glues such as gum arabic and starch paste are very little used now, although they do remain as possibilities should they be required.

Rubber and latex cements must be applied with a brush or spatula to the back of items being stuck down. They can be a little messy to use, and it takes some practice to be able to apply an even coat without excessive wastage and without causing bubbles and blobs to appear in the surface of the artwork or producing excessive seepage from the edges when it is pressed down.

Rubber cements dry comparatively slowly and so allow a good period of working time during which time the work can be repositioned. Even when they have dried completely it is sometimes possible to peel away a cement bond cleanly. In any event the bond can be released by applying solvent to a loosened edge. For a permanent bond the cement is applied to both surfaces and allowed to dry until it becomes tacky; the two are then pressed together and are rolled or burnished lightly to form a perfect bond. In the long term, however, rubber cements cannot always be regarded as completely permanent: some release their bonds eventually as time progresses. Any excess cement can be removed using solvents or by rubbing it away with a special eraser made for removing gum adhesive that has dried.

Dry mounting

Dry mounting is a process by which surfaces are bonded using an interleaved sheet of tissue that carries an adhesive material. There are two distinct versions of this method: the hot dry mounting process and the cold dry mounting process.

The hot dry mounting process is when a sheet of adhesive tissue is cut to match the size of the artwork being mounted. The adhesive on it is activated by heat, and the sheet is tacked in place on the artwork using an iron. When it has been cut to size and trimmed exactly, the backing board, the artwork being mounted, and the adhesive sheet are all lined up and tacked in place. The whole is then put into a special press which heats and presses the work, activating the glue on the dry mounting sheet as it does so. At any time the process is reversible by applying heat once again.

It is important to cover objects being mounted with a silicone release paper or a good brown wrapping paper before they are put into the press, to prevent damage to them. Various presses are available, corresponding to the specific requirements of the user. Smaller ones are hand-operated; larger ones are power-operated. Because materials are only lightly tacked together during the initial stages of the hot dry mounting process, they can be repositioned a number of times before actually being subjected to the final pressing.

The cold dry mounting method involves a similar procedure, but in this case pressure alone, without the aid of heat, activates the adhesive on the sheet. The protective layer is peeled away from a sheet of cold mounting paper; the item being mounted is placed on it and can be repositioned until pressure is applied. When a satisfactory position has been achieved, the back of the cold mounting sheet is rollered or burnished. It can then be peeled away leaving its adhesive on the back of the artwork in question. The artwork is then placed in its correct position on the mounting surface, and pressure is applied to the front this time, again using a roller. A layer of release paper can be placed over the subject to protect it. A firm bond is then made.

Cold mounting sheet can be used together with simple machinery which rolls the subject matter evenly and firmly: the first pass creates a tacking bond, the second pass creates a firm, strong bond.

If dry mounting of a comparatively weighty piece of work is being carried out, or if a subject is being dry mounted onto a rough surface, special adhesive sheets may be required for the hot process and a multiple application of adhesive may be required in the case of the cold process.

Adhesive sticks and pens

To cope with small jobs and applications in which particularly accurate use of glue is required — say, for example, where the shaped edge of artwork has to be followed — there are glues in stick form and in the form of pens. Stick glues are rather like a lipstick of adhesive paste. The paste is rubbed on to the back of the artwork from the stick, and as the stick wears down it is further extended by pushing or twisting the base of its container. Glue pens deliver glue through a shaped point and allow for quite accurate working. Glue pens with heads of different shapes are available.

A similar product is a glue roller, a small bottle of glue with a rolling dispenser head that applies glue direct to the artwork. Such rollers rather resemble the conventional form of the bottle used for packaging deodorants, although the shape of the head differs. Roller applicators can in fact be used to cover quite large areas, but are best suited to small work. Both applicators and pens can be used against a straight edge to deliver measured lines of glue, whereas glue sticks are less suitable for this kind of use.

GLUE STICKS

Stick adhesives include the Pritt Stick from Letraset, Penol Glue Sticks from Faber-Castell and Gluepen from UHU. The Pelifix Glue Stick is suitable for paper, fabric and photographs. UHU supplies glue pens with sponge tips, and Edding supplies three: the C25, the C30 and the C50. 3M supplies the Scotch Glue Pen, and Tombow glue pens and small bottles of liquid glue with a special application tip. Caran d'Ache offers a general-purpose office glue in a slim bottle. Hand-held waxing machines are available from Sam Flax, E. Whitmont & Co, and Langford & Hill. The Lectro Stick Hand Waxer and the Arttec Handy Wax Coater are both hand-held waxing guns with a roller dispenser in their base.

Waxers

Another possibility for mounting artwork, and for general light studio uses of adhesives, is to use a waxing machine. A relatively inexpensive form of waxer is the hand-held waxing gun which has a roller at its base. It is electrically operated and heats up to soften sticks of special wax which are loaded into its top. When the wax adhesive is melted properly it can be rolled out onto the back of artwork so that a fine film of it is deposited. In practice, waxing machines actually lay down the coated wax as minute peaks of adhesive; these are not sticky to the touch, and the artwork can be positioned and repositioned as many times as required during preparation. Applying pressure, however, by rolling or burnishing the surface of the artwork, causes the peaks of wax to bond to the lower surface. The waxes used in waxing machines remain supple almost indefinitely, so that wax-mounted objects can be removed and repositioned at almost any time.

Waxing machines can accommodate mounting jobs involving ordinary boards and paper, and can also be used with light plastics and film products. Because the application of wax is very thin these machines are, in practice, quite economical to use. Bench-top equipment is available as well as the smaller hand-held studio products, and systems are available that cope with artwork in full-page sizes.

Glue sticks and pens with an electric waxer.

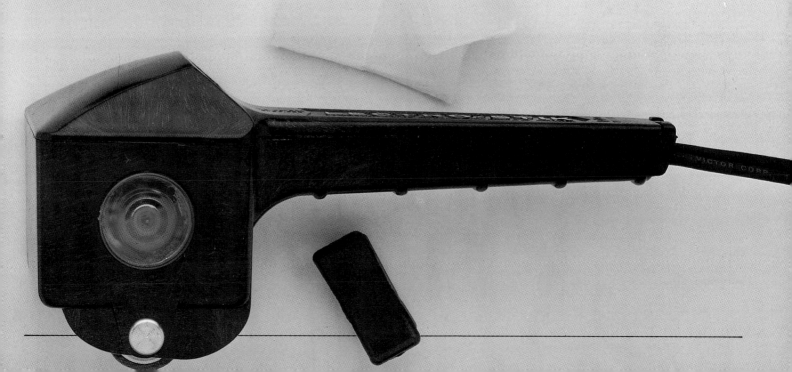

ADHESIVES AND CUTTING EQUIPMENT

SUPPLIER	MANUFACTURER	DISTRIBUTOR	WHOLESALER	RETAILER	Areas where products are available	Local variations in product range	Clear Tape	Masking Tape	Double-Coated Tape	Magic Tape	Rubber Cement	Spray Adhesive	Plastic Putty	Photo Mounting	Dry Mounting	Cold Mounting	Plastic	Metal	Hand-Operated	Electric	Sharpening Stones	Sand Paper	Emery Paper	Scissors	Art Knives/Scalpels	Pocket/Craft Knives	Trimming/Rotary/Parallel Knives	Mat Cutters/Trimmers	Cutting Mats	Paper Cutters
	MANUFACTURER / DISTRIBUTOR / WHOLESALER / RETAILER						**ADHESIVES**										**SHARPENERS**								**CUTTING EQUIPMENT**					
Abelscot-Marchant	•	•	•		W	No	•	•	•	•	•	•	•	•					•											
Alvin	•	•	•		W	No	•	•	•	•		•	•					•	•	•	•	•	•	•	•	•			•	
Art Material International	•	•	•		W	N/S	•																							
Atlantis			•	•	N/S	N/A	•	•	•	•		•	•	•	•			•			•	•	•	•	•	•			•	•
Blair	•				E UK	No						•																		
Conté	•				UK	N/A													•											
Daler-Rowney	•	•			W	No																			•		•			
DRG Sellotape Products	•				W	No	•	•	•	•	•		•																	
Eberhard-Faber	•				C US	No												•												
Edding	•				W	No																			•				•	
Sam Flax		•			W	No					•			•					•	•										
Gaebel	•				S US	Yes															•									
Griffin (Grifhold)	•	•			W	No															•									
Helix	•				N/S	N/A													•	•										
Holbein	•		•		W	No	•																•							•
Jakar International		•			UK	No													•	•										
KIN Rapidograph	•	•			USA C	N/S	•												•		•									
Langford & Hill		•	•	•	W	No	•	•	•	•	•	•	•	•	•	•	•	•	•	•					•	•	•	•	•	•
3M (Scotch)	•				N/S	No	•	•	•	•	•	•	•	•	•	•														
Marabu	•				W	No					•	•															•		•	

SUPPLIER	MANUFACTURER	DISTRIBUTOR	WHOLESALER	RETAILER	Areas where products are available	Local variations in product range	Clear Tape	Masking Tape	Double-Coated Tape	Magic Tape	Rubber Cement	Spray Adhesive	Plastic Putty	Photo Mounting	Dry Mounting	Cold Mounting	Plastic	Metal	Hand-Operated	Electric	Sharpening Stones	Sand Paper	Emery Paper	Scissors	Art Knives/Scalpels	Pocket/Craft Knives	Trimming/Rotary/Parallel Knives	Mat Cutters/Trimmers	Cutting Mats	Paper Cutters
Maimeri		•			UK	N/A						•																		
Mecanorma	•				UK	N/A					•	•		•											•	•				
Microflame			•		N/S	N/S	•	•	•	•	•	•	•	•	•		•	•	•	•	•	•	•	•	•	•	•	•	•	•
M. Myers & Son	•				W	No																					•			
Omnicrom Systems	•				A E UK US	No	•																							
Paragon	•				W	No																			•	•	•			
Pebeo	•				W	No					•	•		•																
H.W. Peel & Co	•	•			W	No																			•	•	•			
Pelltech		•			UK	N/A						•					•		•	•	•	•	•	•	•	•	•	•	•	•
Pilot	•	•			W	No																			•	•	•	•		
Platignum	•				W	No	•							•																
Rexel (Derwent Cumberland)	•				W	Yes	•												•	•	•	•		•			•			•
Rotatrim	•				W	No																					•			•
Rotobord	•	•	•	•	A E UK US	Yes																				•			•	
D. & J. Simons			•		W	No		•				•													•		•	•	•	•
Staedtler	•				W	No													•	•	•									
Talens	•				W	No						•																		
A. West & Partners	•	•			A E S UK	No																				•			•	
Winsor & Newton	•	•		•	W	No		•																						

KEY: A = Australia **C** = Canada **E** = Europe (excluding UK) **S** = Scandinavia **UK** = United Kingdom **US** = United States **W** = Worldwide **N/S** = Not Stated

Other adhesive products

Finally, there are several miscellaneous items that can be used for sticking and mounting in graphic art and design. These include plastic putty, which is a kneadable material rather like modeling clay and which has sufficient tack to hold paper and board to a supporting surface when it is pressed against it. It does not give a close bond, though, and is most useful in mounting posters and displays temporarily. Plastic putty has the advantage here over double-sided tapes or pads in that it is less likely to damage the support to which it is applied. It cannot, however, take very great weight, and because it has only a light adhesive tack it may release its bond in time: but renewed pressure renews the bond. Plastic putty can be reused by kneading it and putting it back in position.

Other unusual materials include dot strips and transfer adhesives. These are both similar products, although one comes in the form of a tape and the other comes as a sheet. Adhesive is printed on their surfaces in the form of tiny dots (often colored in drop-out blue to make use easier). After the protective covering is removed, pieces of artwork can be laid on the adhesive surface face up and lightly rubbed. When the artwork is lifted again the dots of adhesive have transferred to the back of the artwork, which can then be placed on its support and subjected to light pressure to create a bond.

TRANSFER ADHESIVES

Mecanorma Transfer Adhesive and Mecanorma's Roller Col can be used for the accurate mounting of small and intricately-shaped artwork. Roller col is a repositionable and removable transfer adhesive in tape form.

Sharpeners

Various sharpening devices are available. The simplest is the small sharpener consisting of a fixed metal blade mounted lengthwise within a conical slot into which the top of the pencil is pushed. Bench-top versions of the same device are available for office and studio use. Electric versions of this type of machine are also available, and are extremely quick and efficient. In order to reduce mess, larger sharpeners generally have a container of some sort to collect shavings.

All these sharpeners are suited for use with wood-cased pencils only, and give a sharp conical point. However, the very tip of the point is frequently irregular as a result of this type of sharpening and may need to be softened with a few quick strokes on scrap paper before being put to use. Alternatively, it may be sharpened very finely on a sandpaper block which has tear-off strips.

In spite of the popularity and convenience of pencil sharpeners, many manufacturers of wood-cased pencils still recommend that their products be sharpened using a knife. Sharpening in this way can produce a more elongated and even point than with a pencil sharpener, but producing a perfect point with a knife is something of an art. Knives are definitely advisable for sharpening soft-leaded pencils such as charcoal pencils, many types of colored pencil, and pastel pencils.

Special sharpening devices are required for sharpening the leads of leadholders, and these sometimes form an integral part of the pencil itself. Such sharpeners are called lead pointers rather than pencil sharpeners. Special devices are also available for producing an angled point on the leads used in compasses. These consist of a small slot faced by an angled strip of sandpaper, so that when the lead is run down the slot it is ground to an angled point.

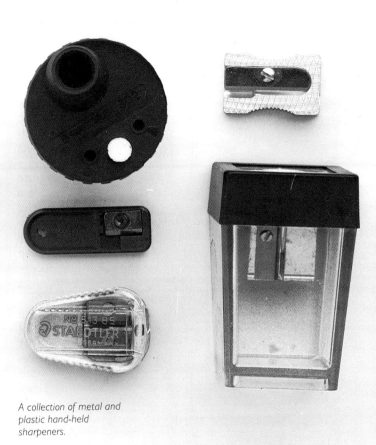

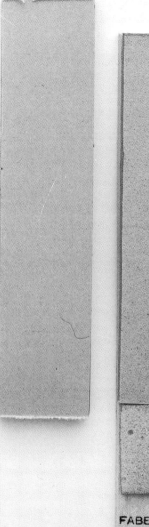

A collection of metal and plastic hand-held sharpeners.

SHARPENERS

Small pencil sharpeners are available from Staedtler, Conté, Schwan-Stabilo, Faber-Castell, Jakar International, Lyra, Helix and Hellerman in metal and plastic versions. Staedtler supplies the Norris 51254 and 51220 pencil sharpeners which are double-holed, as are the Lyra 9579 and the Helix Q04. Desk-top sharpeners are supplied by Hellerman, Lyra, Faber-Castell, Uni, Berol, Staedtler, Tombow and Boston. The Staedtler 50170 is a heavy-duty sharpener for graphite and colored pencils with a built-in point adjuster. The Berol Sword sharpener takes most pencil sizes and has an automatic feed.

Two sandpaper blocks with tear-off sheets, used for very fine pencil sharpening.

*The Dahle automatic
00220 sharpener and the
155 manual sharpener.*

Cutting equipment

Knives and scissors are common items of studio equipment. They are all suited to small cutting operations. Some of these have specialist applications and can cut curves or special shapes easily. For larger straight cuts, paper cutters are used — or more frequently nowadays, a paper slicer or trimmer that has a moving blade guided by a bar along the cutting edge, rather than a large swinging blade which cuts with a downward action.

Paper cutters

Quantities of paper and sheets of board can be cut using desk-top equipment. A paper cutter has a flat base with a straightedge at the top and a blade that swings vertically down and along the right-hand edge of the base. Paper or card is pushed against the straightedge and allowed to overhang the cutting edge by the desired amount. Bringing the blade down produces a cut. With the now rather old-fashioned hinged-blade versions, how-ever, the edge can be miscut if the blade is not sharp enough or if the paper or board is too thick for the cutter's capacity.

Paper trimmers

A more modern version of the paper cutter is the paper slicer, or paper trimmer, which has a circular blade fitted into a holder that runs along a bar above the cutting edge.

Cutting mats and an Olfa mount cutter.

Sometimes paper trimmers have large flat bases like paper cutters, but they are frequently on much smaller bases that consist essentially of the cutting edge and a shallow base just large enough to allow for the positioning of the paper. These again have a straightedge against which the material to be cut can be positioned, and many have the added feature of a flexible plastic strip under which the paper or board is slotted prior to cutting. This holds it in place and makes it unnecessary to apply pressure with the fingers to steady the paper. Pushing the blade holder along the bar cuts neatly and accurately along the cutting edge. Because it is a circular blade it cuts both in the forward and backward cutting motion. Paper trimmers are sometimes freestanding, with a bag slung beneath them to collect scraps.

Cutting mats

To get the best results from knives, professional-quality cutting mats are available. These have a non-slip surface which holds the artwork firmly as the knife cuts, and are generally overprinted lightly with a grid to assist positioning.

The surface of a cutting mat is usually constructed of a special material which can take repeated cutting. As the knife passes through the surface, the surface closes behind it so as not to leave a score mark which might misguide the blade when it next follows a similar path. This feature is referred to as self-healing. Cutting mats can, in spite of this special surface, be damaged by use with heavy-duty cutting knives, and it is best to use them chiefly with X-Acto and other small-bladed instruments. Translucent versions of these cutting mats are available for use on a light-box so that the accurate cutting of film and transparencies can be carried out.

CUTTING MATS

Self-healing cutting mats are offered by Uchida, Olfa, Blundell Harling and Sam Flax. Uchida and Olfa cutting mats are available in translucent white for use over a light-box and in green for general purposes. The Art Mat cutting mat from Blundell Harling and the Sam Flax cutting mat are available in white and blue

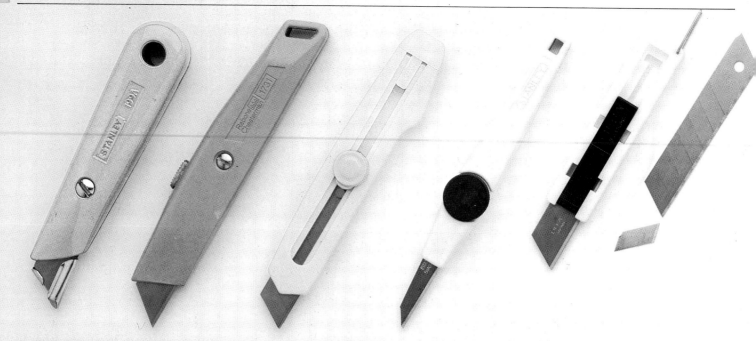

X-Acto and utility knives

X-Acto knives (sometimes called art knives) are ideally suited to very fine cutting and trimming operations. There is a wide choice of blade shapes that go with them to suit almost any requirements. The knife handles themselves are also available in different shapes and lengths. The blades are interchangeable and can be disposed of and replaced as soon as they become blunt. A number of small craft knives and mat knives also make use of similar blades to provide the cutting edge.

Somewhat larger are general-purpose knives which carry a more robust blade, again available in various shapes. These can cut with some accuracy but are too bulky for very delicate work. They are best for cutting in straight lines and for general trimming and shaping of artwork. Some utility knives have blades supplied in strip form. When the part in use becomes blunt it is snapped off along a pre-cut groove and the blade strip is moved forward to give a new cutting edge.

Knives with special applications

For extremely delicate cutting there are knives which are precision-engineered. These knives are often in the form of a pen body with a small blade. Some versions have a retractable blade so that they can be carried safely in the pocket. Others have a swivel head so that the blade can be guided around small curves as it cuts. A dual cutter is a knife with two blades mounted next to each other so that two lines are cut at the same time; these have an adjustment screw which can bring the blades nearer together or farther apart. Blade attachments are also available for compasses for cutting circular or curved shapes.

Scissors

Scissors need to be extremely sharp to cut paper well. For cutting perfectly straight lines and for cutting board, scissors are not particularly useful. Their action does not make production of a perfectly straight cut possible, and they are inclined to wander when cutting heavyweight materials.

However, some high-quality scissors are available for designers, which give above-average performance. Scissors with very long blades tend to be best for straight cuts. For delicate and accurate cutting, needlework scissors or surgical scissors can be very useful — and once you are practiced in their use they can be much quicker than either an art knife or a precision knife.

New forms of scissors are now coming on to the market which employ ceramic blades. These have an extremely sharp edge which effectively does not blunt, and they are strong enough to cut almost anything in sheet form including metals. It is possible that ceramic-bladed scissors may well show potential in the field of graphic art and design in the future.

SCISSORS

Faber-Castell's Kaicut range offers six models, and their Penol range supplies three good-quality pairs of scissors. Dahle makes the Dahle Self-Sharpening Scissors, a product specifically intended for graphic artists. Other respected brands of studio scissors include Fiskar, Alex, Arttec, Alvin and Wilkinson Sword.

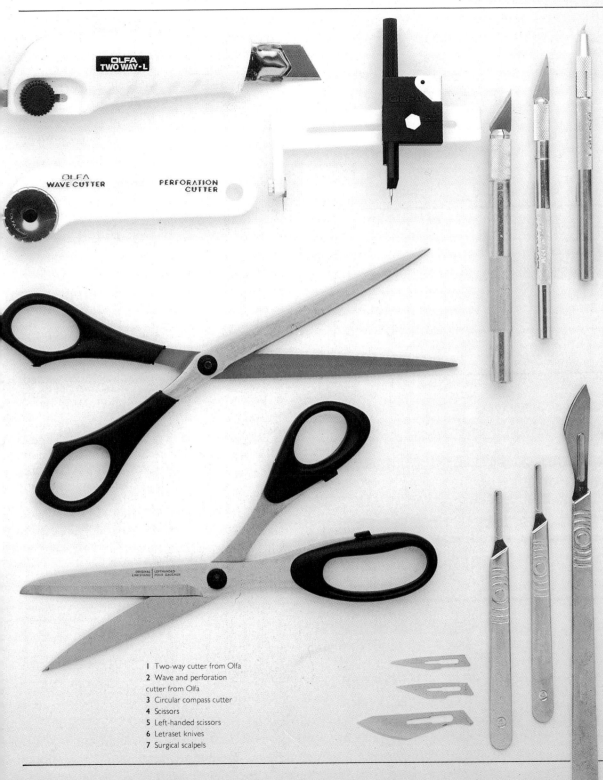

CUTTING INSTRUMENTS

In the U.S., X-acto knives are generally used for studio work. In Britain, surgical scalpels serve this purpose. Swann-Morton and the Paragon Razor Company both make surgical scalpels which can be used in the studio. There are three shapes and sizes of handles available from Swann-Morton and seven available from Paragon. All are metal handles with a slip-on fitting that can take a number of blades. Martor and Dahle supply non-sterile scalpels for use as general-purpose cutting instruments. The Martor range, supplied by Chartwell, provides two with metal handles and two with plastic handles, and folding scalpels which take large or small blades. A designer's art knife is included in the Letraset range. Grifhold offer knives which carry small blades, swivel-headed knives for stencil cutting and delicate work around curved outlines, double-bladed parallel cutters, a compass cutter, and a cutting version of a beam compass. Grifhold knives are supplied by the Griffin Manufacturing Company. The Martor range includes precision cutters, and the Parallelo dual-bladed parallel cutter. Professional designers' knives also appear in the range of Alfac, Mecanorma and Letraset. Alvin offers a small selection of precision knives under the Alvin name, and Maxon includes a designer's knife in their range.

1 Two-way cutter from Olfa
2 Wave and perforation cutter from Olfa
3 Circular compass cutter
4 Scissors
5 Left-handed scissors
6 Letraset knives
7 Surgical scalpels

INSTANT LETTERING AND REFERENCE MATERIALS

Instant lettering and artwork

Instant lettering systems are well known and are extensively used by graphic designers within the studio. However, not all graphic designers may be familiar with the sizes and contents of some of the major ranges. They include large selections of lettering styles — some of which are available in white, in colors, and in metallic finishes, as well as in black — and also large selections of shading, borders, decorative patterns and instant illustrative material in the form of dry transfer or self-adhesive sheets. Lines and borders are also available in the form of strips and in some cases as tapes, for the most part in black.

Many of the dry transfer or self-adhesive sheet products other than lettering are, in fact, aimed at specific applications outside the normal definition of graphic art. Some, for instance, are intended for architects, engineers and cartographers, although they may also be of interest to graphic artists and designers. However, the more decorative products and the general-purpose materials such as shading or texture overlays, should be regarded as graphic artists' materials.

Several ranges include common advertising design motifs and symbols that are in standard use for labeling or product description. These are frequently needed to supplement lettering and hand-drawn artwork, in order to produce a satisfactory end result. A few graphic artists have developed dry transfer and self-adhesive materials as a medium in its own right, and have produced some fascinating work.

In addition to dry transfer lettering there are three other instant lettering systems that should be considered here.

Self-adhesive letters may be used on artwork, although they are more likely to be used on one-off displays or on mock-ups of proposed designs.

Lettering machines are either manually or electrically operated, and typeset onto a strip of self-adhesive tape. These can only cope with modest amounts of text, but are extremely practical and efficient for producing titles and other short pieces of copy.

Computer-controlled typesetting is used extensively in the printing industry. Digital typesetting is increasingly available to graphic artists and designers as a service, though, and some graphic artists consider it as cheap and efficient to have lettering set straight onto film.

DRY TRANSFER SHEETS

Alfac, Mecanorma and Letraset probably offer the most extensive ranges and Zipatone, Cello-tak, Maxon and Edding offer good but less comprehensive ones. Normatype from Conté and Decadry from Alvin are ranges based on popular typefaces.

SYMBOLS AND BORDERS

Mecanorma supplies some borders and corners, but Alfac offers the best selection of characters and designs in strip form. Patterns for frames and borders are also presented in the form of self-adhesive tape on reels. Letraset and Mecanorma supply the most extensive selection of designers' tapes. Letraset are particularly good on standard symbols, e.g. for product labeling. Mecanorma offers graphic sheets for the production of quick, slick, advertising artwork. Alfac is strong on architectural graphics; Maxon offers a good selection of overall patterns; and Zipatone has some extremely decorative borders. All offer dotted and lined screens, including some with graded shading.

LETTERING

Alfac lettering is in three formats: packs are color-coded to indicate if the sheet is A4 or A3. Alfac also offers small-format sheets in packs of five, for small-sized letters and numbers. Mecanorma dry transfer sheets are 12½×16 inches, and upper- and lower-case lettering is generally separable on these sheets. Mecanorma also makes Transfer Cards: smaller-format dry transfer sheets, each surrounded by a rigid frame which makes handling, use and storage much easier. Letraset supplies in one sheet-size only, 10×15 inches. Zipatone lettering is on 8¼×11¾ inch sheets; Cello-Tak offers a 10×13 inch sheet; Maxon uses a 5¾×8¼ inch format; and Edding dry transfer products are on a good-sized sheet measuring 10 inches square.

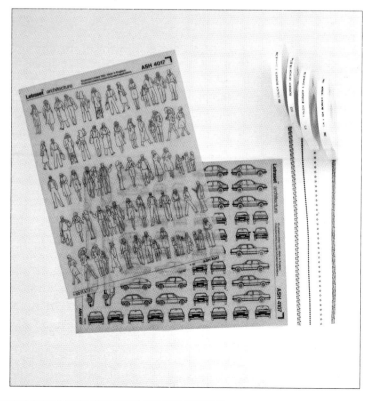

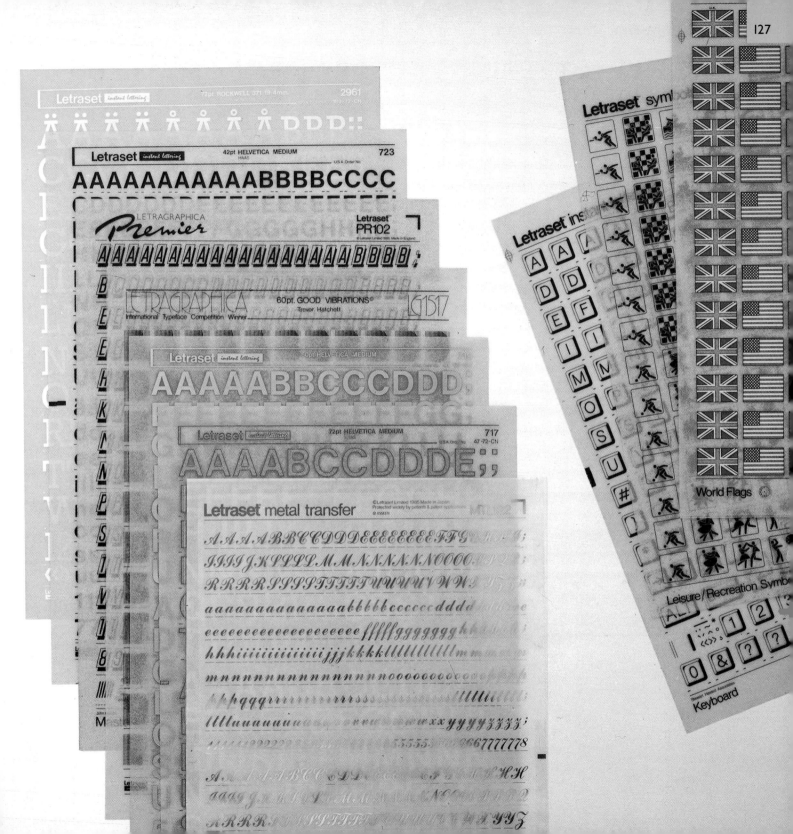

Letraset *instant lettering* 72pt ROCKWELL 371 19.4mm. 2961

Letraset *instant lettering* 42pt HELVETICA MEDIUM 723
HAAS U.S.A. Order No

AAAAAAAAAABBBBCCCC

LETRAGRAPHICA
Premier Letraset™ PR102

AAAAAAAAAAAAAAAAAAAAABBBB;

LETRAGRAPHICA 60pt. GOOD VIBRATIONS® LG1517
International Typeface Competition Winner Trevor Hatchett

Letraset *instant lettering* 60pt HELVETICA MEDIUM

AAAAABBCCCDDD;

Letraset *instant lettering* 72pt HELVETICA MEDIUM 717
HAAS U.S.A. Org. No 47-72-CN

AAAABCCDDDE;;

Letraset metal transfer ©Letraset Limited 1985 Made in Japan
Protected widely by patents & patent applications
® ESSEX

AAAABBCCDDEEEEEEFFG
IIIIJKPLLLMMNNNNNOOOO
RRRRSSSSTTTTTUUUUVWW
aaaaaaaaaaaaabbbbccccddd
eeeeeeeeeeeeeeeeeffffggggggh
hhhiiiiiiiiiiiiiijjjkkkkllllllllmm
mnnnnnnnnnnnnnoooooooox
hhpqqqrrrrrrrrrsss lllll
llluuuuuu ww xxyyyyzzzz
5555 667777778
A A AABCC DD H H
aag g L M N O
RRR SSSTT YYZ

Letraset symb

Letraset *inst*

World Flags

Leisure/Recreation Symbols

Keyboard

Dry transfer sheets

The principle of dry transfer lettering is relatively simple. A typeface or design is printed in reverse on the back of a clear plastic sheet, so that when viewed from the front it is seen the right way around. Flexible inks are used, and the bond between the printing and the plastic sheet is weak. The printed side of the sheet receives a light coating of pressure-sensitive adhesive; when not in use, the sheet is protected by a backing sheet of waxy or silicone-coated paper which does not stick to it, and which protects the delicate type from accidental damage.

The quality of the plastic sheet and the properties of the inks used for dry transfer products vary between one range and another. The best inks do not easily crack or break as they are applied, and are heat-resistant, which means that they are suitable for dyeline or diazo copying. The plastic carrying sheet should be of an appropriate thickness. The best appear to be of polyester

— these withstand the pressures of burnishing very well — but some products are on a thinner material which easily distorts.

The correct method of using dry transfer products is a specific procedure. Firstly a light guideline is applied to the artwork, or sight marks are placed along its edge, so that a ruler can be used as an aid to positioning. For certain applications guidelines in non-reproducing blue may be employed. Remove the protective backing. The transfer sheet, held from the front so that the type or design is seen the right way around, is placed over the artwork and gently maneuvered into the correct position. A burnisher, or any convenient instrument such as a pen or pencil which may be used as a burnisher, is then smoothly and repeatedly drawn over the chosen letter, numeral or design element, making sure that every part of it is well rubbed down. The plastic carrying sheet is then lifted from the artwork with a gentle

peeling action, leaving the print in position on the surface of the artwork.

It is possible to see that the print has transferred before removal of the sheet, because the separation of the printed ink from its carrying sheet causes it to appear gray when viewed through the sheet. If corrections are necessary they should be made at this stage. Dry transfer materials can be removed from smooth non-absorbent surfaces with tape, and from other surfaces with a hard eraser specially made for the purpose.

To complete the whole process, most manufacturers recommend that the silicone backing sheet be then placed separately over the applied lettering and the whole then burnished again to insure a firm bond between the transfer and the artwork. Aerosol sprays or fixatives may be applied in addition if a long-lasting protective surface is required. Guidelines should be removed carefully to avoid damaging the transfer after

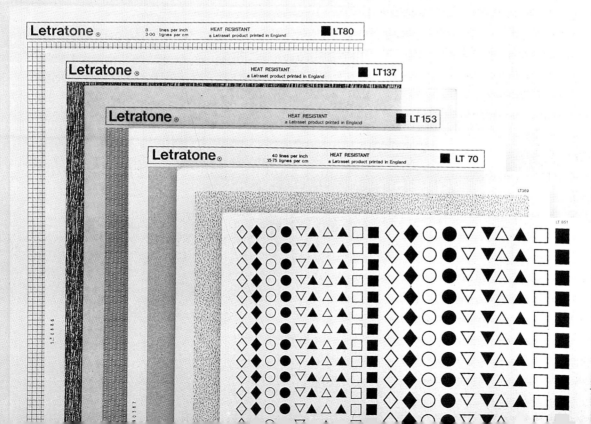

All the major manufacturers offer a range of dotted and lined screens. Some include those with graded shading, as in Letratone (left) Edding offers a small but useful selection of architectural and graphic designs.

it has been applied. (In many circumstances it is not necessary to remove them if they are sufficiently light.) Burnishers are not absolutely essential for the application of dry transfer products, but they are to be recommended for consistently good results.

There are two variants of the dry transfer theme: one is the use of a carrying film, and the other is the use of self-adhesive sheets. In the case of a large or complex design there is a considerable risk of distortion or break-up of the printing ink as it is applied. This may be overcome by overprinting a thin and completely transparent film layer on the back of the sheet, which covers and overlaps the whole character or design. This lies between the printing and the adhesive layer, and when the design is applied, it is held together as a piece by the clear carrying film which supports it.

Self-adhesive film is an alternative way of overcoming the same problem by abandoning the dry transfer process and replacing it with the use of a clear self-adhesive sheet. In the ranges available, the plastic sheet is much thinner and has a low-tack adhesive all over its back, which temporarily bonds it to a waxy or silicone-coated backing sheet from which it is peeled before application. The printing is usually on the front of the sheet, and the inks employed adhere well to it, although they may be scraped off for special effects with the edge of an X-acto knife. Self-adhesive film is applied as cut pieces which overlap their intended area; these are then trimmed back with the aid of a knife. The soft tack of the adhesive allows them to be removed easily for repositioning and permits excess trimmings to be removed without difficulty.

Self-adhesive films are particularly favored for items like borders, and for screen patterns, shading and texture patterns. However, the major manufacturers frequently offer a choice of dry transfer or self-adhesive film versions of such products, where it is feasible to do so. When self-adhesive films are placed in their final position, it is recommended that they are burnished over to improve their hold on the artwork, just as with dry transfer products.

1 Letraset's plastic burnisher
2 Spring-loaded burnisher
  from Chartpak
3 Mecanorma's film/plastic
  burnisher
4 Body type

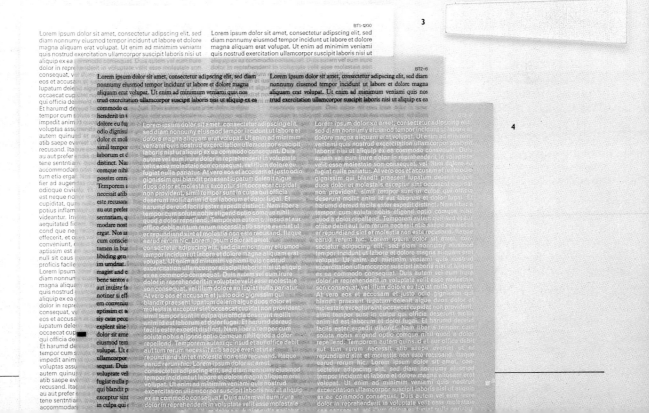

Large self-adhesive letters are die-cut into paper, or more often vinyl sheets, mounted on a protective backing piece. On some products it is best to lift each one out separately, leaving the surrounding scrap in place; other authorities advise that before use the whole of the scrap part of the sheet should be peeled away and discarded, to leave the letters clearly visible and accessible on the backing sheet.

These large letters and numerals are sufficiently self-supporting to be handled on their own, and can be lifted from the sheet by slipping the tip of a knife blade under an edge. They can be carried and positioned in the same manner, on the end of a knife or a special handling spatula, and once in place should be firmly rubbed down to insure that all the air is removed from under them and that they are firmly fixed to the receiving surface. Lettering of this type may be used on large-scale artwork, but more often it is employed for displays and signs, where a one-off product with a professional finish is required.

To assist with the accurate make-up of copy, carrying films may be used with most vinyl lettering. These are specially adapted plastic sheets, sometimes supplied in roll form, on which the vinyl lettering may be assembled face down. Completed text can then be applied as a piece to a surface, so that when the application film is peeled back the design remains in place. A variant on this system is offered by one manufacturer in which the text is assembled on a special grid, from which it can be lifted using a carrying film. The choice of lettering styles available in this form is extremely limited — most ranges offer a choice of basic colors, however. Pictograms and commonly used symbols are also available in a similar form, printed on a backing of self-adhesive vinyl.

Lettering machines carry a disk on which the type style is laid out in low relief. Larger machines have individual type cards which each carry one letter in low relief. The disks are rotated to select the desired letter, or an appropriate type card is slotted in, and when the machine is operated the chosen character is pressed onto a special tape and is neatly printed. The lettering machine insures accurate alignment and spacing, and feeds out the text on a self-adhesive strip. Different typefaces may be accommodated simply by changing the disk. Quite a selection of type styles is available to fit these machines, and a wide selection of tapes, each aimed at a different end use, is also supplied. Lettering may be set in black, white, blue or red, on a backing tape which is transparent, translucent, white, metallic or colored. The tapes are in a convenient cartridge form and are easily fitted. Electric and manual versions of these machines are available.

A similar but cruder version of a lettering machine can be used to punch text onto a tough, self-adhesive plastic strip. This is satisfactory for labeling purposes, and has some possible applications within the realm of graphic art generally, but it is not a suitable product for use on artwork. Proper studio lettering machines are, on the other hand, extremely useful, and are much faster than dry transfer lettering. The adhesive strip that they use is low-tack, which allows for repositioning of whole words or lines of text as the artwork is made up.

Reference materials
Because much graphic design and illustration work has to be produced both within a limited timescale and within a budget, it is not unusual to resort to reference material and instantly available artwork in order to shorten the creative process. A good designer is always creative, but it simply may not be possible for even the best graphic artist to be original all the time.

Reference material enables an artist to draw something which it is not practical to draw from life. It can also provide a starting-point for the creative process. An idea or an image can be extracted from reference material and then worked upon and developed into something quite different. For most artists, graphic artists and designers — and indeed for all creative people — a most important source of reference must be work that they have done before. So the contents of a portfolio represent a valuable source of inspiration. Roughs, sketches and

SELF-ADHESIVE LETTERS

Alvin supplies a range of vinyl lettering called Super-Stick. Letraset supplies the Letrasign range, which includes blanks from which designers may cut their own designs. The best selection of die-cut lettering and symbols is from Zipatone.

even student exercises that have not been put to final use should always be stored there to be called upon again; an idea that didn't quite click last time might do so the next time it is worked on.

More specifically for graphic artists there are also comprehensive visual reference works, each on a particular subject, on which designers may model their drawings and finished artwork. For example, figure drawing can be made relatively easy if it is based on an illustration from a series showing a certain type of figure in a variety of different poses. The finished piece is original, but is more accurate and is more speedily done for being based on reference material.

Copyright-free collections of decorative patterns, motifs and commonly used advertising devices, usually in book form can be drawn from and re-used at the artist's discretion. These again are frequently used as a stimulus to the imagination, but there is nothing to stop artists and designers from copying, cutting and pasting up extracts from copyright-free publications without and alterations. Copyright-free publications are a form of instant artwork, and thus have something in common with the border designs, decorative patterns and other devices that are included in the ranges of dry transfer and self-adhesive materials.

The question of copyright is a delicate one whenever reference material is being discussed. Most countries recognize copyright, and designs may be protected under a number of international agreements. It is generally accepted, however, that certain design devices are in such common use, and have been for so long, that they must be regarded as freely available to whoever wishes to use them. Unless material is offered as copyright-free, or is offered with the actual or implied permission of the owner to be re-used in certain ways, it may not be available as reference material except in its capacity to stimulate creativity.

INSTANT LETTERING

SUPPLIER	MANUFACTURER	DISTRIBUTOR	WHOLESALER	RETAILER	Areas where products are available	Local variations in product range	Dry Transfer Sheets	Line and Transfer Tape	Burnishers	Protective Sprays	Storage Equipment	Lettering Machines	Typesetting programs Equipment	Copyright-free Pictorial Archives	Designer's/Animator's Reference Books	Reference Patterns
Abelscot-Marchant	•	•	•		W	No				•						
Alfac	•				W	N/S	•	•	•		•					
Alvin	•	•	•		W	No	•									
Conté	•				W	Yes	•									
Edding	•				W	No	•									
Sam Flax		•		•	W	No		•	•		•				•	
Griffin (Grifhold)	•	•			W	No			•							
Holbein	•		•		W	No	•		•	•						
Kroy	•				W	No		•	•				•			
Langford & Hill		•	•	•	W	No	•	•	•	•	•	•	•	•	•	•
Locwyn	•				UK US	No					•					
Letraset	•				W	N/S	•	•	•	•	•					
Maimeri		•			E UK	N/A			•							
Marabu	•				W	No				•						
Mecanorma	•				W	N/A	•	•			•					
M. Myers & Son	•				W	N/A					•					
H.W. Peel & Co	•	•			W	No			•						•	
Pelltech		•			UK	N/A	•		•	•					•	
Rexel (Derwent Cumberland)	•				W	Yes	•									
Rotobord	•	•	•	•	W	No	•	•	•	•						

KEY: A – Australia   **C** – Canada   **E** – Europe (excluding UK)   **S** – Scandinavia   **UK** – United Kingdom   **US** – United States   **W** – Worldwide   **N/S** – Not Stated

TYPEFACES

TYPEFACE	Alfac	Decadry (Alvin)	Transfer-Type (Cello-Tac)	Normatype (Conté)	Edding	Letraset	Maxon (Holbein)	Letter-Press (Mecanorma)	Zipatone
Aachen					•2				
Abbey Round									•1
Access							•2		
Advertisers Gothic					•1	•1			
AG Buch Rounded	•2								
Agincourt					•1				
Airkraft					•1				
Akilines A.K.I. Lines							•1		•1
Akzidenz Grotesk					•1		•1		
Albertus	•1				•1		•1		
Alec					•1				
Alexei Copperplate					•1				
Alfac	•6								
Alfereta							•1		
Algerian					•1				
Alte Schwabacher					•1				
Alternate Gothic		•2				•1			
Ambassador					•1				
Ambrose					•1				
Amelia									•1
American Typewriter	•6			•1	•1	•7	•1	•7	•7
American Uncial					•1		•2		
Americana	•3				•1		•3		
Annlie					•2				
Annonce Grotesque					•1	•1			•1
Antikva									•1
Antique	•2	•1					•4		
Antique Olive	•2	•3			•7		•6		•3
Apollo					•1				
Aristocrat					•1				
Arnold Bocklin					•1		•1	•1	
Arrow									•1
Arsis							•1		
Art Deco							•1		
Art Script				•1			•1		
Art World							•1		
Artistik					•1				
Asmyth							•1		
Aster							•3		
Astley					•1				

KEY: The numbers next to the bullets (•6) refer to the number of variants in that typeface.

TYPEFACE	Alfac	Decadry (Alvin)	Transfer-Type (Cello-Tac)	Normatype (Conté)	Edding	Letraset	Maxon (Holbein)	Letter-Press (Mecanorma)	Zipatone
Astra						•1			
Astral							•1		
Augustea						•1			
Aura Script						•1			
Avant Garde			•2				•8	•6	
Avant Garde Gothic	•5				•1	•5	•1		
Baby Arbuckle							•1		
Baby Teeth						•1			
Baker							•3		
Balloon						•2	•3		
Balmoral						•1			
Barbican	•2								
Barcelona	•2						•5		
Barrio									•1
Baskerville				•1		•1	•4		•1
Becka Script						•1			
Belshaw						•1			
Belwe						•5			
Bembo						•1			
ITC Benguiat (Benguiat)	•3					•4	•9		•3

TYPEFACE	Alfac	Decadry (Alvin)	Transfer-Type (Cello-Tac)	Normatype (Conté)	Edding	Letraset	Maxon (Holbein)	Letter-Press (Mecanorma)	Zipatone
Berkeley							•3		
Berling					•3		•3		
Bernhard Antique	•2				•1		•1		
Berthold							•1		
Bertie					•1				
Beton	•2				•5		•6		
Bible Script and Flourishes					•1				
Binner					•1				
Black Shadow							•1		
Blackfriars Roman					•1				
Blackline									•1
Blackmoor					•1				
Blanchard Solid					•1				
Blippo							•2		•2
Block					•1		•1		
Block Schwer					•1				
Block Up					•1				
Blues							•1		
Bobo				•1					
Bodoni					•2	•2	•3	•1	

KEY: The numbers next to the bullets (6) refer to the number of variants in that typeface.

Continued

TYPEFACE	Alfac	Decadry (Alvin)	Transfer-Type (Cello-Tac)	Normatype (Conté)	Edding	Letraset	Maxon (Holbein)	Letter-Press (Mecanorma)	Zipatone
Bolt								•1	
Bombere					•1				
Bookman	•2				•4	•1	•3	•3	
Bottleneck					•1				
Bramley					•5				
Brighton					•4				
British							•4		
Broadway	•1			•1	•2	•1		•1	
Brody					•1				
Brush (Script)					•1	•1	•1	•1	
Bulletin Printer							•1		
Bulletin Typewriter					•1		•1		
Bullion					•1				
Burlington					•1				
Busorama			•1		•1		•1	•3	
Buster					•1				
Buxom								•1	
Cabaret					•1				
Cabarga Cursiva					•1				
Cable					•3				

TYPEFACE	Alfac	Decadry (Alvin)	Transfer-Type (Cello-Tac)	Normatype (Conté)	Edding	Letraset	Maxon (Holbein)	Letter-Press (Mecanorma)	Zipatone
Cairoli	•4	•2							
Caligra							•1		
Calligraphia									
Calliope							•1		
Calypso					•1				
Camellia					•1				
Cancellar esca Script					•1				
Candice					•2				
Candy						•1			
Capone					•1	•1			
Car Plate							•1		
Cardinal					•1				
Carlton			•3		•1				
Carolus					•1				
Carousel					•1				
Caslon	•4				•6	•1	•5	•2	
ITC Caslon					•5				
Cathedra l					•1				
Caxton					•6				
Celtic							•3		

KEY: The numbers next to the bullets (6) refer to the number of variants in that typeface.

TYPEFACE	Alfac	Decadry (Alvin)	Transfer-Type (Cello-Tac)	Normatype (Conté)	Edding	Letraset	Maxon (Holbein)	Letter-Press (Mecanorma)	Zipatone
Celtic Swash	•2								
Century							•5		
Century Old Style	•2								
Century Schoolbook						•2			•2
Challenge						•2			
Champion					•1				•1
Charlston							•1		
Charrette						•1			
Charter						•1			
Cheltenham	•2					•3	•4		•2
Chesterfield						•1			
Chic									•1
Chicago			•1				•1		•4
Chinon							•1		
Chippendale						•1			
Chisel						•1	•1		•1
Choc	•1								•1
Chromium One						•1			
Churchward	•4			•1	•2		•3		
Circus							•1		

TYPEFACE	Alfac	Decadry (Alvin)	Transfer-Type (Cello-Tac)	Normatype (Conté)	Edding	Letraset	Maxon (Holbein)	Letter-Press (Mecanorma)	Zipatone
Cirkulus					•1				
City					•3				
Clarendon				•2	•2	•1		•2	•2
Clearface	•4				•3		•4		•2
Cloister					•1		•3		
Columbian					•1				
Commercial Script					•1		•1		•1
Compacta					•8	•1			
Company					•1				
Compton					•1				
Computer		•3							
Comstock									•1
Condensa	•6								
Condensed			•3						
Conference					•1				
Contest							•1		
Cooper Black	•3	•2		•1	•2	•3	•1	•3	•3
Copperplate							•4	•1	
Coral							•2		
Corinthian					•5				

KEY: The numbers next to the bullets (6) refer to the number of variants in that typeface.

Continued

TYPEFACE	Alfac	Decadry (Alvin)	Transfer-Type (Cello-Tac)	Normatype (Conté)	Edding	Letraset	Maxon (Holbein)	Letter-Press (Mecanorma)	Zipatone
Cornelius	•1								
Cortez					•1				
Countdown					•1				
Crillee					•4				
Croissant					•1				
Crowbar							•1		
Cushing							•4		
Cut-In					•2	•1			
Data 70					•1				
Davida					•1				•1
Decaligra							•1		
Delphin No. 1					•1	•1			
Delphin No. 2					•1				
Delta 4							•1		
Delta 5							•1		
Demian					•1				
Dempsey					•1				
Denby					•2				
Desdemona					•2				
Digita 1							•1		

TYPEFACE	Alfac	Decadry (Alvin)	Transfer-Type (Cello-Tac)	Normatype (Conté)	Edding	Letraset	Maxon (Holbein)	Letter-Press (Mecanorma)	Zipatone
Din 16	•2								
Din 16m					•1				
Din 17	•2				•1				
Din 17m					•1				
Din 1451	•2								
Dom Casual					•1		•1		
Dom Diagonal							•1		
Drafting				•1					
Drafting Standard							•1		
Dubbledik							•1		
Dynamo					•4		•4		
Dynamo Chrome					•1				
Ebbsworth	•2								
Eclat					•1				
Edda					•1				
Edwardian					•1				
Egide							•1		
Egizio	•1	•1							
Egypt		•1							
Egyptian			•1		•1				•1

KEY: The numbers next to the bullets (6) refer to the number of variants in that typeface.

TYPEFACE	Alfac	Decadry (Alvin)	Transfer-Type (Cello-Tac)	Normatype (Conté)	Edding	Letraset	Maxon (Holbein)	Letter-Press (Mecanorma)	Zipatone
Egyptienne	●1					●1	●2		
Einhorn						●1			
El Greco						●1			
Elefont						●1			
Elite						●1			
Emboss									●2
Embrionic									●1
Emilion	●1								
Emporium						●1			
English Tudor						●1			
Engravers (Old English)								●1	●1
Enviro						●1			
Epitaphe						●1			
Eras	●2					●6		●4	
Estella								●1	
Estro								●1	
Etruscan	●1								
Etrusco	●1								
Eurostile	●3	●1	●1	●1	●3	●4	●1	●5	●2
Exeter									

TYPEFACE	Alfac	Decadry (Alvin)	Transfer-Type (Cello-Tac)	Normatype (Conté)	Edding	Letraset	Maxon (Holbein)	Letter-Press (Mecanorma)	Zipatone
Falernus					●1				
Fanfare									●1
Fat Face	●1								
Fat Shadow					●1				
Fencer			●1						
Fenice							●6		
Fette Gotisch					●1				
Fidelio							●1		
Fino					●1				
Flamenco					●1				
Flange		●2					●1		
Flash	●2	●3			●2	●1			
Flint				●1					
Flyer					●2				
Folio	●3	●1	●1	●1	●6	●2	●8		●5
Fontana	●1								
Foreground									●2
Formula One					●1				
Fortune	●1		●1		●2				
Fraktur				●1	●1				

KEY: The numbers next to the bullets (6) refer to the number of variants in that typeface.

Continued

TYPEFACE	Alfac	Decadry (Alvin)	Transfer-Type (Cello-Tac)	Normatype (Conté)	Edding	Letraset	Maxon (Holbein)	Letter-Press (Mecanorma)	Zipatone
Frankfurter					●4				
Franklin Gothic	●5		●1		●4		●3	●3	
Freestyle Script					●2				
Friz Quadrata			●1		●2		●2	●2	
Frutiger					●4		●4		
Full							●1		
Fumo									
Futura	●7		●14	●1	●16	●3	●14	●8	
Gadget Lined									●1
Galadriel					●1				
Gallia					●1				
ITC Galliard					●1		●6		
Garamond		●1			●4		●7		
Garamont							●2		
Garbo							●1		
Garrick					●1				
Gary					●1				
Gay Nineties							●1		
George	●1								
Gill	●6				●12		●6		●2

TYPEFACE	Alfac	Decadry (Alvin)	Transfer-Type (Cello-Tac)	Normatype (Conté)	Edding	Letraset	Maxon (Holbein)	Letter-Press (Mecanorma)	Zipatone
Gillies					●4	●1	●4		
Giorgio									●1
G.K.W. Computer									●1
Glaser Stencil					●1				
Glastonbury					●1				
Glesh Export									●1
Globe							●1		
Glow Worm							●2		
Gold Rush					●1				
Golly									●1
Good Vibrations					●1				
Gorilla							●1		
Gothique (Gothic)	●2	●1					●1		
Gotik				●1					
Goudy	●2				●6		●4	●5	
Graphica	●1								
Graphique							●1		
Graphis					●1				
Grotesk				●1					
Grotesque					●6	●3	●3	●3	

KEY: The numbers next to the bullets (6) refer to the number of variants in that typeface.

TYPEFACE	Alfac	Decadry (Alvin)	Transfer-Type (Cello-Tac)	Normatype (Conté)	Edding	Letraset	Maxon (Holbein)	Letter-Press (Mecanorma)	Zipatone
Grouch							●1	●1	
Hadfield					●1				
Hand Drawn					●1				
Hand Lettering		●20							●5
Handel							●1	●1	
Harlow						●2			
Harrington						●1			
Hawthorn						●1			
Headline (Outline)	●1								
Helvetica	●11	●3	●6	●2	●10	●16	●7	●16	●9
Hepta	●1								
Herkules						●1			
Hermes						·		●1	
Hidalgo		●1							
High Tech								●1	
Highlight						●1			
Hillman								●2	
Hobo									●1
Honey	●1		·						
Horatio						●3			

TYPEFACE	Alfac	Decadry (Alvin)	Transfer-Type (Cello-Tac)	Normatype (Conté)	Edding	Letraset	Maxon (Holbein)	Letter-Press (Mecanorma)	Zipatone
Horndon					●1				
Hot Dog							●1		
Hunter					●1				
Iguana									●1
Impress					●1				
Inga							●1		
Ingrama									●1
Inserat Grotesk			●1						
Intalink	●1								
Isbell	●3						●4		
Isometric					●1				
Isonorm	●1		-		●2			●2	
Italia	●2				●4			●3	●3
Italian Old Style					●1				●3
Italienne				●1					
Jackson							●1		
Jay Gothic									●1
Jenson					●3				
Jim Crow							●1	●1	
Julia Script					●1				

KEY: The numbers next to the bullets (6) refer to the number of variants in that typeface.

Continued

TYPEFACE	Alfac	Decadry (Alvin)	Transfer-Type (Cello-Tac)	Normatype (Conté)	Edding	Letraset	Maxon (Holbein)	Letter-Press (Mecanorma)	Zipatone
Juliet					•|				
Jumbo				•|					•|
Kabel	•|						•3	•4	
Kalligraphia					•|				
Kanina	•|								
Kestrel					•|				
Keyboard					•|				
Knightsbridge					•|				
Koch Fraktur					•|				
Kombi							•|		
Korinna		•3			•4		•3	•3	
Kornelia					•|				
Künstler Schreibschrift				•|					
L & C Stymie					•|				•|
Lamina							•|		
Lando	•|								
Latin		•|							
L'Auriol					•|				
Lazybones					•|				
LCD					•2				
Le Golf					•|				
Le Griffe					•|				
Le Robur Noir					•|				
Lectura					•|		•|		
Leopard							•|		
Lettres Ornees					•|		•2	•|	
Lido		•|							
Limited View							•|		
Lindsay					•|				
Linear					•|				
Locarno Italic					•|				
Locomotive					•|				
Loose New Roman					•|				
Lubalin	•2	•|			•|	•4	•4	•5	
Lucid Shadow					•|				
Lydian		•2							
Machine							•|		
Madame								•|	
Madeleine							•2		
Magnetic							•|		

KEY: The numbers next to the bullets (6) refer to the number of variants in that typeface.

TYPEFACE	Alfac	Decadry (Alvin)	Transfer-Type (Cello-Tac)	Normatype (Conté)	Edding	Letraset	Maxon (Holbein)	Letter-Press (Mecanorma)	Zipatone
Magnificent					●1				
Magnus					●1				
Manin					●1				
Manuscript Caps					●1				
Manuscript Gothic									●1
Marbleheart									●1
Masquerade					●1				
Mastercard					●1				
Media Script							●2		
Melior					●1				●1
Mellissa					●1				
Mendoza					●1				
Mercator							●1		
Mexico Olympic									●1
MGB Patrician					●1				
Michel					●1				
Microgramma					●2	●2	●2	●2	
Mikado							●1		
Milano					●1				
Mirage							●5		

TYPEFACE	Alfac	Decadry (Alvin)	Transfer-Type (Cello-Tac)	Normatype (Conté)	Edding	Letraset	Maxon (Holbein)	Letter-Press (Mecanorma)	Zipatone
Mr Big								●1	
Mistral					●1				
Modern	●1				●1	●1		●1	●1
Modern Gothic									●1
Motter Femina					●1				
Motter Ombra					●1				
Motter Tektura					●1				
Murray Hill	●1		●1		●1				●1
Musica					●1				
NavyCut							●1		
Neil					●1				
Neon	●1		●1		●1			●1	●1
Neptun					●1				
Neuzeit							●1		
Nevison Casual					●1				
New Baskerville							●4		
New York							●1		
News Gothic		●3			●3				●2
Normalise							●1		
Normandia							●2		

KEY: The numbers next to the bullets (6) refer to the number of variants in that typeface.

Continued

TYPEFACE	Alfac	Decadry (Alvin)	Transfer-Type (Cello-Tac)	Normatype (Conté)	Edding	Letraset	Maxon (Holbein)	Letter-Press (Mecanorma)	Zipatone
Nouvea	•2								
Novarese							•4		
Obliq					•2				
Observer	•6								
OCR-A					•1				
Octopuss					•2				
Odin					•1				
Often	•1								
Okay					•1				
Old English			•3		•1	•1			
Olde Toune					•1				
Olive							•7		
One Stroke Script					•1				
Onyx			•1						
Optex					•1				
Optima	•2		•1		•2	•3	•1	•3	•2
Orator							•1		
Orcandia							•2		
Orea							•1		
Ornate			•1						

TYPEFACE	Alfac	Decadry (Alvin)	Transfer-Type (Cello-Tac)	Normatype (Conté)	Edding	Letraset	Maxon (Holbein)	Letter-Press (Mecanorma)	Zipatone
Oxford					•1				
Paddington					•1				
Palace Script					•1	•1			
Palana					•1				
Palatino					•5		•4	•2	
Palazzo							•1		
Pamela					•1		•1		
Paper Clip									•1
Papyrus					•1				
Parisian						•1			
Park Avenue					•1	•1		•1	
Parsons					•1				
Pascal							•1		
Peignot		•1			•3	•1	•3		
Pendry Script					•1				
Perpetua		•1			•1		•3		
Phyllis					•1				
Piccadilly					•1				
Pierrot								•1	
Pinball					•1				

KEY: The numbers next to the bullets (6) refer to the number of variants in that typeface.

TYPEFACE	Alfac	Decadry (Alvin)	Transfer-Type (Cello-Tac)	Normatype (Conté)	Edding	Letraset	Maxon (Holbein)	Letter-Press (Mecanorma)	Zipatone
Pinocchio									●1
Pinto								●1	
Pioneer	●1					●1		●1	●1
Pistilli Roman			●1						
Plantin					●2	●4		●3	
Plastica					●1				
Playbill			●1			●1		●1	●1
Playschool								●1	
Plaza						●4			
Pluto						●1			
Polka								●2	
Poppl-College-1								●3	
Poppl Exquisit	●1					●1		●1	
Portly								●1	
Poster								●1	
Postscript									●1
Premier						●2			
Pretorian						●1			
Primavera									●1
Primitive						●1			

TYPEFACE	Alfac	Decadry (Alvin)	Transfer-Type (Cello-Tac)	Normatype (Conté)	Edding	Letraset	Maxon (Holbein)	Letter-Press (Mecanorma)	Zipatone
Princetown					●1				
Prisma			●1		●1	●1	●2		
Process					●1				
Profil			●1		●1		●1	●1	
Project							●1		
Proteus					●5				
P.T. Barnum			●1						
Pump					●5				
Putty							●1		
Quartermane					●1				
Quartz			●1						
Quay					●5				
Queen	●1								
Quentin					●1				
Quicksilver					●1				
Quirinale							●2		
ITC Quorum	●2				●1		●3		●1
Rage					●1				
Raleigh					●1			●2	
Raphael					●1				

KEY: The numbers next to the bullets (●) refer to the number of variants in that typeface.

Continued

TYPEFACE	Alfac	Decadry (Alvin)	Transfer-Type (Cello-Tac)	Normatype (Conté)	Edding	Letraset	Maxon (Holbein)	Letter-Press (Mecanorma)	Zipatone
Renate					•2				
Renault	•3								
Revue					•1				
RGB's							•2		
Rialto					•1				
Ringlet			•1		•1		•1		
Ritz					•1				
Rockwell					•7		•5	•3	
Rocky	•2								
Roco					•1				
Rodeo					•1				
Roman		•1							
Roman Script					•1				
Romantiques					•1				
Romic					•6				
Ronda							•2	•1	
Rope							•1		
Roslyn					•1		•3		
Roundel							•1		
Round Gothic							•1		

TYPEFACE	Alfac	Decadry (Alvin)	Transfer-Type (Cello-Tac)	Normatype (Conté)	Edding	Letraset	Maxon (Holbein)	Letter-Press (Mecanorma)	Zipatone
Roy						•2			
Roys Tango					•1				
Rubber Stamp					•1				
Ruberta III							•1	•1	
Runnymede					•1				
Rush							•1		
Sachel									•1
Salisbury					•1				
San Script							•2		
Sanideg	•1								
Sans Serif					•1		•2	•1	
Santa Fe					•1				
Sapphire					•1		•1		
Scanner					•1				
Schneidler Old Style					•1				
Scimitar					•1				
Script	•1	•1							
Sea Gull					•1				
Senator					•1				
Serif Gothic			•1		•4		•6	•3	

KEY: The numbers next to the bullets (6) refer to the number of variants in that typeface.

TYPEFACE	Alfac	Decadry (Alvin)	Transfer-Type (Cello-Tac)	Normatype (Conté)	Edding	Letraset	Maxon (Holbein)	Letter-Press (Mecanorma)	Zipatone
Serifa						•1			
Shamrock						•1			
Sharp								•1	
Shatter						•1			
Shelley						•1			
Silva								•1	
Silver Screen						•1			
Simplex	•1								
Sinaloa						•1			
Slipstream						•1			
Slogan	•1								
Society	•1								
Souvenir	•6	•1	•2			•5	•2	•7	•4
Spats	•1								
Spectre						•1			
Spottyface									•1
Spring				•1				•1	
Springfield						•1			
Sprint						•1			
Square								•1	
Squire					•2				
Stack					•1		•1		
Stadia					•1				
Standard					•1				
Steelplate			•1						
Stencil	•1	•1	•1	•1	•1	•1	•2		•1
Steve					•1				
Stilla					•1				
Stilus							•1		
STOP							•1		•1
Stripes									
Stymie		•2					•1		
Sub-Contact									•1
Sully Jonquieres							•2		
Sunday							•1		
Sunshine					•1				
Superfont									•1
Superstar					•1				
Surprise							•3		
Swing									•1

KEY: The numbers next to the bullets (6) refer to the number of variants in that typeface.

Continued

TYPEFACE	Alfac	Decadry (Alvin)	Transfer-Type (Cello-Tac)	Normatype (Conté)	Edding	Letraset	Maxon (Holbein)	Letter-Press (Mecanorma)	Zipatone
Synchro					●1				
Tabasco					●2				
Talisman					●1				
Tango					●1				
Tankard					●1				
Tarragon					●1				
Television							●1		
Tempo									●1
Thalia					●1		●1		
Thorne							●1		
Thunderbird									●1
Tiffany	●2				●3		●3	●4	
Times	●3		●2	●4	●5	●2	●4	●3	
Tintoretto					●1				
Tip Top					●1				
Tiranti					●1				
Titus					●2				
Tonal					●1				
Traffic					●1				
Transmission					●1				

TYPEFACE	Alfac	Decadry (Alvin)	Transfer-Type (Cello-Tac)	Normatype (Conté)	Edding	Letraset	Maxon (Holbein)	Letter-Press (Mecanorma)	Zipatone
Triset					●1				
Trooper Roman					●1				
Trump Graviere		●1							
Tunic	●1								
Tuscan							●1		
Typewriter			●1						
Typo Script									●1
Typos	●1								
Tzigane							●1		
Ultra Bodoni			●1						
Umbra									●1
Uncle Bill									●1
Unitype									●1
Univers	●7	●3	●2	●1	●14	●6	●15		●6
University Roman					●4				
Update							●1		
Upright Neon					●1				
Usherwood							●3		
V.A.G.					●1				
Van Dijk					●1				

KEY: The numbers next to the bullets (6) refer to the number of variants in that typeface.

TYPEFACE	Alfac	Decadry (Alvin)	Transfer-Type (Cello-Tac)	Normatype (Conté)	Edding	Letraset	Maxon (Holbein)	Letter-Press (Mecanorma)	Zipatone
Vegas						•1			
Velfovic							•3		
Vendome					•1				
Venus			•1		•1				•3
Verity	•2								
Via Face Don							•2		
Victorian					•2				
Videotext	•1								
Virility	•1								
Vivaldi					•1	•1	•1	•1	
Voel Beat							•1		
Volta							•1		
Walbaum Fraktur					•1				
Weiß			•1						
Weiß Antiqua							•2		
Weiß Roman					•1				
Weiß Rundgotisch					•1				
Welt					•1				
Western Style	•1								
Westminster					•1				

TYPEFACE	Alfac	Decadry (Alvin)	Transfer-Type (Cello-Tac)	Normatype (Conté)	Edding	Letraset	Maxon (Holbein)	Letter-Press (Mecanorma)	Zipatone
Whitefriars									•3
Whitin								•1	
Wiegand's Renaissance								•1	
Windsor		•1			•6	•1		•2	•2
Wolf Antiqua									•1
Worcester									•2
Xanthus								•1	
YAGI Link Double					•1				
Yankee					•1				
York									•1
Young Baroque					•1				
Zapf Book									•4
Zaph Chancery	•4				•4			•4	
Zelek								•3	
Zentak Grotesque	•2	•1	•1						
Zipper					•1				

KEY: The numbers next to the bullets (6) refer to the number of variants in that typeface.

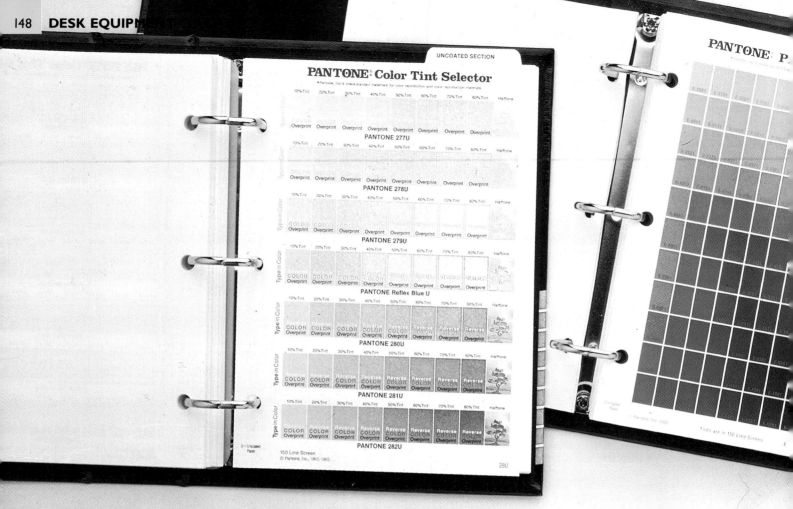

COLOR AIDS AND SPECIFIERS

Graphic artists, fine artists and designers most often work with such media as paints, inks, pencils, pens and crayons. However, there is sometimes also a need for the re-presentation of work done in one form of color in different forms. A design expressed in marker pens, for example, does not look the same when printed by one of the standard printing processes. That may not matter to the graphic artist, who can visualize the finished product, but what that finished product is going to look like needs to be conveyed to both the client and the printer if the idea is to be properly realized. To assist with this, the designer can call upon a number of color aids and specifiers.

Insofar as it is possible to separate these, color aids may be said to assist with imitations of the final product so that it can be assessed in its final form before it is produced, whereas color-specification products are intended to convey actual technical information from graphic artists and designers to printers so that the finished product will match the colors of the original design as nearly as possible. In practice it is common to link color aids at least partly to color-specification systems, so that original artwork and mock-ups can be translated directly into printed products.

COLOR SPECIFIERS

*The PANTONE® * Color Specification System marketed by Letraset offers color-reference and selection products, and a supporting selection of color aids. These can be matched exactly using the PANTONE® * Matching System. The PANTONE® * Color Specifier is a designer's manual with the full range of more than 500 colors available shown on both coated and uncoated paper; a small color square can be*

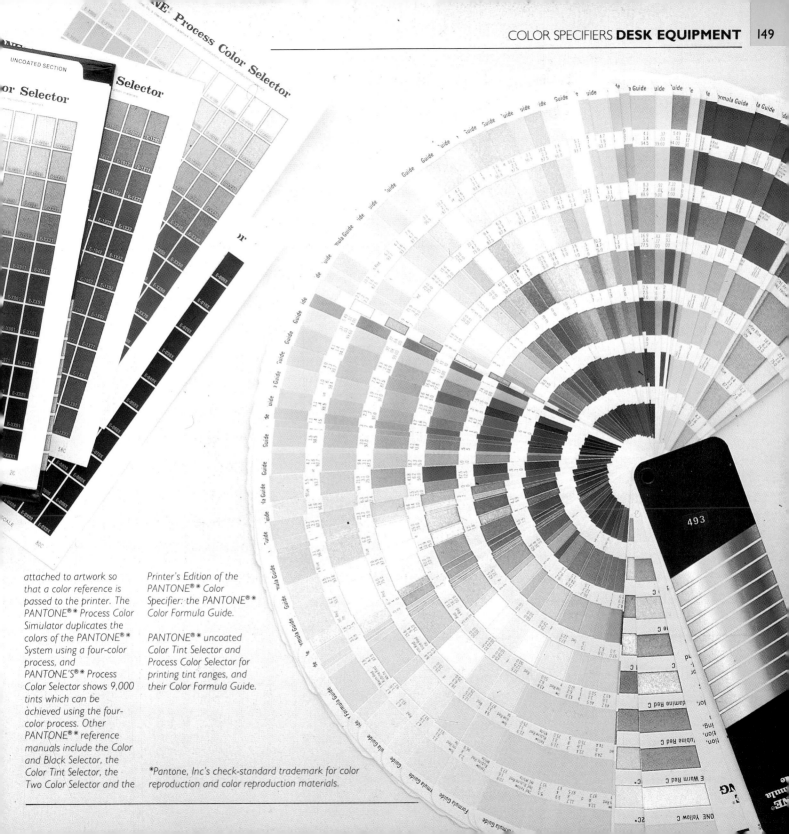

attached to artwork so that a color reference is passed to the printer. The PANTONE®* Process Color Simulator duplicates the colors of the PANTONE®* System using a four-color process, and PANTONE'S®* Process Color Selector shows 9,000 tints which can be achieved using the four-color process. Other PANTONE®* reference manuals include the Color and Black Selector, the Color Tint Selector, the Two Color Selector and the Printer's Edition of the PANTONE®* Color Specifier: the PANTONE®* Color Formula Guide.

PANTONE®* uncoated Color Tint Selector and Process Color Selector for printing tint ranges, and their Color Formula Guide.

*Pantone, Inc's check-standard trademark for color reproduction and color reproduction materials.

Letraset Color Overlay is another way of applying color to well-finished mock-ups, and is available in a choice of 298 colors. Letra Film matt offers a selection of 96 transparent colors matched to the PANTONE®* System. The Coates 50/50 System offers 364 colors, created from 22 basic inks supported by 2 black inks. The Schmincke HKS System offers 84 well-chosen colors as both studio media and printers' inks. HKS Series 25 Designers' Colors are fine-quality gouache paints in a selection of shades that can be matched either by the HKS inks or by four-color process printing. Sericol offers the Seritone matching system, aimed at printers and producing a wide vriety of shades from a very small number of basic inks. Seritone A uses gloss inks based on organic pigments; Seritone B, gloss inks based on chrome and organic pigments; and Seritone C satin and matte inks. The Munsell Color Specification System is a system of color notation in which any color can be accurately described. Internationally, it is regarded as one of the most advanced and reliable systems. Because none of the color-specification systems can claim to be universally accepted, it is common for ink manufacturers and printers to cross-reference the PANTONE®* , Coates, HKS, Munsell and Seritone systems.

*Pantone Inc's check-standard trademark for color reproduction and color reproduction materials

COLOR AIDS

The Omnicrom 2000 produces short runs of color printing, and can be used to simulate oil blocking, for laminating, for thermal binding, and for OHP (overhead projection) transparencies. The Adkins Color Computer specifies colors that are to be printed by a four-color process. It is possible to simulate up to 80,000 colors. Flat Tint Charts are also available for specifying areas of color using the four-color printing process. Color photocopiers can be used for quick low-cost color-imaging, but they do not necessarily reproduce colors accurately. Agfa-Gevaert supplies the Copy Color Photocopying System, and Cannon and Rank Xerox also manufacture color photocopiers. Color-aid papers have a water-resistant surface: corrections can be made by wiping off with a damp cloth. MB Color Shading Papers are graduated colored papers which can be used as background material for finished artwork. Decadry OHP Materials are supplied by Alfac, available as plain colored sheets and as letters, symbols and patterns on either self-adhesive film or dry transfer sheets. Other aids include X Film, a self-adhesive color film which is available from Abelscot-Marchant. Maxon also supplies self-adhesive cut-out color films and color overlays for use in artwork and displays.

Color-specification systems

The principle behind color-specification systems is quite simple: if a designer wishes a printer to produce a particular color, a color sample can be provided against which the printer can match inks. If the sample is of a color about which the designer can offer no additional information except that it is the color desired, whether the printers can match it depends on their knowledge of color-mixing and their ability to assess and evaluate a color by eye. If, however, the graphic artist can pick a color which is of a known specification, the printer can match it exactly by using a known "recipe," and a more or less perfect color match can be not only achieved but repeated.

The leading color-specification systems are therefore linked to a known selection of inks which can be mixed and blended to produce an extensive range of colors. These colors are available to graphic designers and artists as swatch-books, from which colors may be chosen; when a sample of the color, or the color's reference, is communicated to the printer, the corresponding blend of inks can be prepared.

In order to insure the performance of their systems, the manufacturers of color-specification systems retain a rigorous control over the production of both the reference material and the inks. Because ink color may look different on different surfaces, it is usual to include sample swatches in the ranges on a basic choice of paper finishes.

Besides showing colors on different surfaces, color-specification systems also show the permutations that are possible when specified colors are reproduced as percentage tints or in combination with black. Reference material that matches specified colors to the effects that can be produced by four-color process printing is also supplied as part of the major color-specification ranges.

COLOR AIDS AND SPECIFIERS

SUPPLIER	MANUFACTURER	DISTRIBUTOR	WHOLESALER	RETAILER	Areas supplied or in which goods are available	Local variation in product range	Selection Systems	Selection Products	Percentage of Calculators	Proofing/Imaging Systems	Computer Correction Systems	Computer Graphics	Paint Box Systems
Abelscot-Marchant	•	•	•		W	No	•						
Arnold Cook (Graphic Arts)	•	•	•	•	UK	N/S	•						
Art Material International	•	•	•		W	N/S			•				
Colourtech International	•				W	No				•			
Gaebel Enterprises (Stazput)	•				US	Yes		•					
Letraset (Pantone)	•	•			W	N/S	•	•					
Mecanorma	•	•			W	Yes	•	•	•	•			
Quantel	•				W	No						•	•
Rotobord	•	•	•	•	W	Yes			•				
Rototrim	•				W	No					•		
Rotring		•			W	No	•	•					
Schmincke	•				W	No	•					•	
Sky Copy	•	•			UK	N/A				•			

KEY: UK − United Kingdom **US** − United States **W** − Worldwide **N/S** − Not Stated

Color-imaging systems

It is often necessary to produce a final proof for a client's approval before large sums are committed to production. It may also be necessary to produce alternative color suggestions in a highly finished form for final selection by the client. And commercial pressures being what they are, it may in addition be necessary from time to time to produce a near-perfect mock-up of a product for photography prior to the actual production of the finished article. In all these circumstances a color-imaging system is most useful.

Color-imaging systems allow the production of one-off pieces from negatives or from artwork on a translucent base. The available systems vary slightly in the actual procedure and the materials used, but the basic principle of all color-imaging systems is the same. A sensitized ink is applied to a support sheet, or a special pre-prepared color sheet is used. This is put in contact with

the negative and is exposed to ultra-violet light for a short time. An area of color corresponding to the negative is fixed by this process; any excess color can be washed away to reveal a colored print. A multi-colored print is produced by repeating the process several times over.

Most color-imaging systems offer the possibility of producing either a direct print or a transfer print. A direct print is made on a special backing-sheet, where it remains, whereas a transfer print is applied as a dry transfer to any suitable artwork surface. It has to be remembered when producing a transfer print that the image must first be made the wrong way around, because the transfer process will reverse its position.

Some color-imaging systems are linked to color-specification systems. The results of color-imaging systems can be extremely convincing and they are not only quick to produce, but also a fraction of the cost of a printed proof.

*The PANTONE® * Color Coated Selection from Letraset.*

Pantone, Inc's check-standard trademark for color reproduction and color reproduction materials.

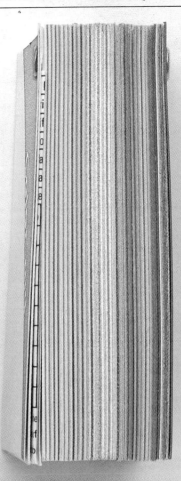

Color specifier from Mecanorma for film.

IMAGING SYSTEMS

Letraset offers the Letrachrome Direct Image System for color imaging, and Color Key is an alternative to Letraset which produces colored images on a clear film. Three types of Color Key film are available: Color Key Opaque, Color Key Transparent and Color Key Photomask. Letraset also offers the Image 'n' Transfer System, used to create dry transfer motifs in a basic selection of colors. Mecanorma's

Creative Color offers a choice of 23 mixable inks from which an extensive range of shades can be produced. Accessories such as the Creative Color Work table are available to complement the system, and complete sets are available for direct-imaging, for transfer-imaging and for ink-mixing. Trans Proof is a color-imaging system by Colortech, and offers a choice of direct-imaging or transfer-imaging.

STUDIO EQUIPMENT

Drawing-Boards • Light-boxes
Studio Furniture • Cameras
Enlargers • Photocopiers
Computer Graphic Systems

DRAWING-BOARDS AND STUDIO FURNITURE

This chapter deals with items of studio furniture that have a practical purpose. Both drawing-boards and light-boxes are considered here, together with storage cabinets and chests, specially-adapted desks, and miscellaneous items such as portfolios, mobile organizers and chairs.

Many of these items make studio spaces more practical to work in, but by no means all of them are as essential pieces of equipment as drawing-boards and light-boxes may be. Some of the examples covered here, moreover, may well be thought less desirable as tastes move on, and may be replaced by other products of the moment. It has to be admitted, however, that some studio furnishings are more valuable for the correct designer image they project than for the functions they perform. Their inclusion is an acknowledgement of the fact that professional image may not merely be both valuable and necessary, but may be part of the creative surroundings that encourage success in commercial design practice.

DRAWING-BOARDS

A firm, flat working-surface is important for virtually all design procedures, ranging from graphic art to technical drafting. And for this reason, most graphic artists make use of a drawing-board. It is essential that the drawing-board be flat, and that it be free from any tendency to warp. Drawing-boards of solid wood have to be very carefully constructed in order to insure that they remain stable. More often nowadays, processed woods or laminated woods are used for drawing boards, therefore, and are often coated to improve their performance and appearance. Plastic drawing-boards also feature in many ranges.

Drawing-boards can be portable, but they are also available as desk-top and free-standing models. In addition to plain drawing-boards, there are many which are equipped with special features. Drafting heads and drawing aids feature on many boards, whereas others are highly adjustable or have features such as parallel motion as an aid to drafting. Some drawing-boards are circular, which makes them particularly versatile in that they can be tilted or rotated in use.

Wood drawing-boards are the simplest, widely used by fine artists and illustrators, and are acceptable items of equipment for graphic artists where a flat surface is all that is required. Wooden drawing-boards are best used with a backing sheet inserted between the work and the board when the work is carried out on light materials such as paper or film. A wooden surface can be rather soft, and can yield and mark easily under the pressure of a heavily-applied pen or pencil. If used for cutting, or if pins are used to secure paper to the board, the surface of a wooden board rapidly becomes marked, and eventually becomes so damaged that drawings cannot be carried out on it without the risk of unintended marks being created. Hard surfaces such as Formica or melamine are commonly applied to the surfaces of drawing-boards to overcome this.

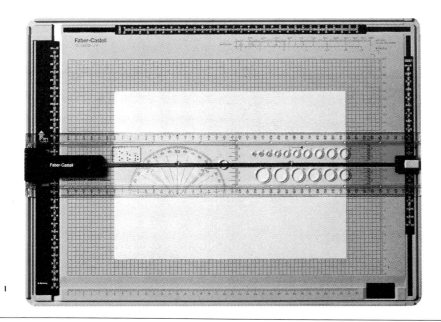

DRAWING-BOARDS

Plain general-purpose boards are available from Helix, Blundell Harling, Hellerman, Langford & Hill, Mayline, Alvin and Sam Flax. Hellerman offers a choice of professional-quality drawing-boards in blockboard and PVC, and melamine-coated. Langford & Hill's boards are in sizes ranging from 16½×22½ inches to 33×47 inches, in plain wood, melamine or green composition finish. Mayline's plain portable board is made in solid wood with a metal edge, or with a melamine finish. Sam Flax and Alvin supply plastic laminated drawing-boards. Blundell Harling offers two ranges.

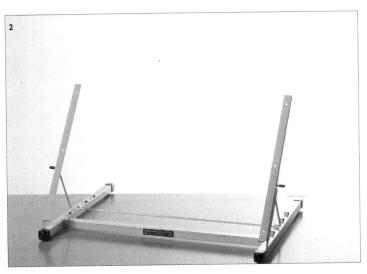

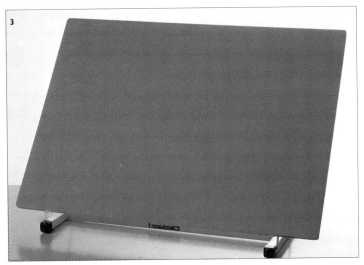

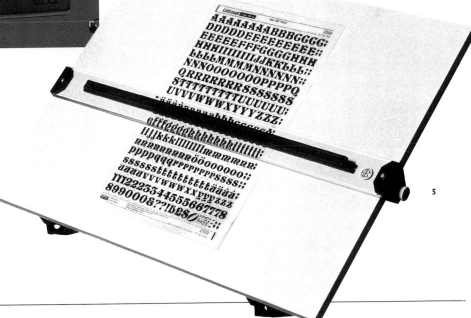

BOARD STANDS

The Mayline Professional Drawing Kit is an adjustable drawing-board with a carrying handle and tilting legs. Hellerman offers three different desk stands for holding or tilting drawing-boards in preset positions. The Sherborne Back Stand from Blundell Harling can be used in any one of four angled positions. Alvin supplies an adjustable drawing-board stand made of wood and Tilt Angled Drawing-boards with short, folding legs and special non-slip tractor feet.

PORTABLE BOARDS

Rotring offers the Rotring Rapid Drawing Board, which is a technical drawing-board, and the Rotring Profil. Faber-Castell supplies TZ Drawing Boards, TZ Plus Drawing Boards and Contura Drawing Boards.

1 The Faber-Castell T2A3+ board
2 Blundell Harling's Trueline stand
3 Trueline stand with A2 wooden board
4 The Rotobord 52
5 Standard Grosvenor drawing board

Portable plastic drawing-boards are generally preferred for technical use. These are dimensionally stable and can be molded with grooves and guides that can accommodate drafting heads and arms. Slightly more sophisticated are desk-top drawing-boards which are adjustable. Some models can be clamped to a suitable surface, while others can offer a number of preset tilt positions. Free-standing drawing-boards are usually quite large and are often called drawing tables. The better models are equipped with sophisticated counter balancing systems, which permit easy adjustment of the height and the board angle by means of weights or springs.

Many of the tables used in technical drafting feature parallel motion. This facility can also be extremely useful in graphic art and design. On a parallel-motion board a straightedge is free to move vertically across the surface of the board. The two ends of the straightedge are connected either to a system of wires and pulleys or to a toothed drive-belt, which insures that whenever the straightedge is moved either up or down, each end of it moves in perfect unison, so that the motion of the straightedge is parallel at all times to its previous position.

Drafting machines, although mentioned in a previous chapter, can also be referred to here. These are often a feature of drawing tables, and consist of a drafting head that can be guided accurately in either a vertical or horizontal direction.

PARALLEL-MOTION BOARDS

Supplied by Blundell Harling, WEB, Hellerman, EDEC, Zucor and Alvin. The Weymouth Parallel Motion System and the Swanage Parallel Motion System are both from Blundell Harling. Professional-quality drafting-machines are supplied by Molin, Tecnostyl, WEB,

Hellerman, Blundell Harling, Molin, Zucor, BFE and Mutoh. The Stratton from Blundell Harling, the BFE8 and BFE, and the new Graphic Compactable from EDEC are probably best suited to general-purpose use in a graphic artist's studio.

ROTARY DRAWING-BOARDS

The best-known rotary drawing boards are made by Rotobord. The Rotobord 52 is a portable rotary drawing-machine which may be used flat or on a desk-top at a tilt. The Two Rotobord 77 models are larger: a manual model, the R77.2, and an electrically-controlled counterbalanced drawing-stand, the R77.3. These boards can accommodate a maximum paper size of $24\frac{1}{2}\times30\frac{1}{2}$ inches on their circular drawing-surfaces.

1 The Stratford Compactable unit
2 The Rotobord 77 free-standing rotary drawing board with built-in cross-hatching device
3 EDEC's Metro 2 with an AO parallel motion board
4 Hulsta Studio Form desk with an A1 Edraft drafting machine from EDEC
5 Hulsta Studio Form desk without drafting machine

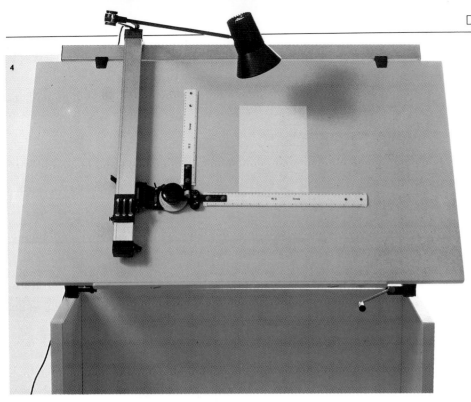

A rotary drawing-board has a circular drawing-surface which is free to move, and, for convenience, the angle of the drawing can be changed instead of the angle of the user and the drafting edge.

Drawing-board accessories

Old and damaged drawing-boards can be protected and revitalized. Hellerman offers Hellerplast Green Vinyl Professional Backing Sheet, a double-sided self-sealing flexible backing-sheet in two-ply vinyl. It can be used to cover drawing-boards, tables, desks and other work-surfaces, and is available pre-cut or on a roll.

Papyrobord is a heavy-duty vinyl material which is constructed in permanently-bonded layers of specially-formulated vinyls. It can be used to revitalize existing work-surfaces and to protect new surfaces, can be applied quickly, easily and effectively, and provides a virtually indestructible surface that is smooth and is said not to crack, chip or peel. There are three types of Papyrobord. Both sides of the standard five-ply product can be used as a working-surface; one side is finished in green and the other in ivory. Five-ply translucent Papyrobord gives a see-through working-surface, and can be used over light-boxes or over desks and tables with well-finished surfaces which it is important not to obscure from view. And, finally, there is a self-adhesive Papyrobord which is light green on one side only and has a strong adhesive layer on the other side.

The Spiroll Drawing Protector is another ancillary product intended for use with a drawing-board. It consists of a tubular metal sheet into which a large drawing can be rolled. It is attached to the bottom of the drawing-board so that the drawing on the roll can be fed out and worked on in stages, thus reducing the risk of damage to very large drawings and also making their handling more practical. If two Spiroll Drawing Protectors are mounted on a board, it is possible to reel an extremely long drawing from one into the other across the board.

STUDIO DESKS

Studio desks are supplied by Hulsta, EDEC, Mayline, BFE, Leuwico and Alvin. Interesting examples are the Hulsta Studio Form Desk, the Tech/Art Drawing Desk from EDEC, the New Angolo from BFE, and the Desk-o-matics from Mayline, All of these have adjustable tops that can be used as a drawing-board. The same manufacturers offer graphic art tables and flat files. BFE and EDEC offer graphic artists' reference-tables on a metal frame with a laminated top. Alvin offers sturdily built reference-tables in solid oak, and flat files in solid oak in a variety of sizes.

LIGHT-BOXES

A light-box can be an important piece of equipment for a design studio. Normally consisting of a shallow tray which carries a lighting source (usually in the form of fluorescent tubes), it has a surface of glass backed by a light diffuser — a sheet of translucent, but not transparent, material which allows light to pass, but splits it in a multidirectional pattern as it does so. Diffusers may be made of opalized plexiglass, or acrylic, or from a sheet of etched or sand-blasted glass. When in operation an evenly diffuse light is shed through the surface of the light-box; items placed over it are lit from behind so that they can be seen clearly.

Light-boxes are used for checking negatives and transparencies, for checking colour separation, and also for color correction. In addition they are used as an aid for transferring drawings from one translucent surface to another by laying and tracing. All these operations demand that the subject is well lit from behind. A light-box may also be used as an aid to registration when artwork is being constructed in a series of overlays: for example, where color separations are being created manually for use in screen printing or for making letterpress blocks.

Light-boxes are mostly designed for table-top use, but there are also wall-mounted versions, portable versions, and light-tables. A light-table offers a large lit area in the form of an adjustable table-top. Light-boxes combined with drawing-boards are also available which make very useful tools for the graphic artist and the designer. Light-cabinets for storing, selecting and checking transparencies are another variation on this theme. These can be ideal for creating transparency libraries in situations where large quantities have to be held available for instant reference.

1 EDEC's Bantam light-box with a 109 stand
2 Tracing frame on a 109 stand from EDEC
3 Illuminated bench unit from EDEC

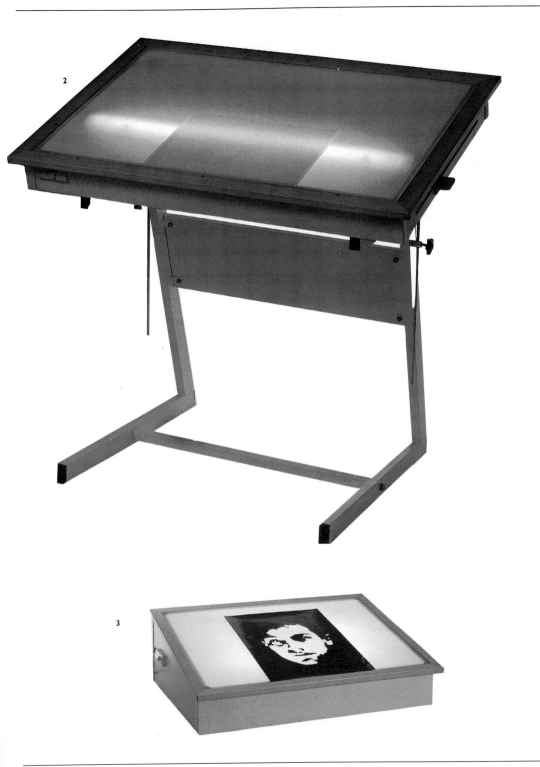

*Light-boxes, light-tables
and light-boards are
supplied by Mayline,
Hancocks, DW Viewboxes,
Vistracan, BFE, Blundell
Harling and Alvin. Mayline
supplies the Forester Lite
Table, the Four Post Lite
Table, which can be tilted
for use as a light-board,
the Futur-matic T/C Lite
Table and the Deskomatic
Lite Table, which are
combination light-boxes
and desks offering a light-
board facility. DW
Viewboxes offers an
economy series of light-
boxes, an executive series,
a portable series, and an
illuminated drafting-table.
DW Viewboxes portable
light-boxes are available in
five different sizes.
Hancocks' light-boxes are
portable, available in a
wide range of sizes and sit
neatly on any flat surface.
Their desk-top light-box is
for viewing transparencies
only. Vistracan light-boxes
are available in four*

different sizes. Vistracan also offers an angled light-box sized 16½×22½ inches. BFE supplies the Lumette Light Box which stands on a rack allowing it to be tilted at various angles. Their Duolite and Opus Light Box are both sophisticated light-boards with drafting-machines. The Rotobord Planner 75 and the Rotobord Planner 100 are large free-standing light-boards. The Tru Line Light Board supplied by Blundell Harling offers parallel motion and a sturdy back stand which can be set at several angles for desk-top viewing in two sizes. Alvin offers Satin Glow Light Boxes and Alvin Tracing Tables. Various light-boxes are also supplied under the brand names of Oakworks, Macbeth, Graphiclit, Porta-trace, Porta-view and Light-mate.

1 Hancock's light-box with Mayline parallel motion
2 Hancock A1, 2, 3 and 4 light-boxes

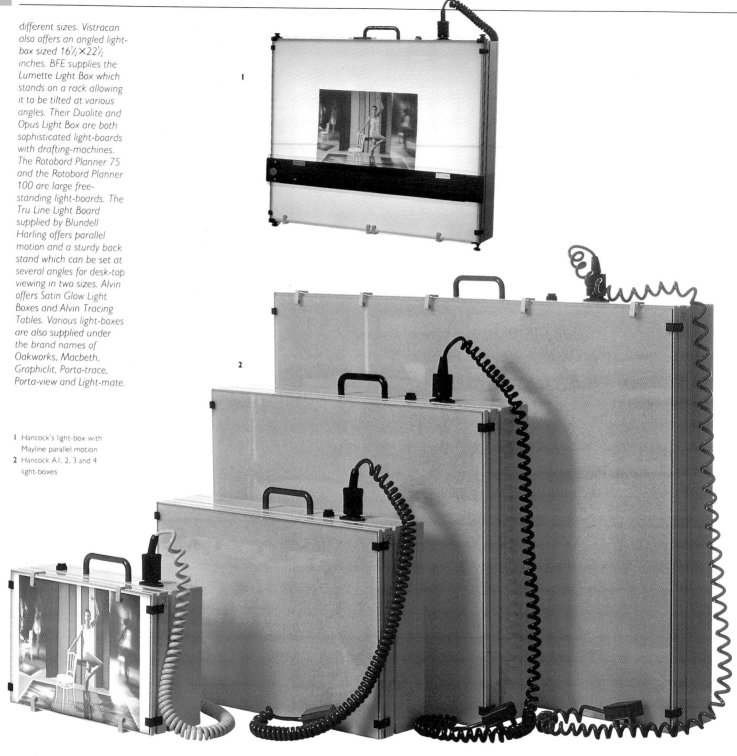

DRAWING-BOARDS AND LIGHT-BOXES

LIGHT-BOXES   DRAWING-BOARDS

SUPPLIER	MANUFACTURER	DISTRIBUTOR	WHOLESALER	RETAILER	Areas where products are available	Local variations in product range	Light-Boxes	Light-Boards	Light-Cabinets	Portable	Wood	Plastic	Plastic-Coated	Desk-Top	Free-Standing	Parallel-Motion Boards	Rotary Drawing Boards	Adjustable Boards
Abelscot-Marchant	•	•	•		W	No	•	•	•	•	•	•	•	•	•			•
Alvin	•	•	•		W	No	•	•	•	•	•	•	•	•	•	•	•	•
Atlantis			•	•	N/S	N/A	•	•	•	•	•	•	•	•	•			•
BFE/Drafton		•	•		E UK US	No	•	•	•	•		•	•	•				•
Arnold Cook	•	•	•	•	UK	N/S	•	•	•									
De Visu (Roger Jullian)	•				E UK US	No					•	•	•	•	•	•		•
Educaid		•			UK	N/A	•	•		•	•	•	•	•	•	•		
Gaebel (Stazput)	•				S UK US	Yes	•											
Graphic Products International		•			S UK	N/S	•											
Hancocks	•				E S UK	No	•											
KIN Rapidograph	•	•			C US	No				•		•						
Kroy	•				W	No	•											
Langford & Hill		•	•	•	W	No	•	•	•	•	•	•	•	•	•	•	•	•
Marabu	•				W	No				•	•	•	•	•	•			•
Pelltech		•			UK	No	•											
Reprodraft		•	•		UK	N/A	•	•								•	•	
Rotobord	•	•	•	•	A E UK US	Yes	•	•	•	•	•	•	•	•	•	•	•	•
Rotring		•			W	No					•	•	•	•			•	•
Staedtler	•				W	No				•							•	
Testrite	•				W	No	•											
A. West & Partners	•	•			A E S UK US	No	•	•	•	•	•	•	•	•	•	•	•	•

KEY: A = Australia   **C** = Canada   **E** = Europe (excluding UK)   **S** = Scandinavia   **UK** = United Kingdom   **US** = United States   **W** = Worldwide   **N/S** = Not Stated

STUDIO FURNITURE

The desk is an important item of any graphic artist's studio. Ordinary desks provide a satisfactory flat surface, but this can be improved upon, from a designer's point of view, by using a desk with a tilting surface that can double as a drawing-board. Large flat tables are also desirable in design studios — many procedures benefit from having sufficient space available to allow a graphic artist or designer to work freely.

A flat file is another desirable piece of furniture in a studio. This is a broad chest with six or eight shallow drawers, each of which can accommodate full-sized sheets of paper, film, board or finished artwork in considerable quantity, cleanly and safely.

Filing cabinets are essential for storing paperwork and can be used for storing large quantities of transparencies and reference material in hanging files.

Vertical storage systems for sheet materials are an alternative to flat files, and are often more convenient when access is required on a regular basis. Locwyn supplies the Megafile System, a simple but practial plan storage system that can be supplied either as single units or as a multi-bay unit. Such systems are often open-plan, however, and cannot usually offer the same protection to the materials that they store; nor can vertical storage systems generally accommodate anything like the amount of material that a flat file can in an equivalent amount of space. For temporary storage of artwork and sheet materials, and for portable storage of artwork, there are portfolios. These come in various sizes and are generally flat in format. A tubular portfolio is easier to carry, but is only for work that can be rolled for transportation.

To accompany desks, drawing-boards and work-surfaces in the designer's studio, many artists often prefer to use specially-designed seating.

A drafting chair may be raised or lowered, and can also have an adjustable back-rest; most have a foot-rest too. A draftsman or designer working at a drawing-board constantly is obliged to adopt an unnatural posture of much of the time, so any support or additional comfort that can be offered is usually welcome.

Drafting stools are also available. Most of the plentiful supply of specially-designed seating for general office use is equally suitable for use in a designer's studio. Designers' mobile organizers are the equivalent of a fine artist's painting-cabinet. They contain drawers and compartments for storing items which are in constant use, and can be wheeled from place to place in the studio.

Desk organizers and paper trays perform a similar function on a graphic artist's desk-top and around work areas. Waste baskets, telephones and desk lights are examples of other items of studio equipment which contribute further to the efficiency and good management of a graphic artist's work space.

FLAT FILES

Both Mayline and EDEC supply a choice of steel or wooden flat files. Plax System also supplies a choice of steel or wooden flat files.

Vertical files are supplied by John Dale, BFE and Mayline, among others. Rouget specialize in vertical plan-filing systems. EDEC supplies wall-mounted and mobile systems which also employ a vertical format.

EDEC Sapele finish 8-drawer

1 EDEC 8-drawer A1 flat file
2 Plax laminated cardboard
  portfolio
3 Locwyn Megafile modular
  storage system

1,2 EDEC Omega chairs, models 2 and 1
3 Zucor Bieffe's mobile organizer
4 Three-door Hulsta pedestal unit

STUDIO SEATING AND MOBILE ORGANIZERS

Sam Flax specialize in studio seating, and offers a very extensive range of drafting-chairs, drafting-stools and well-designed office chairs. EDEC supplies the 30818 Drafting Chair. BFE supplies the Omega Range of draftsmans' chairs and the Wiz Drafting Stools. The Wallis Drafting Chair is another typical studio chair. Adjustable drafting-chairs are also included in the Mayline range. Mobile organizers, also known as bobby trolleys, are included in the ranges of Mayline, EDEC, BFE and Alvin.

STUDIO FURNITURE

SUPPLIER	MANUFACTURER	DISTRIBUTOR	WHOLESALER	RETAILER	Areas where products are available	Local variations in product range	Flat Files	Filing Cabinets	Storage Equipment	Portfolios	Storage Wallets	Storage Boxes	Slide-Holders	Studio/Chest	Studio Chairs	Studio Desks	Studio Stools
Abelscot-Marchant	●	●	●		W	No	●	●	●	●	●	●	●		●	●	
Alvin	●	●	●		W	No									●		●
The Art Factory	●	●			W	No	●		●				●		●		
Atlantis			●	●	N/S	N/A	●										
BFE/Drafton		●	●		E UK US	No	●	●						●	●	●	
Arnold Cook	●	●	●	●	UK	N/S							●				
Cotech Sensitising	●				W	No	●										
De Visu (Roger Jullian)	●				E UK US	No	●	●		●				●	●	●	●
Educaid		●			UK	N/A	●	●									
EXX Projects	●				E S UK	N/S	●			●							
Sam Flax	●	●		●	W	No		●	●	●	●				●		●
Langford & Hill		●	●	●	W	No	●	●	●	●	●	●	●			●	●
Locwyn	●				UK US	No		●	●	●	●	●	●				
Marabu	●				W	No	●	●									
M. Myers & Son	●				W	N/S	●										
Pelltech		●			UK	No				●							
Reprodraft		●	●		UK	N/A	●	●	●	●	●	●	●	●	●	●	●
Rexel (Derwent Cumberland)	●				W	Yes				●	●						
Rhone Poulenc Systems	●				W	No			●								
Rotobord	●	●	●	●	A E UK US	Yes			●								
Simair	●	●			A C E UK US	No	●										
D. & J. Simons			●		W	No				●							
A. West & Partners	●	●			A E S UK	No	●										

KEY: A = Australia **C** = Canada **E** = Europe (excluding UK) **S** = Scandinavia **UK** = United Kingdom **US** = United States **W** = Worldwide **N/S** = Not Stated

CAMERAS, ENLARGERS AND STUDIO MACHINERY

Some design studios contain photographic equipment, studio machinery and machines which convert artwork into a reproducible form. By no means all of this can be regarded as standard equipment for a graphic artist or designer. Indeed, some of it is far more likely to be found in the hands of professional photographers or printers. However, large studios may carry such items, and it is an area in which all graphic artists need some expertise and understanding in order to get the best results from other parties involved in the production and presentation of their ideas.

Of the equipment dealt with here, camera lucidas, projectors and enlargers are the most likely to be found in graphic artists' studios. These are pieces of equipment that actually assist with the production of artwork. Still cameras and their accessories are most likely to be found in the hands of professional photographers. Because they are comparatively small pieces of equipment that are financially within reach of many designers, however, it is not unusual to find them in the hands also of graphic artists. In any event, cameras of the smaller formats are extremely useful for collecting reference material to be used as the basis for artwork created using other media. In fact, many artists, illustrators and designers use photography to provide reference material, and have become professionally involved with photography as a result.

The largest and most complicated equipment, such as process cameras and photomechanical transfer (PMT) machines, are perhaps most likely to be found in graphics studios annexed to printing-houses, where they are used in the production of printing-plates. In the case of photo mechanical transfer machines in particular, though, the potential in such equipment extends far beyond such use, for they can be extremely versatile graphic tools

in the hands of an experienced designer, although the cost puts them beyond the reach of many studios.

Still cameras and accessories
35-mm single-lens reflex cameras, known as SLR cameras, are the most popular cameras. The 35-mm format produces a frame size of 24 mm x 36 mm, which is adequate for collecting reference material, for general-purpose photography, and for some specialist uses. However, where high-quality enlargements are required, larger-format cameras are required.

The single-lens reflex mechanism is to be preferred for all professional purposes because it allows the image to be seen directly through the camera lens as it will appear on the film itself. The wide range of accessories and film types that are available to fit 35-mm cameras means that they are particularly adaptable. In some cases, through the use of an appropriate lens and the correct film, a quality can be achieved which is equal to that of cameras of larger format. In this context it is perhaps worth pointing out that a designer's instructions to a photographer can be an important factor. If a large-format shot is not well planned and has to be substantially cropped for use, it may well be that the area of transparency used is little more than would have been available on a 35-mm camera.

The 120 cameras are most used by professional photographers; these rely on 120-roll film and produce negatives or transparencies in any one of three formats. The most frequently-used size is 60 mm x 60 mm — the old 2¼-inch-square standard. However, it is seldom the case that a square image is used in reproduction, and part of the frame size is inevitably wasted using a "6 x 6". Because of this, two other formats have been developed using 120 film: the 60 mm x 45 mm and the 60 mm x 70 mm. Professional-quality cameras that use these formats are

becoming ever more popular, and the range of available products is likely to increase. Some of the best professional cameras have interchangeable backs and accept more than one of these formats. Most of these larger-format cameras have single-lens reflex mechanisms.

Twin-lens reflex cameras are still used in 6 x 6 format, however, and remain popular with some professionals. The only disadvantage with them is the parallax which occurs because of the distance between the two lenses and is most likely to affect shots taken in close-up. Other camera formats include 4 x 5 inches, which is 100 mm by 125 mm, 7 x 5 inches, which is 175 mm x 125 mm, and 8 x 10 inches, which is 200 mm by 250 mm; 4 x 5 cameras can be regarded as portable, but these extra-large sizes are generally used in studio conditions.

Accessories for professional cameras include motor drive units, which allow a rapid succession of photographs to be taken. These can be used to capture action shots, and are popular with sports photographers. Lenses, light-meters and lighting equipment are among the many other accessories available for professional-quality cameras.

CAMERAS
Well-known and respected manufacturers include Canon, Olympus, Pentax and Praktica. Pentax and Olympus 35-mm SLR cameras can be costly. Zenith cameras offer reasonable quality at a comparatively low cost.

LARGE FORMAT CAMERAS
Hasselblad are the market leaders in this field, and specialize in cameras that accept 120-roll film. Other producers for 120 film are Fujica, Pentax, Maniya

and Rollei. Hasselblad and Maniya produce both single-lens and twin-lens reflex cameras for 120 film models with a top-mounted viewing lens. Pentax produce 120-roll film cameras that resemble enlarged 35-mm SLR cameras. The Fujica Panorama G617 is intended for landscape photography and has an extremely long format. Hasselblad and Horseman produce studio cameras which use extra-large formats.

*Nikon camera, lens and automatic winder (**top**); Hasselblad CM500 camera (**bottom left**); Sinar's latest camera, the P2 (**bottom right**).*

A viewer can be an extremely important item of studio equipment, enabling a designer to enlarge or reduce an image to an exact size. It consists of a stand with a movable copy-board mounted toward its base, above which is an adjustable lens; the machine is topped by a viewing area surrounded by a folding hood. A viewer has its own lighting system, which enables the copy-board to be lit from either above or below. If the subject matter is ordinary artwork, it is placed on the copy-board and lit from above; if a transparency is being used, it is lit from below. To use it, the graphic artist stands at the viewer looking into the viewing area from within the folding hood. Two handles on the front of the viewer enable the copy-board lens to be moved up or down. By turning the handles an image of any size can be produced in the viewing area of the original artwork.

Enlargers and projectors fulfil a similar function for the graphic artist, but they offer the advantage of projection directly onto the work surface for copying, rather than necessitating an intermediate tracing. Downward or front projection directly onto the work surface is very popular with illustrators and fine artists, who find either method extremely convenient when finished artwork has to be produced in an enlarged size from a sketch or photograph. Most of these machines work with both transparencies and solid artwork; some also project three-dimensional objects.

There is some overlap in the terminology used for these machines — it is not unusual for a viewer to be referred to as a "back projector." The projectors and enlargers used by graphic artists should not be confused with projectors and enlargers intended for photographic use, athough they are essentially similar. A slide projector or a photographic enlarger could be used in the same way as a designer's viewer, projectors or enlarger, but the subject matter they can carry is limited to slides, transparencies and negatives.

VIEWERS

Halco Sunbury offer several viewers, including the Capiscanner, which is available in a range of colors. Halco also offers the Copikan, which is a combined camera and viewer. Front-projecting enlargers are usually small and light. Examples are the Artograph AG100, the Arttec Opaque Projector, the Astrascope 5000 Opaque Projector, the Beseler Vu-lyte 3 Opaque Projector, and the Seerite 6-by-6 Opaque Projector. The Gakken Periscope is a small but highly versatile viewer.

*Grant enlargers (**top**) and the Kopyrite enlarger (**bottom**).*

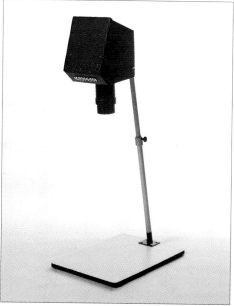

PROJECTORS

The Leisegang Antiskop can be used for horizontal or vertical projection, and the Optiskop, which is a projector, is normally mounted on a floor-to-ceiling support. The Artograph 1000J is a vertical opaque projector which produces precise images directly onto a drawing-surface from above. Artograph also offers the Super AG100, which is another vertical projector. The Kopyrite Opaque Projector is a fairly small projector which fits on a drawing-board. Testrite Instruments offers a selection of projectors in their Seerite range.

(Top) *Rollei slide projector;* **(bottom)** *Overhead projectors from 3M.*

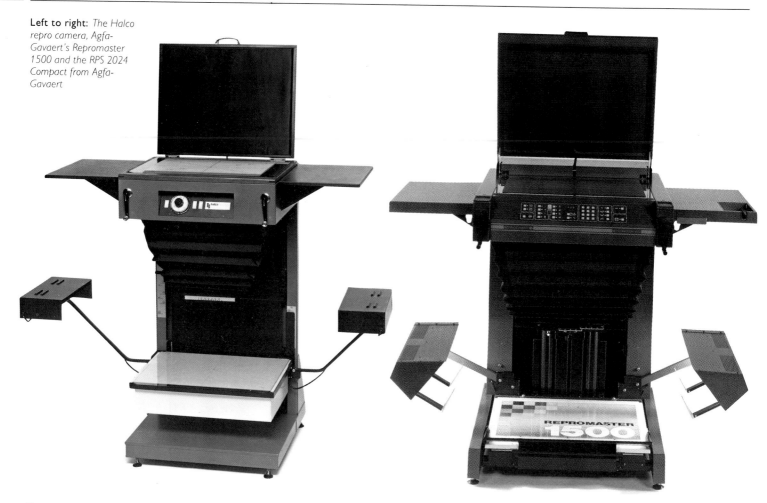

Left to right: *The Halco repro camera, Agfa-Gavaert's Repromaster 1500 and the RPS 2024 Compact from Agfa-Gavaert*

Process cameras, repro cameras and photomechanical transfer machines

Process cameras, repro cameras and photomechanical transfer (PMT) machines are all variants of the same piece of equipment: a camera which enlarges or reduces artwork and converts it into various forms of negative or photographic print.

Process cameras are also called copy or graphic arts cameras, and come in a wide range of sizes and specifications. One of the main uses of a process camera is the production of negatives from which, at a later stage, blocks or prints for printing can be made. The camera itself consists of a lens,

a copy-holder, and a carrier which may be mounted either vertically or horizontally.

In the vertical process, camera copy or artwork is placed in the copy-holder and is held stationary either by the application of pressure or by the use of a vacuum effect between the back of the artwork and the copy-board. Light sources are attached to the copy-holder and the work being reproduced is illuminated ready for photography. Various kinds of light source can be used depending on the particular application — for example, tungsten halogen or metal halide lamps can be used. Once the original copy or artwork is in place on the copy-board, it can be viewed through the lens or through a viewing area

via a system of prisms and mirrors. As with a visualizer, by moving the lens and the copy-board in relation to one another, the user can control the degree of enlargement or reduction in order to produce an image in the desired size.

Horizontal process cameras differ only in that they are able to hold larger pieces of copy or artwork and can accommodate larger film sizes; otherwise they follow the same essential principles. Most process cameras can be used to produce either black and white negatives or color separations for color printing. The focusing and exposure on most modern process cameras is generally done automatically.

For most commercial printing processes, images which are in continuous tones have to be converted into dots or lines for reproduction. (The exception is collotype printing which can reproduce continuous tone perfectly. It is, however, expensive.) Images are converted by screening, which is an effect produced by inserting a special mesh in the process camera so that the image is divided up as it is photographed.

Repro cameras differ very little from process cameras, although the name tends to be applied to slightly more versatile machines. Some repro cameras accommodate three-dimensional objects on the copy-board; others have many of the capabilities of a PMT machine. In any case — as has been said — each of these camera types is a mere variant on a theme, and the terminology is largely at the discretion of the manufacturer.

Photomechanical transfer machines are extremely versatile process cameras. They are mounted vertically and reproduce images without the need for a darkroom, making them a cheaper and quicker means of producing prints and negatives. Among their many functions, PMT machines can change black to white, or white to black, and can produce half-tones via screens. They can also reverse an image from left to right, and can print onto transparent backing-sheets to make overlays for use in artwork.

On some machines, color simulation can be achieved using an image on a film base together with special dyes. It is possible to simulate combinations of most of the principal color effects using a PMT machine at a fraction of the cost of full color-proofing. In the studio one of the most practical uses of a PMT machine is the production of bromides for pasting up camera-ready artwork. The term PMT machine is now in common usage for all such sophisticated process cameras. It should be noted, however, that the name originally referred to one particular manufacturer's product.

Other studio machinery

Three other main types of reprographic equipment may be found in designers' studios. These are photocopiers, facsimile copiers, and diazo printers. Photocopiers are now largely based on electrostatic processes which print onto a variety of paper surfaces or even onto films. The print quality from the most up-to-date machines is very good. The more sophisticated machines also offer enlargement and reduction facilities.

Photocopier results are certainly suitable for rough layouts and preliminary paste-ups for printers to work from, although some quality is lost during the process. In some circumstances, photocopies may make acceptable images for simple reproduction purposes, and even occasionally for finished artwork. Photocopiers, in addition, have various creative possibilities: some designers and illustrators have used them to produce experimental artwork.

Facsimile copiers — known as fax machines — are relatively new pieces of equipment, and are part of the information technology revolution. They may well become increasingly important to graphic artists and designers because of their relationship to other areas of expanding design technology. A facsimile copier instantly transmits information from one location to another by means of electronic links: they can be used, for example, to transmit images directly from a studio to a typesetter.

Diazo printers are more typically found in architects' offices or in the studios of technical draftsmen. Also called dye line machines, they are used for producing small quantities of prints from a transparent or translucent original. Drawings on drafting film, for example, are suited to reproduction by diazo printing.

(**Top**) *Minolta's stylus pen and editing platen from the EP410Z which allows areas to be copied to be outlined;* (**bottom**) *the Minolta EP415Z and* (**right**) *the 3M copier.*

CAMERAS, ENLARGERS AND STUDIO MACHINERY

SUPPLIER	MANUFACTURER	DISTRIBUTOR	WHOLESALER	RETAILER	Areas where products are available	Local variations in product range	Viewers	Enlargers	Grant Enlargers	Projectors	Back Projectors	Overhead Projectors	PMT Machines	Process Cameras	Scanners	Photocopying Machines	Plan Copiers
Agfa-Gevaert	•				W	No	•						•				
Art Material International	•	•	•		W	N/S	•										
De Visu (Roger Jullian)	•	•			E UK US	No		•	•	•	•	•					
Sam Flax		•		•	W	No	•		•	•	•						
Itek Colour Graphics	•				W	Yes									•		
Langford & Hill		•	•	•	W	No	•	•	•	•	•	•	•		•		
MET Graphic Supplies		•			UK	N/A							•	•			
Reprodraft		•	•		UK	N/A											•
Rhone Poulenc Systems	•				W	No								•		•	•
Skycopy	•	•			UK	N/A							•	•			
Testrite	•				E UK US	No				•							
A. West & Partners	•	•			A E S UK	No	•										
A. Wirr	•	•	•		W	No		•	•	•	•	•					

KEY: A = Australia **C** = Canada **E** = Europe (excluding UK) **S** = Scandinavia **UK** = United Kingdom **US** = United States **W** = Worldwide **N/S** = Not Stated

COMPUTER SYSTEMS

The future of graphic art and design lies with the computer. The same is true of technical design procedures such as architecture, engineering and industrial design, and of the industry at which so much graphic art is aimed — the printing industry. The use of computers in graphic art and design and in related areas is a complex and fast-changing subject, but this book would be incomplete if no attempt were made to summarize the present situation.

As yet, really sophisticated technology in the field of graphic art is still expensive and beyond the reach of many studios. However, the current trend is one of falling prices in both computers and software, associated with increased machine speed and capacity and greater ease of use, at all levels of the market. The indications are that this trend will continue, and that computer technology will become available for general studio use as a result.

Computers and the associated peripheral devices and software that can be used for graphic design purposes presently range from very expensive systems which claim to duplicate the work of an entire studio to relatively inexpensive items which are perhaps of questionable value to the professional designer. Although cost is relevant, it is not necessarily the most important criterion when it comes to selecting a suitable computer system for graphic design: any graphic artist seriously considering the installation of such a system would be well advised to examine the market in detail before making any commitment.

A vast range of computer products is available, particularly in the field of programming. Consequently, in this chapter an attempt has been made to consider what might be relevant to a graphic artist working in a typical studio. Cost, quality of output, and ease of use — although not necessarily in

that order — have been chosen as yardsticks, but it has been felt necessary also to include several items of equipment that graphic artists and designers are unlikely to possess or, for that matter, want, which are, nevertheless, relevant because of the likelihood of their coming into contact with them. In addition there is the possibility that graphic artists may need to modify some of their design procedures in order to fit in with the use of computer and computerized technology in other fields.

In graphic design itself, the available equipment touches both extremes. A Cray Supercomputer, for example, can produce stunning graphics — but at a staggering cost. This would not be an item for an average, let alone an about-average, studio, even supposing that the studio-owners have the finance for it and somewhere large enough to keep it. At the other extreme, there are graphic design packages which are available for the very lowest run of computers: the personal computers, which are primarily intended for educational and domestic use. In this context, an entire system including the software can cost less than a good typewriter — but, as might be expected, the capabilities of such packages are strictly limited and they are in consequence of little use to a professional or even to an advanced amateur. The products most likely to be of use, both now and in the future, lie somewhere in between these extremes.

It is a feature common to most computer-graphics systems and their explanatory literatures that they avoid the technicalities of programming and adopt the so-called user-friendly approach: they use "drop-down menus" which offer a choice of instructions to the computer-operator in plain language, so there is no need to be conversant with any of the esoteric computer languages. Most graphic computer systems and programs go further, in that

they attempt to copy the designer's usual manner of working even to the extent of including representations of familar studio equipment such as drawing-boards and pens as their mean of control, and having operational modes which imitate the effect of pens, pencils, paintbrushes, airbrushes, and the equipment for cutting and pasting.

The Aesthedes graphic CAD system.

Turnkey graphics systems

Some of the most advanced systems available to graphic artists and designers are based around microcomputers and are called turnkey systems. The term "turnkey" refers to the fact that these systems are usable as soon as they are switched on they are not computer systems on top of which the software or any separate form of programming has to be installed for each operation. They are machines used solely for graphic design (or for other kinds of design) and cannot be used for other purposes. These are closed systems.

In this type of system the computer itself may form an integral part of the manufacturer's product, or it may be a general-purpose machine which has been adapted to give it greater capacity in the field of graphics by the addition of extra circuit boards, special residual software and peripheral devices. This statement needs some clarification. In a personal computer the circuitry is almost entirely on one large circuit board, which is usually referred to as the mother board. Further room is provided within the computer for a number of expansion boards which can modify and improve the capacity of the computer. External controls and specialized peripheral devices are likely to require an expansion board to annex them into the computer system. An expansion board in the case of a graphic artist's computer would provide the extra sophistication required to create artwork of a professional standard.

On turnkey systems, artwork or component elements of artwork can be originated in various ways. The designer can sit at the computer and use a special pen-like instrument on a digitized drawing-board, and can proceed as if he or she were in a normal studio. The computer "senses" and follows the movements of the pen, and produces a drawn or "painted" image on the screen in front of the designer. By selecting different operational modes the designer can thus work as if he or she were using ordinary studio equipment.

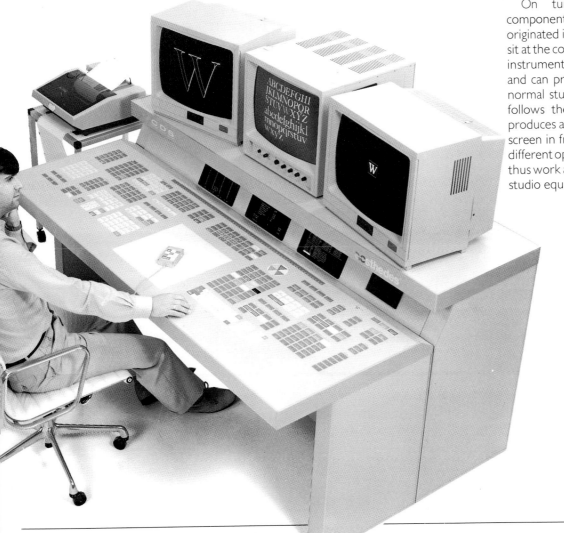

GRAPHIC SYSTEMS

The Letraset Illustrator and the Artron Computer from Graphic Products both offer a palette of over 16 million colors. Other turnkey graphics systems include Aesthedes from Claessens International, Pluto from 10 Research, Electronic Arts, P1, Pisa, the Digisolve Ikon Pixel Engine, Picturemaker, Artonics, Aurora, Video Data Systems, and Siggraphs. Agfa has the Business Graphics GX 2500 System on offer, and Rotring offers two drafting machines, the NC Drafting System (which is a computer-aided design system) and the NC Scriber 10.

The fact that operating designers can produce work in virtually their normal manner is one of the most distinctive and important features of sophisticated turnkey graphics systems, and it diffentiates them from the cheaper "mouse"-driven versions that offer a lower degree of control. A mouse, incidentally, is an externally separate control device for a computer, operated by movement of the user's hand: a more detailed description is given later in this chapter.

On turnkey systems, however, artwork can also be fed into the computer by input from a video-camera or by scanning an image — that is, feeding the information in serially; in this way such an image might be a photograph or transparency, a printed page or a piece of artwork. What is more, several different inputs can be combined on screen. This allows greatly increased flexibility over conventional working methods, and makes it possible to complete complex procedures such as photo-retouching and color-correction in a fraction of the normal time. These factors, together with the general benefits of using a computer, enable work of a startling quality to be produced on these machines.

The use of a computer also brings a designer a number of highly desirable extras. For instance, once an image has been created or input from another existing source, it can be worked upon in whatever way the graphic artist wishes. But if that is not successful, the original image can be re-trieved instantly, and the process started again using either the same or a different operational mode. In other words, a designer can try out his or her work in different media in very little time, and because of the computer's memory those images can be retained for comparison or further modification.

The benefit of being able to store a piece of work at each stage in its production is self-evident. If a mistake is made, or if it becomes necessary to make a change to the artwork,

the designer can simply go back to a previous stage in the preparation of the work and continue in a different direction from that point on — there is no need to made a fresh start. Work may thus take much less time to complete — a factor that obviously has a direct bearing on costs and profitability.

In addition to straightforward graphics, turnkey systems also offer controlled shading, the ability to pan and zoom, perspective drawing (both solid and wire), three-dimensional modeling with different light sources, and the rotation and synthesizing of images based on the input from photographs or video-cameras. When it comes to putting the image out, turnkey systems can be equally versatile. It is possible to translate the image into video-tape, into film taken by a conventional camera, into transparencies or reflection copies, or directly into color separations for use in plate-making for four-color process printing. It goes without saying that not all of the features described for turnkey systems are

available on one single machine or system.

There are considerable variations in the degrees of sophistication offered by different computers. However, virtually all the features discussed here are available on some systems, and if graphic artists want an entire studio at the touch of a button, the technology is available if the costs can be met.

The Quantel Paint Box **(below)**, *introduced in 1982, has become the industry standard for the production of television graphics. However, final artwork has to be created separately. The Graphic Paint Box is a turnkey graphics system which simulates a normal studio setting in which the designer works with a pen and a drawing-board. The drawing-board is an electronic touch tablet, and its accompanying pen is a pressure-sensitive stylus.*

Other microcomputer-based graphics systems

Although most of the systems so far outlined are based around microcomputers, there are also less specifically-directed products which have a graphics capacity. These are general-purpose machines which have not been specially adapted for use as graphics systems by the addition of extra circuitry, but which can be used for graphic design purposes by running graphics software — graphics computer programs — on them. The type of software that these machines accept is generally far less expensive than any used on the turnkey systems. Standard microcomputers with graphics software packages are therefore far more accessible to the ordinary designer. However, it is fair to say that these systems often fall short of being a professional designer's tool although they certainly have some useful applications and are an excellent introduction to the possibilities of computer designs.

Typically, these systems give a much lower screen resolution than a turnkey system, and are much more likely to be mouse-driven. The mouse — as has already been stated — is the small hand-operated control device that is linked to the computer. It has a small ball within it which protrudes slightly from its underside. Moving the mouse on a flat surface causes the ball to move, and the movements of the ball are relayed by the mouse to the computer. This converts the mouse's movements into instructions and moves the small pointer (called the cursor) around the screen. The cursor represents the point of activity on the image, and in most graphics systems it changes its appearance according to the selected mode of operation (for example, whether it is imitating a pencil or a brush).

Most computer mice have one or two buttons as well, which can be pressed to sellect items, techniques or tools. But in every operation selected from the drop-down menu offered upon the computer screen, it is less easy to operate a mouse accurately than it is to use a pen on a drawing-board — so the same degree of control over work cannot be achieved with mouse-driven systems as can be achieved with expensive digital drawing-board and pen systems.

As has been stated, the resolution available on most of these microcomputer design packages is generally low, but there are some on the market which do make use of the full 300-dots-per-inch of a laser printer, making possible fairly good output results. As with turnkeys, the facilities offered by microcomputer graphics packages vary between one product and another. Most include the automatic creation of lines, rectangles, circles, tones and patterns, as well as facilitating freehand work. Other features might include fonts, erasure, zooming in, scrolling, and possibly special effects such as perspective and distortions. They may also offer operational modes such as pencil, paintbrush or airbrush, but the effects are likely to be somewhat cruder than on sophisticated turnkey systems.

In short, microcomputer-based graphics systems can offer many of the features of a professional design package, but the degree of control over the creation of the artwork and the quality of the output to some extent limits their appeal and potential.

*The Apple Mackintosh machines (**left**) have a good range of software available, including MacDraw, MacPaint, MacDraft, CricketDraw and Superpaint. MacDraft has zoom, pan and resizing facilities. The IBM PC Standard is very compatible with the Apple, and its programs include GemGraph, GemDraw, PC Paintbrush, WindowDraft, Freelance and GemPcint. Also available for the IBM PC is Drafix from Foresight Resources.*

Computerized typesetting and desk-top publishing

Computerized typesetting systems and desk-top publishing systems are methods for producing text and illustrations for publication.

Computerized typesetting systems are intended primarily for those involved in the production of newspapers and magazines. Some of the computer systems available, however, possess features which might make them of interest to a graphic designer. In any event, it is technology that already has considerable bearing on the activities of many graphic artists, and it is an area with which all of them will have to become increasingly familiar in future. As with turnkey graphics systems, computer typesetting systems come either as a complete system using an integral computer, all produced as a unit by a manufacturer, or as a microcomputer which has been modified for this use.

Digital typesetting is extremely fast and it cuts out many of the traditional processes associated with the production of printed text. In addition to setting the type, typesetting by computer typically allows page-by-page layout to be undertaken on the computer screen, integrating text, line and half-tone illustrations in a simple operation. In this process the text and graphics are merged onto pre-created masks composed of grids and templates.

Other features that may be available on computerized typesetting systems include the placing and cropping of graphics and, on some systems, the use of tints, the production of enlargements or reductions, and electronic retouching and airbrushing. Digital typesetting systems can carry extensive selections of typefaces on memory, which can be recalled for use by simple operating procedures.

Desk-top publishing and computerized typesetting have many similarities, especially in the way in which pages are created. The differences are similar to those described between turnkey graphics systems and microcomputer-based graphics systems: differences in capacity, control and quality of output.

A desk-top publishing system usually consists of a microcomputer, desk-top publishing software, and a laser printer, although some software packages drive a dot matrix or an ink-jet printer.

Although desk-top publishing equipment might not be considered a professional designer's tool, there are circumstances in which it could be put to good use. In any case,

*Scantext 1015 Image scanner (**left**) with Scantext 2000 Commander.*

desk-top publishing systems are worth the attention of graphic artists and designers in that they allow the creation of documents with both text and graphics without having recourse to a designer, typesetter or printer.

Many of these systems are relatively expensive, and it is possible that they will be used to a significant extent in future in areas where work is now still directed to graphic artists and designers. To be blunt, they pose a threat to the livelihoods of some small design studios and to some small typesetting and printing businesses. There is some satisfaction, however, in the knowledge that desk-top publishing systems are merely practical tools, and that without creative input the artistic quality of the documents they produce is likely to be low, so it is probable that there will be a demand for designers who can work the systems as they come into more general use.

Text and graphics are best originated elsewhere on word-processing and graphics software, although almost all desk-top publishing software itself has some capability for creating both, depending upon its degree of sophistication. As would be expected of a computerized system, any desk-top publishing system shows an image of what is being created on the monitor screen. Some systems show only a reduced-size image, which can be misleading when the output is to be of different dimensions; other systems allow actual size and enlargements of artwork to be viewed. Text and graphics are either entered directly onto the page shown on the monitor or "pasted in" electronically, having been created elsewhere. A page layout once created on computer can be altered and amended at will until the desired result is obtained. It is then realized as a finished document by instructing the system to print.

The more advanced desk-top publishing packages also offer facilities such as kerning and leading (creating space) between the lines; extra fonts may be available to expand the system.

TYPESETTING SYSTEMS

The Scangraphics Scantext 2000 can produce and integrate text and line and half-tone illustrations. Other systems are the Bertholds Magic Text and Graphics System, AM Varitypes, Penta, Epics-XL, Compugraphic, and Autologic. Many computer typesetting sytems are based around the IBM PC.

DESK-TOP PUBLISHING

The Apple Mackintosh dominates the market, and the main software package is probably Pagemaker from Aldus, which is now available for the IBM PC System as well. Also available on the IBM PC System is Ventura Publisher. Other desk-top publishing programs and systems available include the Canon Personal Publishing System, Fleet Street Editor and Fleet Street Publisher, Book Machine, Frontpage, Jetsetter, Ready Steady GO 3, and Fontasy. Fontasy is economically priced and particularly good value, since it includes some sophisticated facilities such as kerning.

Hewett-Packett's desk top publishing system, including software.

Scanners, printers and plotters

One of the ways in which images or text can be captured and used in a computer graphics system is by means of a scanner.

Scanner machines are based on both photocopier and facsimile machine technology. The image is scanned using a light beam, and the information is digitized serially — meaning it is converted into code which can be held and read by the computer. When decoded it appears on the computer screen as the original image. Different types of scanner exist: images can be scanned either on a drum scanner or on a flat-bed scanner. On a drum scanner, the artwork is scanned as it rotates on a cylinder or drum; because the artwork is wrapped around the drum, it must be on a thin and flexible support. The two different types of scanner can scan text either line by line or a page at a time. At the output end of most computer systems there are printers and plotters which translate the computer's digital information into "hard copy" (as it is referred to in computing).

These are available in a wide range of types and sizes, and offer black-and-white or color to different resolutions. Graphic designers are generally more concerned with high-quality results than are most computer users, at least as an option, so many computer printers are simply not acceptable for their purposes.

Daisy-wheel printers, for example, although offering high-quality type, are nevertheless restricted to that role alone, and for that reason will receive no further consideration here. Dot matrix printers — included by reason of the fact that they can print graphics — are not usually of great use in a computer graphics system because the quality is not high enough. They are, however, improving. The printers that are most used as outputs for computerized systems are lasers, ink-jets and thermal transfer printers.

Laser printers are closely related to the technology of the photocopiers, and use toner in a similar manner. They have the advantage of being clean and easy to use, but they do limit the resolution to the fineness of the toner itself. This toner comes in cartridges and typically lasts for around 3,000 to 4,000 prints, depending on the prints themselves and the amount of coverage they require.

Because most laser printers operate at around 300 dots per inch, they are not a real challenge to the average typesetter operating at approximately 1,250 dots per inch. There are, however, some laser printers now on the market which operate at the much higher resolution of between 1,270 and 2,500 dots per inch. The use of laser printers has been closely related to the growing interest in desk-top publishing for which they offer one of the best outputs.

Ink-jet printers work by firing very fine jets of ink through nozzles onto the paper as they print. The computer controls the nozzles, and so forms them in different combinations into characters or designs, a process that has advantages and disadvantages. Of importance to the graphic designer is the fact that ink-jet printers can produce outstanding color quality in the printed image; they are also fast, and compared to other printers they are very quiet. Unfortunately, in the past they have been plagued with difficulties because of the way in which they work: the ink tends to clog and then splatters across the paper, spoiling the print as it does so. Manufacturers have for long sought ways of overcoming this problem — they have, for example tried firing the ink as a vapor, and tried having it in a solid form which is then melted onto the paper. The ink-jet printers' capacity for color graphics obviously makes them suitable for use with graphic design packages, but they can also be used for general word-processing and produce prints of a high standard.

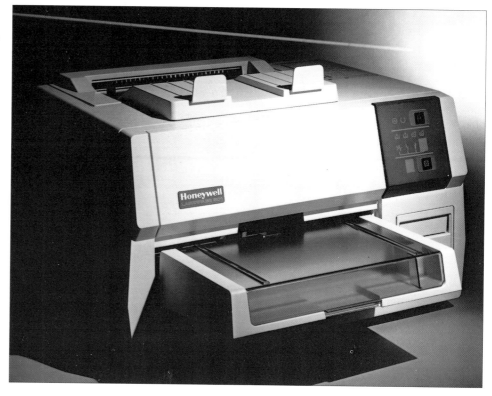

Thermal transfer printers work by electrically heating a special print head, which then melts ink held on a coated ribbon. As with ink-jet printers, the quality of color-printing from thermal transfer printers is very good. However, they do tend to be comparatively expensive items, and a further drawback for the graphic artist is that a special paper is often required for use with them. (This also applies to some ink-jet printers.)

Dot matrix printers work by passing a matrix of wires — usually between 9 and 24, depending on the quality of the printer — over a ribbon of ink rather like a conventional typewriter. The characters or the image is formed by using different configurations of wires to produce a composite series of dots that make up a chacter or line. In the case of color, using a dot matrix printer the image is produced by the juxtaposition and superimposition of four colors; red, yellow, blue and black — a process which resembles conventional color-printing.

A problem which arises with dot matrix color printers is that it is easy for color from one band of the ribbon to dirty the other hues, thus leading to an inaccurate or confused color reproduction. The printing quality of dot matrix generally would render one of little use to a graphic designer if high-quality results are required. Even with the better-quality printers offering color, it would not compare with an ink-jet or thermal transfer printer. However, dot matrix printers are being constantly improved, and could perhaps be considered for some application in which the quality of the final output was not so critical.

Plotters, unlike printers which produce sectional images, draw in continuous lines as one would draw by hand. In fact, they use

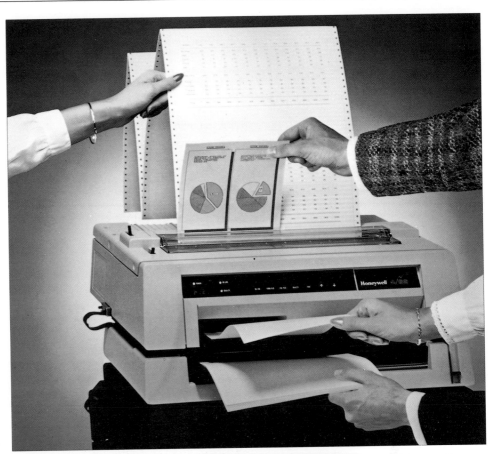

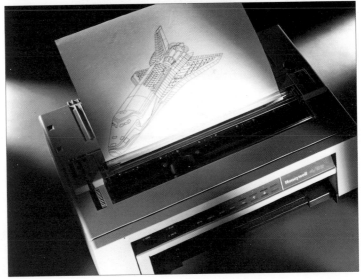

*Laserpage 801 printer from Honeywell (**left**).*

*Honeywell's 4/66 color marker printer (**top**); and their 4/66P printer/plotter (**bottom**).*

PRINTERS

The HP Laserjet is from Hewlett Packard, which also produces the Series II and Laserjet 2000. Apple Computers produces the Laser Writer and the Laser Writer Plus. Other laser printers on the market include the OKI-Laserline 6, Centronics PP-8, the QMS K8 Laser and PS 800, the DEC LN03 and LN03 Plus, the Hitachi Koki LB028, in addition to printers from Canon, Konica and Ricoh. Xerox also produces laser printers. Advanced Colour Technology produces one of the most useful ink-jet printers.

plotting points which are very similar to technical pens. This makes them very useful for certain areas of design, in particular where the end result requires a crisp linear approach. The number of colors available on the plotter depends on the number of pens that the plotter can accommodate at any one time. Typically this is between four and eight. Paper sizes can sometimes be a problem with plotters because they tend to work only in certain formats. Plotters are not strictly a graphic designer's tool, but they are intended for use with computer-aided design systems and are ideal for the automatic production of technical drawings and plans.

Computer-aided design (known as CAD) is an aspect of computer technology which is of most interest to architects, engineers and technical draftsmen. In many ways the CAD systems resemble the other design-oriented computer systems that have been described so far. They are not dealt with in detail here because their main use falls outside the scope of most graphic artists' activities.

DOT MATRIX PRINTERS

Dot matrix printers available for use with computers include the Panasonic KX P1091, the Epson LX-80, the Star SG10, the Centronics GLP, and the Riteman F+. Good dot matrix printers are also available from Honeywell Bull.

The best computer plotters produce drawings to 11¾×16½ inch format.

The Roland DXY 980 works to this size and has eight pens as well as an electrostatic paper-hold. Microperipherals produce the Sekonic SPL-420. Other plotters are the Penman, the Astron MCP-80, the Epson HI-80, and the Folex Computer Plotter. Plotter supplies are available from technical pen manufacturers such as Rotring, Faber-Castell and Staedtler.

3M's four-color dot matrix 7500 printer/plotter (in blue, red, green and black).

Television and animation programs

Some of the most sophisticated turnkey graphics systems are in part derived from computer-controlled systems developed for use in television and video production. In fact, the only practical difference in some cases is that the finished results can be seen only on a television screen when produced by a television graphics computer, although they can be translated into print using an ordinary computerized graphics system. The revolution that has taken place in both television presentation and video production has been substantially based on the availability of computer technology.

The facilities for mixing and distorting images on television and video are now extremely advanced: stunningly fantastic imagery has become a feature of some of even the most mundane television productions. Insofar as this affects advertising and the design process leading up to television advertisements, it is relevant to a certain section of graphic artists and designers. It is more generally important because of its spinoffs in the field of ordinary computerized graphic design, but it is also of interest because it offers the possibilities of new areas of non-static graphics which have yet to be developed.

Computer animation exploits facets of both television graphics systems and ordinary turnkey graphics systems. Here an image once fed in can be moved, rotated, and generally directed so as to imitate the apparent movement of a real object. Because computer animation systems can create convincing three-dimensional effects which cast shadows precisely as they should, the results can sometimes be incredibly lifelike. Computer animations are, as yet, expensive, but they are less costly and more sophisticated than the nearest equivalent animations done by hand. They are currently being used in television advertising, but some experimental animated films have been made by computer as film sequences in their own right, and it is quite likely that the field will develop further.

The main drawback with computer animation systems is the large amount of accurate information that must be fed in concerning the images before they can be animated. This is very time-consuming and requires a great deal of programming.

COMPUTER GRAPHIC SYSTEMS

SUPPLIER	MANUFACTURER	DISTRIBUTOR	WHOLESALER	RETAILER	Areas where products are available	Local variations in product range	Graphic Design Programs	Computer Paintboxes	Animation Software	Desk-Top Publishing Systems
Aesthedes Ltd	•	•	•		W	No	•	•	•	
Cannon	•				W	No				•
Digisolve	•				N/S	N/S	•	•	•	•
Filmsales	•				N/S	No			•	
Graphic Products International		•			S UK	N/S	•	•		
Mackintosh	•				W	No				•
Pisa Graphics		•		•	N/S	N/S	•	•	•	•
Quantel	•				W	No		•	•	•
Video Data Systems	•				W	N/S	•	•	•	

KEY: A = Australia **C** = Canada **E** = Europe (excluding UK) **S** = Scandinavia **UK** = United Kingdom
US = United States **W** = Worldwide **N/S** = Not Stated

APPENDIX

Paper weights and sizes

The following information is designed to aid conversions between the metric and imperial systems of basis paper weights.

The weight of paper is expressed either in grammes per square meter — the more modern expression of its substance — or in pounds weight, which is the old Imperial system. The term "pounds" refers to the weight of a ream (500 sheets) of the paper in Imperial sheets (30 in x 22 in). A description of a particular paper as 90 lb or 300 lb does not refer to a specific quality of the sheet, therefore, but is a general indication of its density and thickness.

The international metric paper-size range (**ISO** series) is based on economics, in that any smaller sizes in the series can be cut without waste from one large basic sheet. The anomalies of the Imperial system have largely been overcome by referring to the basis weight of a single sheet of paper in grammes per square metre weight, expressed as **Gm²**.

To convert paper in **Gm²** into the approximate equivalent in pounds per ream weight:

150-160 Gm²	: 2.08 = Imperial	**72 lb**
	: 2.81 = Royal	**54 lb**
180-200 Gm²	: 2.08 = Imperial	**90 lb**
	: 2.81 = Royal	**68 lb**
240-250 Gm²	: 2.08 = Imperial	**120 lb**
	: 2.81 = Royal	**90 lb**
285-300 Gm²	: 2.08 = Imperial	**140 lb**
	: 2.81 = Royal	**106 lb**
410-425 Gm²	: 2.08 = Imperial	**200 lb**
	: 2.81 = Royal	**150 lb**

Note that one tonne (metric) paper = 1000 kg weight and that one tonne (Imperial) paper = 2,240 lb weight.

To convert traditional weights to metric weights:

Weight in lb × per ream	4.06 Large Post	
	3.57 Demy	
	3.40 Medium	= **Metric weight**
	2.81 Royal in Gm²	
	2.34 Double Crown	
	2.08 Imperial	

For example, a **90lb** sheet of Double Crown size paper = (90 × 2.34) = 210 **Gm²**.

ISO series metric sizes

Many countries have already decided to adopt the International System of Units — Systéme International d'Unités — as the only legally acceptable classification of measurement. The **ISO** series includes three denominations — **A, B** and **C**. The '**A**' series is used to denote paper sizes for general printing matter, '**B**' is primarily for posters and wall charts and '**C**' is specifically for envelopes.

Denominations	Metric (mm)	Imperial (inch)
A0	841 × 1189	33.11 × 46.82
A1	594 × 841	23.39 × 33.11
A2	420 × 594	16.54 × 23.39
A3	297 × 420	11.69 × 16.54
A4	210 × 297	8.27 × 11.69
A5	148 × 210	5.83 × 8.27
A6	105 × 148	4.13 × 5.83
A7	74 × 105	2.91 × 4.13
A8	55 × 74	2.05 × 2.91
A9	37 × 55	1.46 × 2.05
A10	28 × 37	1.02 × 1.46
4A0	1682 × 2378	66.22 × 93.52
2A0	1189 × 1681	44.81 × 66.22

Denomination	Metric	Imperial
B0	1000 × 1414	39.75 × 55.67
B1	707 × 1000	27.80 × 39.40
B2	500 × 707	19.60 × 27.80
B3	353 × 500	13.80 × 19.60
B4	250 × 353	9.80 × 13.80
B5	176 × 250	7.00 × 9.80
C0	917 × 1297	36.20 × 51.00
C1	648 × 917	25.50 × 36.20
C2	458 × 648	18.00 × 25.50
C3	324 × 458	12.75 × 18.00
C4	229 × 324	9.00 × 12.75
C5	162 × 229	6.40 × 9.00
C6	114 × 162	4.50 × 6.40
C7	81 × 114	3.25 × 4.50

ISO series untrimmed stock sizes

The untrimmed paper sizes of the **ISO** '**A**' series trimmed to '**A**' sizes after printing, are made in the following denominations:

The '**RA**' series (addition of an '**R**' to the '**A**' series) for non-bled printing and includes approximately an extra 10-20mm onto the '**A**' size which is trimmed off after the printing has taken place.

The '**SRA**' series (addition of an '**SR**' to the '**A**' series) is used when printed work is bled off the edge of trimmed size and an extra 40-60mm is allowed on the '**A**' size for trimming after printing is completed, eg:

A2 420 × 594 mm
RA2 430 × 610 mm
SRA2 450 × 640 mm

DIRECTORY OF MANUFACTURERS/ DISTRIBUTORS OF GRAPHIC DESIGN EQUIPMENT

KEY D = Distributor **M** = Manufacturer **W** = Wholesaler **R** = Retailer

ABELSCOT-MARCHANT LTD
Unit 9
Guinness Road Trading
  Estate
Guinness Road
Manchester M17 1SD
UK

D/M/W Graphic materials,
airbrush equipment

ADIT S.p.A.
Via Segrino 8
20098 Sesto Ulteriano
Milan
Italy

D/M Studio furniture

AGFA-GAVAERT LTD
Mac Systems Division
27 Great West Road
Brentford
Middlesex
UK

M Enlargers, PMT machines,
process cameras

THE AIRBRUSH COMPANY
13 Woodcote Road
Leamington Spa
CV32 6PZ
UK

D/W Airbrush equipment

ALVIN & CO, INC
P O Box 188
Windsor
CY 06095
US

D/M/W Graphic materials

**ANDROMEDA SOFTWARE
UK LTD**
200 Brent Street
Hendon NW4 1BH
UK

M Graphics software

THE ART FACTORY LTD
Unit 6
Blackwell Trading Estate
Lanrick Road
London E14 0JS
UK

D/M Graphic materials

**ART MATERIALS
INTERNATIONAL**
Boschstrasse 8
D-2358 Kaltenkirchen
WEST GERMANY

D/M Graphic supplies,
airbrush equipment

ATLANTIS PAPER COMPANY
Gullivers Wharf
105 Wapping Lane
London E1 9RN
UK

R/W Graphic materials

**BADGER AIR BRUSH
COMPANY**
9128 W. Belmont
Franklin Park
IL 60131
US

M Airbrush equipment

BARCHAM GREEN & CO LTD
Hayle Mill
Maidstone
Kent ME15 6XQ
UK

M Handmade papers

BEROL LTD
Oldmedow Road
King's Lynn
Norfolk PE30 4JR
UK

M Pencils, pens, ink

BLAIR ART PRODUCTS
PO Box 286
8282 Boyle Parkway
Twinsburg
OH 44087
US

M Adhesives, varnishes,
coatings

J BLOCKX FILS sprl
Route de Liège 39
B 5291 Terwagne
BELGIUM

M Paints

BURTON HOLT LTD
PO Box 3
Cranbrook
Kent TN17 2LR
UK

M Charcoal

**BUSINESS FURNITURE &
EQUIPMENT (BFE) LTD**
Unit 9 Armstrong Way
Great Western Industrial
  Park
Windmill Lane
Southall
Middlesex UB2 4SD
UK

D/W Graphic materials

CALDER COLOURS LTD
Nottingham Road
Ashby de la Zouch
Leics LE6 5DR
UK

M Graphic materials

CANNON & WRIN LTD
68 High Street
Chislehurst
Kent BR7 5BL
UK

D/M Drawing materials

CARAN D'ACHE SA
Chemin du Foron 19
PO Box 169,
1226 Thonex-Geneva
SWITZERLAND

UK agent:
JAKAR INTERNATIONAL

M Pencils, pens, paints

CHARTPAK LIMITED
14-17 Station Road
Didcot
Oxfordshire OX11 7NB
UK

D/M Graphics materials

P. H. COATE & CO
Meare Green Court
Stoke St. Gregory
Taunton
UK

M Charcoal

**COLOURTECH
INTERNATIONAL LTD**
Europa House
Bower Hill
Epping
Essex
UK

M Colour proofing/imaging
systems

**CONOPOIS INSTRUMENTS
LTD**
39 Littlehampton Road
Worthing
Sussex BN13 1QJ

D/M R/W Airbrush
equipment

CONTE LTD
Park Farm Road
Park Farm Industrial Estate
Folkestone
Kent CT19 5EY
UK

M Graphics materials

COTECH SENSITISING LTD
Unit 15
Tafarnaubach Industrial
  Estate
Tredegar
Gwent NP2 3AA
UK

M Filing cabinets

**CRESCENT CARDBOARD
COMPANY**
100 W. Willow Road
Wheeling
Illinois 60090
US

M Papers and boards

DALER-ROWNEY LTD
PO Box 10
Bracknell
Berks RG12 4ST
UK

D/M Graphic materials

DEKA-TEXTILFARBEN GmbH
Kapellenstrasse 18
D-8025 Unterhaching
WEST GERMANY

M Acrylic paint

**THE DEVILBISS COMPANY
LTD**
Ringwood Road
Bournemouth
Dorset BH11 9LH
UK

M Airbrush equipment

DE VISU INTERNATIONAL
rue Ampère BP 33
91430 Igny Zai
FRANCE

M Graphic materials

ALOIS K. DIETHELM AG
Zurichstrasse 42
Postfach
CH-8306 Bruttisellen
WEST GERMANY

M Acrylic paint

DIGISOLVE LTD
Aire & Calder Works
Cinder Lane,
Castleford
West Yorkshire WF10 1WU
UK

M Computer systems

DRG SELLOTAPE PRODUCTS
Elstree Way
Borehamwood
Herts
UK

M Adhesive tape

EBERHARD FABER INC
Crestwood
Wilkes-Barre
PA 18773
US

UK agent:
John Heath Company
230 Bradford Street
Birmingham B12 0RJ

M Pencils, pastels and pens

C. W. EDDING LTD
North Orbital Trading Estate
Napsbury Lane
St Albans
Herts AL1 1XQ
UK

M Pens, pencils, knives

EDUCAID LTD
Lychgate
Albion Road
Pitstone
Leighton Buzzard
Beds LU7 9AY
UK

D Drawing aids, rulers, light-
boxes

EXX PROJECTS
72 Rivington Street
London EC2 3AY
UK

M Plan chests, portfolios

FILM SALES LTD
145 Nathan Way
Woolwich Trading Estate
London SE28 0BE
UK

D Film

**FLAMBEAU PRODUCTS
CORPORATION**
PO Box 97
15981 Valplast Street
Middlefield
OH 44062
US

M Art storage boxes

SAM FLAX
111 Eighth Avenue
New York
NY 10011
US

D Graphic materials

GAEBEL ENTERPRISES INC
100 Ball Street
PO Box 276
East Syracuse
NY 13057
US

D/M Drawing equipment

**GRANT EQUIPMENT
SUPPLIES**
Grant South
Kingston House Estate
Portsmouth Road
Surbiton
Surrey
UK

M/D/R/W Grant projectors,
PMT cameras, processors

GRAPHIC ARTS
Riverside Maltings
Stanstead Abbotts
Ware
Herts SG12 4HG
UK

D/R Colour systems, light-boxes, furniture

**GRAPHIC BOOKS
INTERNATIONAL LTD**
PO Box 349
rue de Goddards
Castel, Guernsey
Channel Islands
UK

M/D/W/R Reference materials

**GRAPHIC PRODUCTS
INTERNATIONAL LTD**
43/45 Dorset Street
London W1H 3FN
UK

D Rulers, light-boxes, computer systems

**THE GRAPHIC WAREHOUSE
LTD**
1-11 Rayfield Grove
Swindon SN2 1HD
US

W Graphics equipment

**GRIFFIN MANUFACTURING
COMPANY**
PO Box 308
1656 Ridge Road East
Webster
NY 14580
US

M/D Drawing boards, light-boxes

HABICO
Kunstlerpinselfabrik Hans
Bieringer & Co
Liebersdorferstr. 4
D-8809 Bechhofen adH
WEST GERMANY

M Brushes

HALCO SUNBURY CO LTD
Staines
Mddx TW18 2BS
UK

M Enlargers, cameras, light-boxes

HAMILTON & CO LTD
Brush House
Rosslyn Crescent
Harrow HA1 2AE
UK

D/M Brushes

HANCOCKS LTD
114 Welsbach House
The London Production
Centre
Broomhill Road
London SW18 4JQ
UK

M Light-boxes and tables

A. S. HANDOVER LTD
Angel Yard
Highgate High Street
London N6 5JU
UK

M Brushes

HELIX LTD
PO Box 15
Lye
Stourbridge
West Midlands DY9 7AJ
UK

M Drawing equipment

HEWLETT PACKARD LTD
Miller House
The Ring
Bracknell
Berkshire RG12 1XN
UK

JOHN HEYER PAPER LTD
Chronicle House
Sheldon Way
Larkfield
Kent ME20 6SE

D Paper

ESMOND HELLERMEN LTD
Hellerman House
Harris Way
Windmill Road
Sunbury on Thames
Middlesex TW16 7EW
UK

D/M Drawing office
equipment

**HOLBEIN ART MATERIALS
INC**
2-2-5 Ueshio
Minami-ku
Osaka-542
JAPAN

M/W Graphic materials

HONEYWELL BULL LIMITED
Honeywell House
Great West Road
Brentford
Mddx TW8 9DH
UK

M/R Computer graphic
systems

INSCRIBE LTD
Woolmer Industrial Estate
Bordon
Hants GU35 9QE
UK

W Art materials

ITEK COLOUR GRAPHICS
Princess Elizabeth Way
Cheltenham GL51 7RD
UK

M Scanners

JAKAR INTERNATIONAL LTD
Hillside House
2-6 Friern Park
London N12 9BX
UK

D Graphic materials

KEUFFEL & ESSER COMPANY
900 Lanidex Plaza
Parsippany
NJ 07054
US

D/M Graphic materials

**KOH-I-NOOR RADIOGRAPH,
INC**
100 North Street
Bloomsbury
NJ 08804
US

D/M Art materials

KROY LTD
Worton Grange
Reading
Berks RG2 0LZ
UK

M Graphic materials

LANGFORD & HILL LTD
10 Warwick Street
London W1
UK

D/R/W Graphic materials

LANGNICKEL INC
229 West 28th Street
New York
NY 10001
US

M Brushes

LASCAUX FARBENFABRIK
Alois K Diethelm AG
Zurichstrasse 42
Postfach
CH-8306 Bruttisellen
WEST GERMANY

M Paints

LERCHE BÜROSTAHLWAREN
Postfach 180164
D-5650 Solingen 18
SWEDEN

M Cutting equipment

LOCWYN LTD
North Lane
Weston-on-the-Green
Oxon OX6 8RG
UK

M Filing systems

**LUKAS ARTISTS' COLOURS &
MATERIALS**
PO Box 7427
Harffstr. 40
D-4000 Dusseldorf 1
WEST GERMANY

M Art materials

3M UK plc
3M House
PO Box 1
Bracknell
Berks RG12 1JU
UK

M Adhesives

**MAIMERI ARTISTS MATERIALS
LTD**
Hartlebury Trading Estate
Hartlebury
Nr Kidderminster
Worcs DY10 4JB
UK

D Graphic materials

MARABUWERKE
Erwin Martz GmbH & Co
D-7146 Tamm
WEST GERMANY

M Graphic materials

MARCUS ART PTY LTD
218 Hoddle Street
Abbotsford
Victoria 3067
AUSTRALIA

M Pencils, paints, inks

MECANORMA LTD
10 School Road
North Acton
London NW10 6TD
UK

M Graphic materials

MET GRAPHIC SUPPLIES
13 Charter Street
Leicester
UK

D Paper, PMT machines,
process cameras

MICROFLAME LTD
Vinces Road
Diss
Norfolk IP22 3HQ
UK

W Graphic materials

M MYERS & SON plc
PO Box 16
Oldbury
Warley
West Midlands B68 8HF
UK

M Storage equipment, rotary
cutters

**ALBERT NESTLER
VERKAUFSGESELLSCHAFT
mbH & Co**
PO Box 1920
Alte Bahnhofstr. 10
D-7630 Lahr-Schwarzwald
WEST GERMANY

M Graphics equipment

NOVA ITALPLASTIC spa
Via Verga 18
22077 Olgiate Comasco
Como
ITALY

M Canvases

OMNICROM SYSTEMS LTD
Tonge Bridge Way
Bolton BL2 6BD
UK

M Colour systems, paper,
film

ORAM & ROBINSON LTD
Cadmore Lane
Cheshunt
Herts EN8 9SG
UK

M Papers and boards

**OSMIROID INTERNATIONAL
LTD**
Fareham Road
Gosport
Hants PO13 0AL
UK

M Pens, inks

**THE PARAGON RAZOR
COMPANY**
Nursery Works
Little London Road
Sheffield S8 0UJ
UK

M Cutting equipment

PEBEO SA
St. Marcel BP 12
13367 Marseilles
Cedex 11
FRANCE

M Graphic materials, paints

H. W. PEEL & CO LTD
Norwester House
Fairway Drive
Greenford
Middlesex UB6 8PW
UK

D/M Graphic materials

PELLING & CROSS LTD
93-103 Drummond Street
London NW1 2HJ
UK

D Cameras and enlargers

PELLTECH LTD
Station Lane
Witney
Oxon OX8 6YS
UK

D Drawing office equipment

PENTEL LTD
Wyvern Industrial Estate
Beverley Way
New Malden
Surrey KT3 4PF
UK

M Pencils, pens, pastels

THE PILOT PEN COMPANY LTD
9 Bethune Road
North Acton
London NW10 6NJ
UK

D/M Graphic materials

PISA GRAPHICS LTD
Gibbs House
Kennel Ride
Ascot
Berks SL5 7NT
UK

D/R Computer systems

PLASTIC SUPPLIERS
2400 Marilyn Lane
Columbus
OH 43219
US

D/M Films

PLATIGNUM PLC
PO Box 1
Royston
Herts SG8 5XX
UK

M Pencils, pens, crayons, adhesive tape

QUANTEL LTD
31 Turnpike Road
Newbury
Berks RG13 2NE
UK

M Computer systems

RAPHAEL
Ets Max Sauer
2 rue Lamarck
BP 204
22003 Saint-Brieuc
FRANCE

M Brushes

REPRODRAFT LTD
34 Buckingham Road
West Industrial Estate
Weston Super Mare
Avon BS24 9BG
UK

D/W Studio equipment

REXEL LTD
Gatehouse Road
Aylesbury
Bucks HP19 3DT
UK

D/M Graphic materials

RHONE-POULENC SYSTEMS LTD
High Street
Houghton Regis
Beds LU5 5QL
UK

M Plan printing equipment and dyeline materials

ROTATRIM LTD
35-43 Dudley Street
Luton LU2 0NP
UK

M Colour systems, cutting equipment

ROTOBORD LTD
Stanmore Industrial Estate
Bridgnorth
Shropshire WV15 5HP
UK

D/M/R/W Graphic material, drawing boards

ROTRING
Building One
GEC Estate
East Lane
Wembley
Middx HA9 7PY
UK

D Graphic materials

SALIS INTERNATIONAL, INC
4093 North 28th Way
Hollywood
Florida 33020
US

M Pens, paints, inks, airbrush equipment

SCANGRAPHIC VISUTEK LTD
Caxton House
Randalls Way
Leatherhead
Surrey KT22 7TW
UK

R Typesetting equipment

SCHLEICHER & SCHUELL GmbH
Grimsehlstrasse 23
Postfach 246
D-3352 Einbeck
WEST GERMANY

M Papers and boards

H SCHMINCKE & CO
Otto-Hahn-Str. 2
D-4006 Eerkrath-
Unterfeldhaus
WEST GERMANY

M Graphic materials

SCHOELLERSHAMMER
Heinr. Aug. Schoeller Sohne
GmbH & Co
Postfach 1 47
D-5160 Düren
WEST GERMANY

M Papers and boards

PAPERFABRIEK SCHUT BV
Kabeljauw 2
Postbus 1
6866 ZG Heelsum
HOLLAND

M Papers and boards

SCHWAN-STABILO
Postfach 4553
Maxfeldstrasse
8500 Nürnberg 1
WEST GERMANY

M Graphic materials

SENNELIER
rue de Moulin à Cailloux
Senia 408 Orly
94567 Rungis Cedex
FRANCE

M Art materials

SIMAIR GRAPHICS EQUIPMENT LTD
Park Mill House
47 Stanningley Road
Leeds LS12 3LR
UK

D/M Airbrush equipment, plan chests, cameras and enlargers

D. & J. SIMONS & SONS LTD
122-150 Hackney Road
London E2 7QL
UK

W Graphic materials

SKYCOPY LTD
412-420 The Highway
London E14 8ED
UK

D/M studio machinery, colour systems and film

WILLIAM SOMMERVILLE & SON plc
Dalmore Mill
Milton Bridge
Penicuik
Midlothian
UK

M Papers and boards

STAEDTLER LTD
Pontyclun
Mid Glamorgan
UK

M Graphic materials

ROYAL TALENS BV
PO Box 4
Sophialaan 46
7311 PD Apeldoorn
NETHERLANDS

M Brushes, paints, pencils

TESTRITE INSTRUMENTS CO INC
135 Monroe Street
Newark
NJ 07105
US

M Light-boxes, projectors

AMERICAN TOMBOW INC
5352 Sterling Center Drive
Westlake Village
CA 91361
US

M Pens and pencils

TOMBOW PEN & PENCIL GmbH
Eupener Strasse 161
D-5000 Koln 41
WEST GERMANY

M Pen and pencils

TWO RIVERS PAPER COMPANY
Rosebank Mill
Stubbins
Ramsbottom
Bury
Lancs
UK

M/R Handmade paper and board

PRODUCTOS VALLEJO
PO Box 53
Villanueva Y Geltru
Barcelona
SPAIN

M Acrylic and water-based paints

VIDEO DATA SYSTEMS LTD
Studio 6 Intec 2
Wade Road
Basingstoke
Hants RG24 0NE

M/R Computer systems

A WEST & PARTNERS LTD
684 Mitcham Road
Croydon CR9 3AB
UK

D/M Graphic materials

WHATMAN PAPER LTD
Springfield Mill
Maidstone
Kent ME14 2LE
UK

M Paper and board

WINSOR & NEWTON
Whitefriars Avenue
Wealdstone
Harrow
Middx HA3 5RH
UK

WINSOR & NEWTON INC
555 Winsor Drive
Secaucus
NJ 07094
US

D/M/R Art materials

INDEX

Pages numbers in *italic* refer to the illustrations and captions.